The Radial Method of the Middle Wittgenstein

Also available from Bloomsbury:

Certainty in Action, by Danièle Moyal-Sharrock
Ethics after Wittgenstein, edited by Richard Amesbury and Hartmut von Sass
Wittgenstein and the Problem of Metaphysics, by Michael Smith
Wittgenstein, Religion and Ethics, by Mikel Burley

The Radial Method of the Middle Wittgenstein

In the Net of Language

Piotr Dehnel

BLOOMSBURY ACADEMIC
LONDON • NEW YORK • OXFORD • NEW DELHI • SYDNEY

BLOOMSBURY ACADEMIC
Bloomsbury Publishing Plc
50 Bedford Square, London, WC1B 3DP, UK
1385 Broadway, New York, NY 10018, USA
29 Earlsfort Terrace, Dublin 2, Ireland

BLOOMSBURY, BLOOMSBURY ACADEMIC and the Diana logo are
trademarks of Bloomsbury Publishing Plc

First published in Great Britain 2023
This paperback edition published 2024

Copyright © Piotr Dehnel, 2023

Piotr Dehnel has asserted his right under the Copyright,
Designs and Patents Act, 1988, to be identified as Author of this work.

Cover image: kristof lauwers / Alamy Stock Photo

All rights reserved. No part of this publication may be reproduced or transmitted
in any form or by any means, electronic or mechanical, including photocopying,
recording, or any information storage or retrieval system, without prior permission
in writing from the publishers.

Bloomsbury Publishing Plc does not have any control over, or responsibility for, any
third-party websites referred to or in this book. All internet addresses given in this
book were correct at the time of going to press. The author and publisher regret any
inconvenience caused if addresses have changed or sites have ceased to exist,
but can accept no responsibility for any such changes.

A catalogue record for this book is available from the British Library.

A catalog record for this book is available from the Library of Congress.

ISBN: HB: 978-1-3502-5733-7
        PB: 978-1-3502-5737-5
        ePDF: 978-1-3502-5734-4
        eBook: 978-1-3502-5735-1

Typeset by Integra Software Services Pvt. Ltd.

To find out more about our authors and books visit www.bloomsbury.com
and sign up for our newsletters.

For Amelia

Contents

Preface	viii
Abbreviations	xv
Introduction: The radial method of the middle Wittgenstein	1
1 The phenomenological turn	13
2 Verification: 1929–31	41
3 Wittgenstein's critique of Frege in the notes from 1929 to 1932	55
4 'A clever man got caught in this net of language!': Wittgenstein's attack on set theory	75
5 *The Big Typescript* as a middle-period work	107
6 PS: Understanding, expecting, wishing, etc.	123
7 Magic, rituals and philosophy: Wittgenstein on Frazer's *The Golden Bough*	133
8 Wittgenstein as a philosopher of culture	163
Notes	180
References	196
Index	204

Preface

This book explores the middle period in the development of Ludwig Wittgenstein's philosophy, stretching between his return to Cambridge in 1929 and the drafting of the first version of his *Philosophical Investigations* (MS 142) in late 1936 and early 1937. It took some time until scholarship came to regard this timeframe as representing a tolerably distinguishable and consistent whole. This process of recognition unfolded in stages which were fuelled by the gradual release of Wittgenstein's abundant writings and notes from his lectures. Today, to talk about 'the middle Wittgenstein' is somewhat of a commonplace among researchers even though some scholars claim that splitting his work into early, middle and late periods is an ill-advised approach. They insist that there was just one Wittgenstein, although his thought indeed radically evolved, in particular throughout the period I explore in this book.[1] Disputes and discussions on this period are still rife as there is no consensus on what makes it distinct and distinctive as compared with Wittgenstein's early views presented in the *Tractatus Logico-Philosophicus* (1922) and his late philosophy encapsulated in the *Philosophical Investigations* (1953). The matter is made all the more complicated by the fact that Wittgenstein never wrote a similar book to outline his position in the 1930s.[2]

Wittgenstein came back to Cambridge at the beginning of 1929, after a hiatus of fifteen years following the time he had spent studying philosophy under Bertrand Russell. His return to Cambridge thus marked his return to philosophy. He obtained a research grant at Trinity College and vigorously applied himself to intensive research work. In February 1929, he also resumed recording his ideas in diary entries. The very first entry contains his confession:

> At Cambridge again. Very strange. It seems as if time had gone back. I make these notes with some apprehension. I don't know what lies ahead. We'll see! If I don't lose the spirit. I'm circling anxiously, but I don't know around what point yet. Indeed, my time here should be or is to be a preparation for something. I should clearly realize something.
>
> (MS 105, 2)

Wittgenstein numbered his manuscripts as volumes from I to X, additionally giving some of them titles of their own, such as *Philosophische Bemerkungen*,

Philosophische Betrachtungen, Bemerkungen zur philosophischen Grammatik and *Philosophische Grammatik*. He even took care to place an epigraph at the beginning of the first volume. Based on these manuscripts, Wittgenstein dictated typescripts for later use in his further work. The typescript marked as TS 209 served as the source of *Philosophische Bemerkungen*, the first selection of Wittgenstein's notes from the 1930s, edited by Rush Rhees in 1964. Four years later, Rhees published *Philosophische Grammatik*. Its first part contained the revised text (*Umarbeitung*) of the initial eight chapters of what came to be known as *The Big Typescript* (i.e. TS 213); its second part comprised seven unrevised chapters on the philosophy of mathematics from TS 213. In 2000, Michael Nedo edited the whole of *The Big Typescript* as the eleventh volume of the *Wiener Ausgabe*. Even though some of these publications, in particular those edited by Rhees, have invited some criticism from scholars, they add up to a representative repository of knowledge about the middle period in Wittgenstein's philosophy. Other useful resources are available as well. Starting in early 1930, Wittgenstein gave regular lectures in which he evoked and discussed issues directly related to the focal areas of his studies at respective moments. George E. Moore, who attended almost all of those lectures, took meticulous notes, which offer us a faithful record of the themes and topics that Wittgenstein addressed in them.[3] Additionally, in 2020, Arthur Gibson and Niamh O'Mahony edited the previously unstudied manuscripts of Francis Skinner from 1932 to 1941 (cf. Gibson, O'Mahony 2020), which may shed a new light on the evolution of Wittgenstein's philosophy between the *Tractatus* and the *Investigations*. Between 1934 and 1935, Wittgenstein dictated two texts, which are known today as *The Blue and Brown Books*, in English to a group of selected students, because he concluded that the audience of his lectures had grown too large and it would be useful to first make the content of the lectures available to the chosen few and later discuss it with the rest. The texts soon began to circulate among his students as stand-alone works in their own right.

Between 1929 and 1936, Wittgenstein would spend half a year at Cambridge and the rest of his time in Vienna. The stints in his hometown did not entail putting his work on hold as Wittgenstein often used this time to make typescripts and discuss things with Moritz Schlick and Friedrich Waismann, members of the Vienna Circle, a habit they had already developed in the second half of the 1920s. These conversations were written down by Waismann and are now an invaluable source of information about Wittgenstein's beliefs at the time (cf. WVC).

As increasingly larger portions of Wittgenstein's manuscripts and typescripts from the 1930s were being made available, scholars began to realize that it was misguided to divide his philosophy into two essentially different periods and that the middle period did not simply involve a repudiation of the positions embraced in the *Tractatus* for the sake of the concepts outlined in the *Investigations*. More and more studies highlighted the continuity and dynamics of Wittgenstein's philosophical development.[4] Yet the major problem associated with the middle period of Wittgenstein's work is not related to the continuity/rupture dichotomy but to the challenge of resisting the temptation to view this period as a transition from the *Tractatus* to the *Investigations*, a passage envisaged as a conceptual conversion which had a clearly defined starting point and an equally clearly defined end. Of course, solving the Tractarian difficulties was indeed one of Wittgenstein's aims after his return to philosophy, which was natural enough since, resuming his systematic philosophical work, Wittgenstein needed something to start with – a point of reference from which to bounce off. At the same time, entirely new thematic concerns appeared in his thought, along with entirely new areas of interest, especially those associated with philosophy of mathematics, which did not necessarily lead straight to the *Investigations*. Wittgenstein's manuscripts from that time evidently imply that his thinking did not develop in a linear manner in the middle period, that thoughts did not follow neatly one upon another, that insights did not directly ensue one from another and that his ideas did not form a smoothly interlocking sequence. Wittgenstein's innumerable notes are a testament to ongoing, multidirectional explorations, experimentation and trial-and-error ventures. They form a tangled maze of thoughts, intuitions, allusions and sometimes profoundly personal remarks, where one would indeed be hard-pressed to identify points where discourse is crystallized. Wittgenstein probes multiple fields at the same time, with his discourse sprawling in several directions at once, as if radially; or, to use a chess metaphor, he plays a simultaneous exhibition on multiple boards. If anything, this is the signature characteristic of Wittgenstein's philosophy in this timeframe.

My book is designed to provide an overview of this radial sprouting of Wittgenstein's middle thought by addressing themes that exemplify sudden shifts in his standpoint and those that he did not develop along a consistently linear trajectory but interrupted abruptly or abandoned for some time only to revisit them in other contexts. My aim in doing this is to portray the wealth and diversity of Wittgenstein's enquiries, including those centred around worldview questions. This aim is to be furthered by a certain asymmetry of the themes I examine. While the first four chapters of this book focus on the problems resulting from the *Tractatus Logico-Philosophicus*, the following ones feature new threads in Wittgenstein's preoccupations. The volume consists of an introduction and eight essays. The Introduction seeks to clarify what I mean by the titular radial method of the middle Wittgenstein and how, if at all, the indisputable fact that the middle period in Wittgenstein's work was a transitional phase between the *Tractatus* and the *Investigations* can be reconciled with the notion that this period boasts an autonomy and distinctiveness of its own and should not be regarded merely as an attempt to overcome his early position or as a harbinger of his late one to come.

In Chapter 1, entitled 'The Phenomenological Turn', I discuss the idea of creating phenomenology and a phenomenological language, which Wittgenstein developed directly after returning to Cambridge in 1929. In all probability, he learned about Ernst Mach's version of phenomenology during discussions with the members of the Vienna Circle. However, he harnessed it to his own ends, which were related to the problems spawned by the *Tractatus*, primarily to the colour exclusion issue and thus to the very thesis of the independence of elementary propositions. Wittgenstein still upheld the idea that language could be delimited by establishing in what combinations words were meaningful and in which they were not. The problem of colours, which he tackled in 'Some Remarks on Logical Form' (1929), made him realize that the logical analysis of language was not a viable means to this end and that the logical analysis of phenomena themselves was needed instead. This prompted his idea of a phenomenological language, which was to be created as a perspicuous symbolism. Such a phenomenological language, one which would depict direct experience and steer clear of the ambiguities of ordinary language, quickly enough proved impossible to construct. As a result, Wittgenstein discarded the idea of crafting a phenomenological language and, with it, relinquished the belief that a perspicuous notation was fundamental to philosophy. Linguistic confusion could be dispelled without having to construct a new symbolism. How this actually could be achieved was the question that Wittgenstein would spend the coming years trying to answer, but throughout the period of developing phenomenology he would explicitly refer to grammar as a survey of the rules governing the use of language.

In Chapter 2, entitled 'Verification, 1929–31', I investigate Wittgenstein's views on verification. Initially, Wittgenstein talked about verification in the context of mathematical propositions and identified it with proof. This idea was cast in doubt when he began to perceive that language could function in many various ways. Nevertheless, verification more frequently surfaced in the context of phenomenology and phenomenological language, where it referred to immediate experience. My argument is that, from the very beginning, Wittgenstein leant toward a grammatical interpretation in his version of verificationism from 1929. Perhaps, for some time, he did not object to the interpretation endorsed by the members of the Vienna Circle, who linked verification to the empiricist theory of meaning, demarcation, protocol sentences and so on, but were not really interested in epistemological issues. Nevertheless, when Wittgenstein re-engaged in systematic philosophical practice and revisited the problems occasioned by the *Tractatus*, his thinking had already taken a different course than the ideas propounded by Schlick and his collaborators.

In Chapter 3, entitled 'Wittgenstein's Critique of Frege in the Notes from 1929 to 1932', I show that Wittgenstein's defence of formalism against Frege's criticism paved the way for the concept of language as a family of 'language games', which is known from the *Philosophical Investigations*. While this defence not always did justice to Frege's theories, it was not geared to determining once and for all who was right; rather, it sought to bring into relief the idea that served to convey the prescriptive (normative) quality of mathematical propositions. In his defence of formalism against Frege's objections, Wittgenstein continued some formalist reasoning of the *Tractatus*, notably standing by the general belief that in talking about propositions of mathematics, one should not step beyond the realm of signs and their use. In Wittgenstein's notes from 1929 to 1932, this belief is reasserted and honed in the formalist comparison of mathematics to a game where the notions of rules and use are accorded ultimate precedence.

Chapter 4, entitled '"A Clever Man Got Caught in "This" Net of Language!": Wittgenstein's Attack on Set Theory', discusses a relatively underexamined area of Wittgenstein's philosophy of mathematics, specifically, his critique of set theory. My account of this criticism is chiefly based on Wittgenstein's manuscripts and *The Big Typescript*. In relating Wittgenstein's ideas, I venture beyond my central timeframe to look into the second part of the *Remarks on the Foundations of Mathematics*, which elaborates on his earlier notions. I depict and assess Wittgenstein's objections against the theories of Dedekind and Cantor, such as the confounding of extensional and intensional contexts, the faulty definition of infinite set as infinite extension and the failings of Cantor's diagonal method. I also address the ideological aspect of Wittgenstein's critique as epitomized in his query: 'Where is Cantor's infinity $\aleph_0$ to be used?' The question, as it were, denounces the fashioning of such bold visions as transgressing the boundaries of what makes sense, of ordinary language use in a given 'language game' based on a set of shared rules and ways of life. The concepts of set theory produce a discourse that takes us beyond the horizon of the everyday, of the common, beyond the known and the familiar. Lured by this discourse, we cannot but abandon the realm of social practices and leave home and community, which entails breaking our bonds, losing our bearings and living in solitude.

Chapter 5, entitled '*The Big Typescript* as a Middle-Period Work', revolves around the middle Wittgenstein's intention to write a second book to follow the *Tractatus*. My major focus in these considerations is whether TS 213 can be viewed as a book project or whether it is only a somewhat ordered ensemble of resources, compiled to help Wittgenstein advance with his work. I trace the genesis of *The Big Typescript*, look into its structure and outline its axial preoccupations. The abundance of subjects and the extensive thematic compass of *The Big Typescript* defy any simple general categorization. Nonetheless, I believe that it is possible to identify an overarching idea that emerges in the early 1930s and permeates *The Big Typescript* as a whole. This idea, I argue, is the concept of language as a calculus, a game or a system of rules. Wittgenstein tended to use these terms interchangeably. Framing language in this manner was supposed to yield a perspicuous account of 'grammar', that is, of grammatical rules which determine the limits of sense, and to point out where and how language sets metaphysical traps for us.

Chapter 6, entitled 'PS: Understanding, Expecting, Wishing, Etc.', is a continuation of Chapter 5 that examines the psychological notions discussed by Wittgenstein in *The Big Typescript*. I consider these concepts pivotal because they arrestingly reflect the stage which Wittgenstein's philosophical thinking had reached by that time. On the one hand, he was prompted to explore them by his growing interest in concrete phenomena of everyday language and endeavoured to describe their grammar, and on the other, he analysed them within a general framework of the picture-conception of language promulgated in the *Tractatus*. In this chapter, I highlight the fact that the notions of understanding, thinking and meaning are stripped from their meta-logical quality in *The Big Typescript*, becoming just words as any other ones.

Wittgenstein's notes from the 1930s contain some remarks about the books he was reading at the time, specifically about two very particular volumes: Ernst Renan's *Histoire du peuple d'Israël* and James George Frazer's monumental *The Golden Bough*. In Chapter 7, entitled 'Magic, Rituals and Philosophy: Wittgenstein on Frazer's *The Golden Bough*', I depict and scrutinize Wittgenstein's critical insights concerning Frazer's study, along with their interpretations proposed by Frank Cioffi, Peter Hacker and Marco Brusotti. I also seek to establish what position these notes took in the development of Wittgenstein's philosophy and whether they left any lasting imprint on his later thought, beyond the notion of a 'perspicuous representation'. I argue that the relevance of 'Remarks on

Frazer's *Golden Bough*' primarily lies in articulating Wittgenstein's belief that the human world must be comprehended in its unique and autonomous fashion. This corresponds to Wittgenstein's anti-scientistic worldview, which forms an organic whole with his ideas of language and meaning.

Chapter 8, the last one in the book and entitled 'Wittgenstein as a Philosopher of Culture', glimpses beyond the timeframe of the middle period but takes as its starting point Wittgenstein's ideologically inflected notes from the 1930s, chiefly his drafts of prefaces to a future book, which are to be found among his other remarks. I argue that it was in this period that Wittgenstein's worldview was shaping up. I also address the existing interpretations of Wittgenstein as a philosopher of culture, primarily those offered by Stanley Cavell, and in the last part I propose an answer to Georg Henrik von Wright's question whether and, if so, to what extent Wittgenstein's ideas about language are conceptually interrelated.

This volume certainly neither provides a comprehensive interpretation of all the facets of the middle period in Wittgenstein's philosophical development nor encompasses all the issues that he pondered at that time. Rather, I treat Wittgenstein's writings from 1929 to 1936 as an expression of the multiple views he held over these years in the belief that the essence of this period can be better grasped by attending to particular questions. The essays that make up this book's consecutive chapters may be read separately since following my argument in any of them does not require having read any of the remaining ones. This having been said, only when read together do they substantially illumine Wittgenstein's notions between the *Tractatus* and the *Philosophical Investigations*. It is in this sense that the chapters form a certain whole.

Piotr Dehnel

Abbreviations

Ludwig Wittgenstein's works:

BB *The Blue and Brown Books* (Oxford: Blackwell, 1958).

BT *Big Typescript: TS 213*, German – English Scholars' Edition, edited and translated by C. Grand Luckhard and Maximilian A. E. Aue (Oxford: Blackwell, 2005).

CV *Culture and Value*, edited by G. H. von Wright. Revised edition of the text by A. Pichler. Translated by P. Winch (Oxford: Blackwell Publishing, 1998).

LCA *Lectures and Conversations on Aesthetics, Psychology, and Religious Belief*, edited by C. Berrett (Oxford: Basil Blackwell, 1967 [2007]).

LE 'A Lecture on Ethics'. *The Philosophical Review*, Vol. 74, No. 1, 1965.

LWL *Wittgenstein's Lectures, Cambridge 1930–32, from the Notes of John King and Desmond Lee*, edited by D. Lee (Oxford: Blackwell, 1980).

NB *Notebooks 1914–1916*, edited by G. H. von Wright and G. E. M. Anscombe (Oxford: Basil Blackwell, 1961).

PG *Philosophical Grammar*, edited by R. Rhees, translated by A. Kenny (Oxford: Basil Blackwell, 1974).

PI *Philosophical Investigations*. The German text, with an English translation by G. E. M. Anscombe, P.M.S. Hacker and J. Schulte. Revised 4th edition by P.M.S. Hacker and J. Schulte (Oxford: Wiley-Blackwell, 2011).

PR *Philosophical Remarks*, edited by R. Rhees (Oxford: Basil Blackwell, 1975).

RFM *Remarks on the Foundations of Mathematics*, edited by G. H. von Wright, R. Rhees and G. E. M. Anscombe, translated by G. E. M. Anscombe (Oxford: Basil Blackwell, 1967).

RGB   'Remarks on Frazer's *Golden Bough*'. In Ludwig Wittgenstein, *Philosophical Occasions 1912–1951*, edited by J. Klagge and A. Nordmann (Indianapolis & Cambridge: Hackett Publishing Company, 1993), pp. 115–56.

SLF   'Some Remarks on Logical Form'. In Ludwig Wittgenstein, *Philosophical Occasions 1912–1951*, edited by J. Klagge and A. Nordmann (Indianapolis & Cambridge: Hackett Publishing Company, 1993), pp. 28–36.

TLP   *Tractatus Logico-Philosophicus*, translated by D. F. Pears and B. F. McGuinness (London: Routledge & Kegan Paul, 1961).

WVC   *Wittgenstein and the Vienna Circle*, edited by B. McGuinness, translated J. Schulte and B. McGuinness (Oxford: Basil Blackwell, 1979).

Z   *Zettel*, 2nd edition, edited by G. E. M. Anscombe and G. H. von Wright, translated by G. E. M. Anscombe (Oxford: Basil Blackwell, 1967).

MS and TS: manuscripts and typescripts as classified by Georg Henrik von Wright. Cf. G. H. von Wright, *Wittgenstein* (Oxford: Basil Blackwell, 1982).

Introduction

The radial method of the middle Wittgenstein

As mentioned in the Preface, the major interpretive difficulty upon which one stumbles when studying the middle period in the development of Ludwig Wittgenstein's philosophy lies in attempting to present this period as a tolerably autonomous and separate whole and, at the same time, as a transition for the *Tractatus* to the *Philosophical Investigations*.[1] To reconcile these two perspectives is a genuine challenge to any author on the middle Wittgenstein who aspires not to treat the philosopher's post-1930 texts exclusively as a testimony to abandoning his earlier philosophical ideas and a harbinger of his mature thought and simultaneously seeks to identify moments that bespeak the transformation of his philosophy. Such an approach is predicated on establishing what it actually is that is distinctive to the middle Wittgenstein's writings on language, phenomenology, verification, the mathematical infinite and/or Frege's theory, as compared with the *Tractatus* period, and to his texts on grammar, philosophy and/or mental content in comparison with the *Investigations*. Whether we consider the years between 1929 and 1936 to be a transitional period or 'a phase in its own right', the identity of the middle Wittgenstein is invariably premised on the relation in which it stands to those of the early and late Wittgenstein.

Peter M.S. Hacker (Hacker 1986: 128–34), one of the most eminent researchers of Wittgenstein's philosophy, interprets the trajectory of his thought in the middle period as gradually passing from the concept of language as a calculus (*Kalkül*) to the concept of language as a family of 'language games' (*Sprachspiele*). In the *Tractatus*, Wittgenstein insisted that ordinary language had the structure of a formal calculus as a system of symbols, the use of which was governed by the rules of logical syntax. Understanding language as a calculus means being able to use this calculus, that is, to operate its signs, in the same way as, for example, putting down the result of multiplication involves an operation on signs. Thus, a proper account of the understanding of symbolism requires an appropriate depiction of the structure of the calculus. In Hacker's view, the comparison of language to a calculus was gradually losing its power in the 1930s as the very comparison called for an explanation. Such an explanation was becoming particularly urgent for the notion of following the rule, a key idea in the calculus vision of language. Wittgenstein began to explore this question in a range of contexts, which eventually resulted in replacing the concept of language as mutually interrelated propositional systems (*Satzsysteme*) with the concept of language as 'something used in speech or writing, in human activities which take place and have significance only against complex contexts of human forms of life and culture' (Hacker 1986: 132).

This account of the evolution of Wittgenstein's philosophy in the middle period seems to be on the mark if it is contemplated from a distance, that is, from the perspective of his mature philosophical stance. But if the angle is slightly changed so that PI does not eclipse the entire image and Wittgenstein's remarks are scrutinized from close-up, one unmistakeably notices that the ideas of language as a calculus from the TLP period and the middle period are certainly not the same thing[2] and that Wittgenstein tended to use the terms 'calculus' and 'game' interchangeably. As a matter of fact, he continued to do so even in the *Investigations*: 'In philosophy we often *compare* the use of words with games, calculi with fixed rules, but cannot say that someone who is using language *must* be playing such game' (PI, §81). Admittedly, further in this paragraph Wittgenstein delivers a statement which some interpreters[3] construe as evidence of the critique of the concept of language as a calculus:

> All this, however, can only appear in the right light when one has attained greater clarity about the concepts of understanding, meaning and thinking. For it will then also become clear what can lead us (and did lead me) to think that if anyone utters a sentence and *means* or *understands* it he is operating a calculus according to definite rules.
>
> (PI, §81)

However, the word 'calculus' may as well be replaced with 'game' in this context, as games – for example, chess – are known to be based on definite rules, too. Of course, it is not about words as such but about what they express. In Hacker's interpretation, the concept of language as a calculus is a concept of language as a system of rules that are codified without any reference to their applications and, as such, independently of how language is really used 'in speech or writing'. However, as shown by Andrew Lugg (Lugg 2013), Wittgenstein continued to approach language as a calculus in the *Investigations* as well. He depicted both calculi and games predominantly in terms of their underlying rules. In Lugg's view, the notion of calculus may be explained in terms of a game, and the notion of game – for example, chess, which was Wittgenstein's classic, go-to example in the 1930s – can be explained in terms of a calculus. This is very clear in BT 108, tellingly headlined as 'Mathematics Compared to a Game', where Wittgenstein ponders whether and, if so, to what extent comparing mathematics to chess makes sense. Amidst his reasoning, he states:

> Calling arithmetic a game is just as wrong as calling the movement of chess pieces (according to chess-rules) a game; for that can be a calculation too.
>
> So one ought to say: No, the word 'arithmetic' is not the name of a game. (of course once again this is trivial). – But the meaning of the word 'arithmetic' can be explained by the relationship of arithmetic to an arithmetical game, or also by relationship od chess problem to the game problem.
>
> But in doing so it is *essential* to recognize that this relationship is not of a tennis problem to the game of tennis.
>
> (BT, 534/5)

Whether and how Wittgenstein uses the terms 'calculus' and 'game' depend on the context. If he seeks to state, for example, that propositions of mathematics do not express any thought, that they are about nothing, he equates mathematics either with a game or with a calculus, without any difference: 'Because mathematics is a calculus and therefore is really about nothing, there isn't any metamathematics' (BT, 532). At the same time, he realizes that there are limits to such comparisons: 'If you want to say that mathematics is played like chess or patience, and the point of it is winning or going out, that is obviously incorrect' (BT, 531).

Lugg also does not endorse the idea that it was around the mid-1930s that Wittgenstein started talking about words and propositions as intertwined with their applications in everyday life. In any case, the account of language as a calculus does not deny its applicability. Again, BT comes in handy, as in chapters 112 and 114 Wittgenstein addresses the applicability of arithmetic (mathematics) and concludes that:

> At this point we can say: arithmetic is its own application. The calculus is its own application. In arithmetic we cannot make preparations for a grammatical application. For if arithmetic is only a game, its application too is only a game, and either the same game (in which case it takes us no further) or a different game – and in that case we were already able to lay it in *pure* arithmetic.
>
> (BT, 556)

In other words, the middle Wittgenstein does not sever the calculus from its application. Given this, it is not his idea that the application of a calculus in the grammar of real language imbues this calculus with a tangibility it did not have before: 'No, a calculation with applies is essentially the same as a calculation with lines or numbers' (BT, 555).

My point is not that this and other observations undermine the interpretation of the evolution of Wittgenstein's philosophy in the middle period as the dismissal of the concept of language as a calculus for the concept of language as a multiplicity of language games. I am not tempted to engage in 'passage-hunting', to use Hans-Johann Glock's coinage (Glock 1990: 152), and to comb Wittgenstein's texts for quotations that suitably corroborate a given interpretation. The truth is that, in the later period, Wittgenstein more frequently relied on the *comparison* of language to a game than to a calculus, and he also more frequently referred to the use of words in everyday language practice, treating this practice as intertwined with a form of life. Still, when examined from close-up, under the microscope as it were, Wittgenstein's statements do not seem to speak to a genuinely dramatic shift in his conceptions. Alois Pichler has recently shown that the fact that Wittgenstein often fell back on the calculus analogy in the early 1930s does not actually mean that he 'defend[ed] and promote[d] that analogy in ways that committed him to *holding* a calculus conception of language' (Pichler 2018: 45). Along with Joachim Schulte, David Stern and Mauro Engelmann, Pichler is one of the group of scholars who emphasize a certain autonomy and distinctiveness of Wittgenstein's middle philosophy.[4]

Among this group, Engelmann has presented what is perhaps the most comprehensive interpretation of this period in Wittgenstein's work (Engelmann 2013). In his view, the philosophy of the middle Wittgenstein should be conceived in terms of 'a constant struggle, as he adapts and overcomes old conceptions by means of newly invented tools and methods' (Engelmann 2013: 2). This struggle progresses in four major stages: phenomenology, grammar, the genetic method and the anthropological view. According to Engelmann, the aim of the *Tractatus* – that is, defining the limits of language and thinking – persisted until the composition of *The Big Typescript* in 1933 although the methods and tools for achieving this aim were evolving in the meantime. Early in 1929, Wittgenstein came to believe that the logical symbolism of the *Tractatus* would not suffice to attain the goal and consequently came up with the idea of crafting a phenomenological language. Still, at the end of the same year, he discarded the idea of phenomenological language as essentially faulty and proceeded to focus on grammar, which determines the limits of language and thinking.

At the end of 1930, his struggle with the pictorial conception of language and with Russel's causal theory of meaning pushed him in two directions: towards the genetic method, which first appeared in *The Blue Book*, and towards the idea of the autonomy of grammar grounded in the calculus conception of language. However, this concept alone was not enough to explain the origin of philosophical problems, in particular how 'the puzzles of philosophy' come into being in the first place. The genetic method was supposed to reveal which false steps (primarily, deceptive language analogies) make us pose philosophical questions. For its part, the notion of 'grammar' led to the conception of language as a calculus, which found its complementary idea in the genetic method designed to eliminate philosophical problems by establishing how they arise.

Wittgenstein's last step towards his late philosophical views involved dismissing the concept of language as a calculus and adopting an anthropological approach. Engelmann argues that by embracing this viewpoint Wittgenstein was able to resolve the tension between the genetic method, which called for philosophical neutrality, and the idea of 'grammar' as a set of rules for the use of language that makes sense, which was a philosophical concept only espoused in *The Big Typescript*. Finally, *The Brown Book* brought together the genetic method and the anthropological point of view, a unification that attained its final form in the first version of the *Philosophical Investigations in* 1937.[5] At the same time, Engelmann avers that '[i]t is only in this later stage that the major goal of the philosophy of the T is abandoned and a completely new philosophy is created' (Engelmann 2013: 2).

Engelmann's interpretation is very important as he is one of the few scholars to have attempted to grasp the specificity of Wittgenstein's middle philosophy with its hallmark of constant clashes between the old and new ideas and, at the same time, to explain how these frictions were implicated in the evolution of Wittgenstein's position from the *Tractatus* to the *Investigations*. Nevertheless, the latter inclination – that is, assessing the middle Wittgenstein from the perspective of his mature thought – prevails. Engelmann himself admits that his 'whole book might be seen as an introduction to the PI' (Engelmann 2013: 5). One ramification of this attitude is Engelmann's portrayal of Wittgenstein's path towards the *Investigations* as a series of philosophies that followed upon one another as discreet stages, each of them ensuing from essential changes in Wittgenstein's thinking. All the problems of such an interpretation (e.g. those related to the 'genetic method' to be discussed later) aside, this perspective inevitably deprives us of something meaningful. Specifically, if we treat Wittgenstein's writings from the 1930s as a journey to PI, we will fail to pay due attention to issues that his opus magnum left out, notably, the philosophy of mathematics, though it was the focus of a bulk of Wittgenstein's middle writings. This failure is patent in Engelmann's interpretation, which does not picture the philosophy of mathematics as an organic part of Wittgenstein's development. In this approach, remarks concerning the philosophy of mathematics are not recognized as a focal area in its own right and are relegated beyond the main developmental trajectory of Wittgenstein's philosophy, instead of being acknowledged as its integral part. We will not comprehend Wittgenstein's critique of set theory, which I discuss in Chapter 3, if we wrench his remarks on this issue from a broader context of considerations on language, meaning, grammar and ways of life. If these remarks are construed as assertions pertaining to a narrowly circumscribed field of the philosophy of mathematics, they may easily be misinterpreted and too hastily judged.

In interpreting the development of Wittgenstein's middle philosophy as a series of successive philosophies, we stumble upon yet another difficulty. Attempts at revealing a clear-cut evolutionary path in his thought between 1929 and 1936 will always collide with something that lies outside of this path and must be passed over, deliberately or inadvertently. Towards the end of 1929, Wittgenstein wrote that he was rejecting the idea of phenomenology, but he devoted a whole chapter to it in *The Big Typescript* in 1933. Admittedly, he stated at the very beginning that 'phenomenology is grammar', but this was also what he had already done in one of the first entries in early 1929: 'Thus phenomenology would be the grammar of the description of those facts on which physics builds its theories' (MS 105, 5; PR, 51). Wittgenstein returned to phenomenological grammar, framed as the grammar of expressions describing sense data, at the end of BB,[6] when he revisited the problem of solipsism and the grammar of words depicting mental actions: seeing, hearing and feeling. In doing this, he referred to the phenomenological notions of 'Euclidean space' and 'visual space', offering the same examples as in BT. Evidently, the ideas of phenomenology and phenomenological language that Wittgenstein entertained in early 1929 were neither completely discarded nor entirely replaced with new notions; rather, they underwent a transformation. Something – precisely speaking, the idea of phenomenological language – was relinquished while something else was continued in a new form, that of the grammar of expressions referring to sense data.

A similar process is visible in Wittgenstein's critique of Frege from the early 1930s. Its echoes – in fact, more than echoes, rather analogous formulations of its main insights – reverberate across his various writings, for example, in a chapter on 'Understanding' in BT and in BB. The opening of what has come to be called *The Pink Book* also refers to this criticism, but comments on Frege and signs on paper – saying that they are insignificant and that only their meaning matters – are woven into more general reflections on meaning and use.[7] Metaphorically speaking, these are individual thoughts and ideas that crop up here and there as single-coloured threads amidst the multicoloured texture of a thick fabric. In a way, the philosophy of middle Wittgenstein is a tangled knot of various motifs, ideas, thoughts, notions and concepts that refuse to neatly fall into place in a linear order and where novel insights do not oust older ones. For example, Pichler has convincingly argued that as early as in the first chapter of BT Wittgenstein criticizes the calculus concept of language and pits an anthropological conception of language against it. This would mean that these two frameworks were engaged in a dialectical discussion already from the early 1930s on. In Pichler's view, the calculation concept is not characteristic of the middle Wittgenstein, which runs counter to the common belief. Instead, the signature feature of this period is 'that he permits *the struggle between the calculus and the competing anthropological conception* (as well as other struggles) to emerge fully' (Pichler 2018: 59). Pichler rebuts the linear approach in which Wittgenstein's middle philosophy is envisaged as a series of successive steps – 'first a, then b' – on the way towards the *Investigations* and, instead, advocates a polyphonic approach, where 'while a and b are both present in Wittgenstein's thought, it is the weighting and rating which each receives that changes' (Pichler 2018: 59).

I share the latter viewpoint, because I similarly believe that Wittgenstein's philosophy did not evolve in a linear manner in the middle period. Some thoughts did not simply replace others, and his new ideas did not chase old ones away; rather, Wittgenstein's reasoning spread radially along various vectors at the same time. Wittgenstein developed his discourse simultaneously in multiple areas and in diverse directions. This can easily be discerned if we attempt to identify central notions typical of the 'middle Wittgenstein'. This is a very helpful method for capturing the core of a philosophical system, an epoch or an individual work. Whereas the central notions of the *Tractatus* and Wittgenstein's entire early philosophy legitimately include 'logical form', 'depiction', 'elementary proposition', 'internal relations' and 'logical syntax', and the corresponding central notions of the *Investigations* and Wittgenstein's later thought comprise 'language games', 'use', 'rules' and 'following the rule', 'perspicuous representation' and 'family resemblances', we would be hard-pressed to pinpoint equally characteristic and pivotal notions in the middle Wittgenstein.

What we could do instead would be pointing out his two major aspirations. One of them involved striving to solve the difficulties arising from the *Tractatus*, first and foremost, the problem of the independence of elementary propositions, as posed by Ramsey. The other enterprise centred on writing a new book, as implied by the drafts of prefaces and primarily by the typescript known as TS 213, that is, *The Big Typescript*, which will be discussed in detail in Chapter 5. Nevertheless, these general ventures on which Wittgenstein embarked headed in multiple directions. Wittgenstein's philosophical work in the middle period represents a maze of conceptual explorations, in which he tried out new solutions for old issues and faced up to new problems as they continued to emerge. This stream of thinking practically never stopped, but neither was it self-confident; it did not accumulate the truths at which it had arrived into a whole but abandoned them, instead, ever so often only to recapture them in other contexts. Some of the themes explored by Wittgenstein after his return to Cambridge can certainly be regarded as attempts at overcoming the challenges engendered by the *Tractatus*. This is the case, for example, with his project of phenomenology. However, to establish whether he quickly relinquished this project or perhaps continued it in a different form is far from straightforward, which I discuss in Chapter 1. It is also true that most notions characteristic of Wittgenstein's late philosophy were forged in this period, as exemplified by 'a perspicuous representation' (*die übersichtliche Darstellung*). Yet it is equally true that this term appeared among Wittgenstein's remarks on Frazer's *The Golden Bough* in 1931, when the philosopher's views were still very different from his position in the *Investigations*, and the notion itself did not refer to language or its grammatical rules. Without a doubt, the development of Wittgenstein's thought was also marked by a gradual change in his approach to language which may be associated with a particular moment. While this could serve us as the only clear clue indicating the path of Wittgenstein's thinking, it does not indisputably designate the onset of his late philosophy.[8] For better or worse, this moment is represented by Wittgenstein's eschewal of the project of creating a phenomenological language: 'We have to make do with our ordinary language and just understand it correctly' (MS 107, 176). Thus, Wittgenstein concludes, our everyday language – the forgotten source of sense, as it were – is the only thing with which we are left. From this moment on, he incrementally foregoes the abstract approach to language and begins to analyse particular phenomena in language and to describe the uses of some language expressions. Nevertheless, when Wittgenstein examines, in *The Big Typescript*, the use of words such as understanding, thinking, commanding, intending, wishing and/or expecting, he goes about it equipped within a general, *Tractatus*-like framework of the proposition (language) as a picture of reality: a command and its execution, a wish and its fulfilment, an intention and the pursuit of it. To him, language continues to be a picture of reality rather than a tool in human life, though this picture admittedly no longer reflects a logical form but itself casts a shadow on that which it is the picture of. A new thought seems to be sprouting, but it is not there yet.

I have dubbed the polyphonic quality of Wittgenstein's philosophy *the radial method*, which begs the question of what this method essentially consisted in. To answer this question, let me evoke Wittgenstein's first lecture in the academic year 1930/1931, when he talked about a fundamental change in philosophy, one comparable to the germination of chemistry from alchemy or to Galileo's discoveries.[9] While Wittgenstein equated this change with the invention of a new method, George Moore[10] observed that Wittgenstein had never explained what this method actually involved in his lectures. Instead, he offered some hints, saying:

> Such a remark as 'This is one of the most typical problems of philosophy' would be a hint. This remark may set you on the right track in solving a problem. But I could leave out all the hints and just treat special problems.... All you need to do is to observe what we do, which will be the same sort of thing each time.
> (Wittgenstein 2016: xlvi)

Wittgenstein's hints imply that his method lay not so much in solving philosophical problems, as rather in dissolving them through a meticulous analysis of the facts we know. At the same time, Wittgenstein declared: 'But I could leave out all the hints and just treat special problems.' Therefore, the gist of the middle Wittgenstein's radial method can be grasped by studying the way in which he approached the philosophical problems, and in the 1930s this way did not unfold in a natural and uninterrupted sequence of one thought segueing into another. It was no coincidence that Wittgenstein's notes addressed a panoply of topics from varied and remote fields that he tackled issues only tangentially, if at all, connected with each other and that his thoughts unfurled radially.

It is an utterly intriguing question how this radial expansion of Wittgenstein's ideas suddenly came to be channelled in one direction in the *Philosophical Investigations*. How did the polyphony of insights transfigure, as if in an abrupt leap, into a work which spins its thoughts in a naturally ordered sequence? A work, notably, which bears no resemblance, either in content or in form, to anything that Wittgenstein wrote in the 1930s. As already mentioned, having returned to Cambridge and philosophy, Wittgenstein planned to write his second book, but the road from intent to fruition was long and winding. His roadmap split into multiple paths, which intersected and spiralled into an intricate mesh of ideas, remarks and often entirely disconnected thoughts. With PI, we suddenly and rather unexpectedly find ourselves in a conceptual space whose structure Wittgenstein sketched out and presented in an admittedly loose form of an album, but leafing through this album one can appreciate its clear design. He professed in the 'Preface': 'Originally it was my intention to bring all this together in a book whose form I thought of differently at different times. But it seemed to me essential that in the book the thoughts should proceed from one subject to another in a natural, smooth sequence' (PI, 3). Never before had Wittgenstein managed to articulate his thoughts 'in a natural, smooth sequence'. Of course, this was not an instance of *creatio ex nihilo*. A few paragraphs later, Wittgenstein confessed that the publication of this work had been directly and, as it were, externally prompted by the realization that as his insights circulated among students, they tended to be misunderstood or distorted. What he had in mind was, in all probability, BB, which immediately preceded his work on the first version of the *Investigations* and which Rhees would furnish with the subtitle 'Preliminary Studies for the *Philosophical Investigations*'. If so, is it justified to talk about a 'sudden leap'? BB and the materials from the Skinner-Archive, which have recently been published by Gibson, certainly embody Wittgenstein's attempts at ordering and clearly channelling his thoughts, but I do not believe that they deserve to be treated, either content-wise or formally, as a prior step or stage from which the next one – that is, PI – straightforwardly ensues. Rather, to continue, the metaphor, they stand for a run-up to the leap.

The Brown Book – or, more precisely speaking, its first part (1934) – is the most consistently arranged and linear of these resources. It analyses examples of increasingly complicated language games; however, having begun working on the translation of *The Brown Book* into German, Wittgenstein soon stopped to deplore: 'Dieser ganze "Versuch einer Umarbeitung" von Seite 118 bis hierher ist *nichts wert*' ('This whole "attempt at a revision", from the start right up to this point, is *worthless*') (MS 115, 292). While various reasons have been cited for Wittgenstein abandoning the work on the German version of *The Brown Book* and denouncing the text as having no merit, the dominant position holds that it was not the matter of form or style alone, even though this is suggested by Wittgenstein's letter to Moore, saying that the author found the text 'boring &

artificial'.¹¹ Engelmann claims that in Wittgenstein's view *The Brown Book* was not underpinned by a proper method (i.e. the genetic method), one applied in MS 142:

> Wittgenstein does not talk about the right method, but about conveying a concept of his method. This is done in two different ways, both absent in the BrB and in the BrBG. *First*, by explicitly stating his method:
> > One of our most important tasks is to express all false trains of thought so true to character that the reader says, 'Yes that's exactly the way I meant it.' To trace the physiognomy of every error.
> > We can never bring someone away from a mistake unless he acknowledges this
> > expression as the correct expression of his feeling.
> > Only if he acknowledges it as such it is the right expression. (Psychoanalysis).
> > What the other acknowledges is the analogy that I'm presenting to him as the source of his thought (MS 142 (UF) §§121; TS 220 (FF), §106; TS 239 (BFF), §139).
>
> (Engelmann 2013: 209)

The problem is that the passage Engelmann quotes is dated on no other day than 29 June 1931 and was later incorporated into BT (see BT, 410), where Wittgenstein rounded it up with the last sentence, which is not to be found in the original version.¹² This implies that the genetic method was explicitly formulated as early as in 1931, rather than in the first version of PI from 1936 to 1937 (MS 142). If so, the genetic method could not possibly be used (though unnamed) for the first time in BB. Furthermore, this casts in doubt Engelmann's narrative of the middle Wittgenstein's philosophical thought developing in four major phases: phenomenology, grammar, the genetic method and the anthropological approach. Rather, all these perspectives overlapped and alternated without coalescing into any linear continuity. An impression of such a continuity only arises if Wittgenstein's notes produced in the 1930s are interpreted from the perspective of his mature stance. If this lens is applied, hurried ideas and provisional remarks are goaded into seeming familiar and well-grounded solutions to us. Still, even if we did look at *The Brown Book* in this way, we could not but realize how much it differed from PI. This was already pointed out by Rhees in his preface to the 1958 edition of BB, in which he called attention to one of the most fundamental dissimilarities. In *The Brown Book*, the depictions of various language games follow as stages in the reasoning aimed at grasping what language is. They are supposed to shed light on the relation between words and what they represent. In the *Investigations*, Wittgenstein is mainly interested in the concept of meaning that underlies such a manner of viewing language and that expresses a certain tendency causing philosophical puzzles to arise. Thus, the argument in the *Investigations* seeks to demonstrate in what way descriptions of 'language games' may help us explain what a philosophical problem is. What was 'boring & artificial' to Wittgenstein in *The Brown Book* can be deciphered as the sense of there being no natural connection between language issues and philosophy, no insight into how the use of some words generates so-called philosophical problems. For example, the use of the word 'meaning' as a name may lead to the philosophical conclusion that it denotes a certain 'object' in the mind. Briefly, Wittgenstein found himself disaffected with *The Brown Book*, because it did not present thoughts in their natural and uninterrupted sequence from object to object.[13] For quite a while, specifically from the dictation of the first part of *The Brown Book* in 1934 until the last attempt at correcting its German version in August 1936, Wittgenstein seemed pretty content with the effects of his work and even planned to have *The Brown Book* published.[14] However, he eventually deemed it 'worthless' and hence began to work on an entirely new project – the first version of the *Philosophical Investigations* (MS 142) – in November 1936. He no longer relied on *The Brown Book* as his fundamental resource, but instead used a collection of remarks from the early 1930s, that is, *The Big Typescript*,[15] even though he was mostly dissatisfied with its content. Does this mean that he entirely discarded the 'Versuch' text? By no means, and this is easily recognizable by the textual similarities between MS 142 and MS 115, but, as observed by Pichler (Pichler 2004: 139), the 'Versuch' text inspired Wittgenstein in a negative manner, that is, as something that must be relinquished. Thus, what I have dubbed a 'sudden leap' – the shift from a radial multitude to a natural and uninterrupted sequence – took place between August and November 1936. The fact that in order to effect this transition Wittgenstein deployed BT, which is a collection of notes drafted between 1929 and 1932, may be seen as confirming this conclusion, which does not in the least mean that TS 213, many remarks from which were transplanted into the *Investigations*, anticipated the position Wittgenstein assumed in this mature work. Wittgenstein's philosophical thought is rather associated with constant tension and dynamic change; nothing in it is a plain continuation or a simple revision of prior views. His thinking harbours a mystery.

1

The phenomenological turn

Upon his return to Cambridge in January 1929, Ludwig Wittgenstein resumed recording his ideas in a diary after a hiatus of ten years. His phenomenology-related notes were not widely known for a long time and only became more accessible when Rush Rhees published the typescript known as TS 209, that is, *Philosophische Bemerkungen*, in 1964. Wittgenstein used the collage method to piece together typescript TS 209 by cutting out and gluing in fragments of typescript TS 208 and adding handwritten notes to this assemblage of excerpts. TS 208 had been dictated on the basis of manuscripts produced in 1929–30 as a report on Wittgenstein's research pursuits up to that moment, which Wittgenstein had been requested to submit by Moore via Russel to have his research grant at Cambridge extended. Nonetheless, many scholars believe that *Philosophische Bemerkungen* edited by Rhees (i.e. TS 209) does not fully or adequately render the thematic content of Wittgenstein's manuscripts from the period.[1] Against the intentions of Wittgenstein himself, who did not consider TS 209 to be a complete book ready for printing, Rhees published the typescript in exactly that form and fitted it with a peculiar 'Foreword', sourced as a matter of fact from outside the corpus of *Philosophische Bemerkungen*. Another serious flaw of this publication lies in that it strays from the chronological order of TS 208, a deviation which is particularly glaring in remarks on phenomenology and causes a great deal of content- and theme-related confusion. One example is enough to illustrate this. At the very beginning of the *Philosophical Remarks*, the second note reads: 'I do not now have phenomenological language, or "primary language" as I used to call it, in mind as my goal. I no longer hold it to be necessary. All that is possible and necessary is to separate what is essential from what is inessential in our language' (PR, 1). In the manuscripts, this insight is recorded under 25 November 1929 (MS 107, 205), whereas Wittgenstein embarked on his phenomenological project in February 1929, and most of his notes on this subject, which were passed over in TS 209, come from the period between February and October 1929. Yet some later notes from the time after the dropping of the phenomenological project were included in the *Remarks*, towards the end of the book, where, among others, a note made on 26 December 1929 (MS 107, 40) is to be found. Similar examples abound.

While acknowledging Rhees's editorial merits, we must remember that the *Philosophical Remarks* does not offer a sufficient and comprehensive source of Wittgenstein's views from the middle period of his philosophical development. If any analysis of the textual legacy of this period should first and foremost be grounded in the manuscripts and typescripts that add up to what is known as *Nachlass*, this is a sine qua non for the study of Wittgenstein's phenomenology.

Admittedly, some papers exploring Wittgenstein's philosophy in the context of phenomenology had appeared before PR was released, but they had only concerned general questions and mostly referred to the *Tractatus* and the *Philosophical Investigations*, Wittgenstein's two works widely known at that time. One of these studies compared the conceptions of philosophy and philosophical method in Wittgenstein and Husserl.[2] In another, Thomas W. Munson, who searched for mediation points between continental and analytic philosophies, labelled Wittgenstein's philosophy as phenomenology, or, more precisely speaking, called his approach to meaning phenomenological. In Munson's view, this approach was founded on Wittgenstein's rejection of both the interpretation of meaning as a mental entity and the possibility of grasping it through examining the formalized relations between the sign and the signified. Consequently, the only adequate solution to the problem of meaning was by describing the actual use of words in everyday language practice.

For understandable reasons, neither of the papers referred to Wittgenstein's phenomenological passages registered in 1929–30 or addressed his proper phenomenology. The publication of PR radically redirected research into this issue. Four years after the publication of PR, Herbert Spiegelberg wrote 'The Puzzle of Wittgenstein's Phänomenologie (1929–?)',[3] a paper devoted to *Philosophische Bemerkungen*. Spiegelberg, a student of phenomenologist Alexander Pfänder, was acquainted with Husserl and had contact with other members of the phenomenological movement. In his study, Spiegelberg asked six questions about Wittgenstein's phenomenology, which have lost none of their relevance and kept as a matter of fact not very numerous group of dedicated scholars intrigued and busy ever since.[4] Spiegelberg's questions are:

> 1.What did Wittgenstein really mean by 'Phänomenologie'? 2. When did he adopt it? For what reasons? What were his relations to the Phenomenological

Movement of the time? 3. How far did he abandon this *Phänomenologie*? When? For what reasons? 4. What was its role in Wittgenstein's development? 5. What is its philosophical merit? 6. What is its significance for other phenomenologists?

(Spiegelberg 1968: 244)

Spiegelberg sought to answer all these questions in his paper, but as he had no access to copious but yet-unpublished resources (both manuscripts and typescripts), his investigations could not but be fragmentary. This notwithstanding, his study has proven impactful on later research.

My argument below focuses on the genesis and essence of Wittgenstein's phenomenology and the ways it affected his later philosophy, which corresponds to the initial four questions posed by Spiegelberg. Despite some progress in research, certain facets of these issues still remain underexamined. As a caveat, I do not venture into the relations between Wittgenstein on the one hand and Husserl and other phenomenological philosophers on the other, because this would require a separate study of its own and a more systematic approach.[5]

1. The genesis of Wittgensteinian phenomenology

Establishing what Wittgenstein meant by phenomenology is premised on understanding its origin. The major question is where he actually took the very notion from, given that it did not have a wide currency in the prevalent philosophical language in England in his day. An apparently obvious answer would be that Wittgenstein was inspired by the writings of Edmund Husserl and/or other members of the phenomenological movement.[6] This theory would be corroborated by the fact that Husserl's name was mentioned in a conversation between Schlick and Wittgenstein in December 1930. Schlick asked: 'What answer can one give to a philosopher [Husserl] who believes that the statements of phenomenology are synthetic *a priori* judgements?' (WVC, 67). Wittgenstein replied:

> Now suppose the statement 'An object cannot be both red and green' were a synthetic judgement and the word 'cannot' meant logical impossibility. Since a proposition is the negation of its negation, there must also exist the proposition 'An object can be red and green.' This proposition would also be synthetic. As a synthetic proposition it has sense, and this means that the state of things represented by it *can obtain*. If 'cannot' means *logical* impossibility, we therefore reach the consequence that the impossible *is* possible.

Here there remained only one way out for Husserl – to declare that there was a third possibility. To that I would reply that it is indeed possible to make up words, but I cannot associate a thought with them.

(WVC, 67–8)

This conversation about Husserl has prompted deliberations on whether Wittgenstein knew and/or had read his *Logische Untersuchungen*, which Schlick referenced during the talk. Regrettably, no reliable proof of this has been found so far. Nowhere in his notes does Wittgenstein mention the name of the founder of phenomenology. Spiegelberg, who researched this issue, cites an exchange John N. Findlay's had with Wittgenstein in 1939, in which Findlay said that he was working on a translation of *Logische Untersuchungen*, and, in response, Wittgenstein reportedly 'expressed some astonishment that he was still interested in this old text' (Spiegelberg 1968: 247). This circumstantial evidence is too meagre to convincingly imply that Husserl formatively affected Wittgenstein's understanding of phenomenology. As no such impact is corroborated by the *Nachlass*, it is quite implausible that Husserl's phenomenology was Wittgenstein's inspiration.

Spiegelberg posits in his paper that Wittgenstein's phenomenology could stem from Rudolf Carnap's *Der Logische Aufbau der Welt* (1928).[7] When living in Buchenbach in the vicinity of Freiburg between 1922 and 1925, Carnap attended Husserl's seminar and was deeply impressed, though apparently not so much by what Husserl taught as by his personality and committed manner of philosophizing. Carnap's *Der Logische Aufbau der Welt* features five references to the *Logical Investigations* and *Ideas*. Although Carnap forged his own notion of phenomenology and identified it with a 'theory of objects', wherein he often used the terms *die Phänomenologie* and *die Gegenstandstheorie* interchangeably, he shared with Husserl the evocation of basic experiences (*Erlebnisse*) in the analysis of the content of consciousness and the constitution of the object. For example, Carnap envisaged a phenomenology of the humanities that aimed to establish what mental processes (experiences) constituted so-called primary cultural objects and a phenomenology of values that explored the properties of elementary value experiences of the different types of values.[8] Spiegelberg, who is aware that talking about 'influences' of other thinkers is highly problematic in the case of Wittgenstein, is rather inclined to conclude that phenomenological themes and their conceptualization were part of the scholarly atmosphere of Vienna in the 1920s and that this atmosphere could have affected Wittgenstein's thought.[9] Still, even such an indirect and mediated influence of Carnap on Wittgenstein seems little probable, given the utterly different temperaments of the two thinkers.[10] This aside, there is no textual evidence whatsoever to support Carnap's impact on Wittgenstein.

On the whole, Spiegelberg appears to be right when supposing that Wittgenstein had come in touch with the phenomenological approach before he arrived in England. However, his mind was swayed to embark on the phenomenological trajectory by discussions in Schlick's seminars, whose themes included the relation between mathematical constructs in the form of physical theories and sense data, rather than by the Vienna Circle's debates on Carnap's project in the winter of 1925 or the publication of *The Logical Structure of the World* three years later. Regarding the former, Schlick and the other members of the Vienna Circle tended to follow Ernst Mach, who applied the phenomenological framework to physics.[11] In Mach's view, the senses were the only source of the legitimate description of physical phenomena, and all abstract terms should be reduced to sensory experience. However, Wittgenstein was an attentive reader of *Die Prinzipien der Mechanik* by Heinrich Hertz and approached the relation between the empirical and a priori elements of theory in his spirit. Hertz clearly distinguished the external structure of mathematical models of mechanical phenomena from their applicability in experience, that is, from the extent to which they could be used to describe the world perceived in the daily observation of phenomena. In Mach's view, sense data (i.e. impressions) set the external boundary of a physical theory. Whatever could not be conveyed in the language of impressions (phenomenological language) was not suitable for describing the empirical world. According to Hertz, the boundaries of a theory were internal boundaries, meaning that a theory as a set of possibilities charted uncrossable limits within which physical phenomena and processes could take place. Importantly, Wittgenstein is known to have studied Ludwig Boltzmann's *Populäre Schriften*, one chapter of which dealt with the recent developments in theoretical physics, including Mach's concepts.[12] Boltzmann's discussion of Mach's ideas was fair, albeit critical, and he often used the term 'phenomenology' in this context. Following Hertz (and Boltzmann), Wittgenstein claimed that no system of formal laws – understood as a system of possibilities in a 'logical space', a 'way of presentation', a 'symbolism' or simply a 'language' – could be converted into an empirical description of the world by virtue of its own rules (cf. TLP, 6.342). Nevertheless, the members of the Vienna Circle did not consider Mach's programme and the *Tractatus* philosophy to be materially incompatible. In their view, Wittgenstein's work availed itself of the symbolism of the *Principia Mathematica* to provide logical foundations of the positivist theory of knowledge, mainly in the form of logical atomism theory. For its part, Mach's theory fleshed out the formal skeleton of empiricism with content by equating 'atomic facts' with impressions. As a result, 'elementary propositions' from the *Tractatus* morphed into *protocol sentences* ostensively linked to the content of our sense impressions. Wittgenstein's phenomenological – or primary – language may partly at least be understood as an attempt at taking a position on the immediate description of phenomena, one that refers to sensory perceptions.

To sum up, the sources of Wittgenstein's phenomenology of 1929 elude any straightforward identification, and if we were to point out any, we should in my view pick Mach's phenomenology. As a matter of fact, Mach's name appears time and again in Wittgenstein's notes and, to boot, in the context of phenomenological considerations on visual space and possibilities of describing it. This indicates that Wittgenstein was familiar with the term and notion of phenomenology as they appeared in Mach's and Boltzmann's writings. Still, as will be seen, Wittgenstein re-cast it in ways prompted by the problems resulting from the *Tractatus*.

2. Phenomenology: 1929–9

What then did Wittgenstein mean by 'phenomenology', and what place did it take in his intellectual development? As early as in his first remarks noted down after the return to Cambridge, Wittgenstein observed:

> There is a lot to suggest that the representation of visual space (*Gesichtsraum*) by physics is indeed the simplest one. This means that physics would be real phenomenology. An objection to this, however, would be that physics strives after truth, that is, correct predictions of events, whereas phenomenology does not do *that*. It strives after *sense* not *truth*.
>
> It can be said: physics has a language and formulates propositions in this language. These propositions may be true or false. They constitute physics and grammar or phenomenology.
>
> (whatever we call it)
>
> Physics differs from phenomenology in that it is concerned to establish laws. Phenomenology only establishes possibilities. Thus phenomenology would be the grammar of the description of those facts on which physics builds its theories.
>
> To explain is more than to describe. But every explanation contains a description.
>
> (MS 105, 1–9; PR, 51)

The juxtaposition of physics and phenomenology can suggest that the latter concerns a more elementary level of description, that is, immediate sensory experience, and in this sense forms the basis of physics. However, the passage first of all highlights the difference between the two disciplines. While truth is the realm of physics, sense is the domain of phenomenology; the former seeks to formulate laws, and the latter only identifies possibilities. This begs a fundamental question: What is it that phenomenology aspires to capture the sense of – phenomena as such or their language representations? The equating of phenomenology with grammar seeks to immediately settle this: phenomenology is defined as the grammar of the description of the facts on the basis of which physics constructs its theories. Besides, knowing how Wittgenstein understood the sense of a proposition in the *Tractatus,* we can assume that phenomenology demarcates the sphere of possibilities within which propositions can be either true or false (i.e. bipolar). This is the reason why Wittgenstein insisted that phenomenology pursued sense rather than truth. Hence, phenomenology was in his view identical with logical syntax or grammar, and not with the description of direct sensory experience, itself conceived as self-evident and intrinsically true. This notion is substantiated by Wittgenstein's profoundly Tractarian question: 'What is the general form of spatial statements (*der räumlichen Aussagen*)?' (MS 105, 11). This is only followed by some suggestions:

> It seems to me that a specific property of spatial statements is that space apparently cannot be described without a reference to time. For example, I can say 'I see a red circle on a blue background now.' It is a proposition. But I cannot say: 'a red circle [is on] a blue background.'
>
> Basically, it is probable from the beginning that time cannot (additionally) enter into the description of visual space as an embellishment. ...
>
> Colours are similar in this respect.
>
> Colours and space interpenetrate.
>
> The way in which they interpenetrate produces a visual field (*Gesichtsfeld*).
>
> (MS 105, 11–13)

These remarks imply that phenomenology would also deal with the description of what Wittgenstein referred to as the visual field. This seems to confirm his idea of constructing a phenomenological language which was supposed to be 'the description of immediate sense perception', as he later put it in *The Big Typescript*.[13] Wittgenstein first mentions such a language in a note which probably dates back to mid-June 1929:

> Phenomenological language describes exactly the same thing as ordinary, physical language. It must only limit itself to what is verifiable.

Is it at all possible?

We must not forget that physical language also only describes the primary world, and not, for example, a hypothetical world. Hypothesis is only a supposition concerning the practical (right) manner of presentation.

(MS 106, 108–10)

The dating of this remark is important insofar as it suggests that the idea of phenomenological language was related to the problem of the mutual exclusion of colour propositions raised by Frank Ramsey in his review of the *Tractatus*.[14] Wittgenstein addressed this problem in his paper 'Some Remarks on Logical Form'. Generally speaking, the point was that if the proposition 'A is red and A is blue' was a contradiction, both parts of this conjunction – that is, 'A is red' and 'A is blue' – could not be elementary propositions because, as the *Tractatus* had it, these propositions were mutually independent and the conjunction of two elementary propositions could not be a contradiction. This conclusion was highly troublesome, because what other propositions, if not those having the logical form of 'A is x', were to be the elementary propositions? If we realize that a similar problem pertains to all the elementary propositions that ascribe specific properties to an object, it would be difficult to imagine how the ascription of such properties could be reconciled with attributing other properties to this object at the same place and time. Evidently, the problem was indeed serious. It could be solved in two ways. One way was to consider propositions such as 'A is red' not to be elementary propositions and to be breakable into even simpler propositions meeting the condition of logical independence, and consider 'red' and 'blue' not to be the names of simple objects (assuming they are objects). The other way was to reject the entire conception of the independence of the elementary propositions along with the principle of extensionality, both of which were fundamental notions of the *Tractatus*. Wittgenstein was first inclined to espouse the former option, but he eventually dropped it as faulty, possibly under Ramsey's influence. This did not mean that he embraced the latter solution, entailing the negation of the central tenets of the *Tractatus*, which was understandably difficult to its author. In 'Some Remarks on Logical Form', Wittgenstein advanced another argument which involved modifying the rules of logical grammar governing logical conjunctions. He stated that whereas the elementary propositions could not be mutually contradictory, they could be mutually exclusive. 'A is red' does not contradict 'A is green', but the two statements exclude each other, that is, they want to attribute colours red and green to an object at the same place and time, while there is only 'room' for one colour. The function that asserts the existence of something at a given place and time leaves room for one entity only. This exclusion of colours takes place at the level of the elementary propositions and regrettably cannot be eliminated through logical analysis. At the same time, this means that the rules of logical syntax cannot not be derived from an analysis of the propositions of ordinary language. These rules ought to be established so as to preclude such difficulties through eliminating certain T and F constructions, which should be effected in the ultimate phenomenological analysis – a posteriori, as it were. Although Wittgenstein did not refer to phenomenological language as such in 'Some Remarks' at all, this was exactly the language he meant: one free from the difficulties of colour exclusion. Such a language would not permit constructions such as 'A is red and A is green', because they would be precluded by the syntax (grammar) of phenomenological language in the same way that syntax (grammar) does not allow responding 'It is twenty-three degrees Celsius, but it is not twenty-five degrees Celsius' to the question 'What temperature is it outside?' and the way we answer the question 'What time is it?' without adding what time it is not.

A phenomenological analysis should make us realize that the structure of the elementary propositions cannot be predicted in advance, which is what our everyday language encourages us to do by its subject–predicate and relational forms. The fact that these forms exist must not make us draw conclusions about the real logical form of the facts being described. Propositions such as 'This book is boring', 'God exists', 'It'll rain tomorrow', '2 + 2 = 4', etc. have nothing in common, but they are all subject–predicate sentences which ostensibly share the same form. In reality, however, 'we project in *ever so many different* ways *ever so many different* logical forms' into our language (SLF, 30–1). To adequately describe these forms requires a logical analysis of the phenomena themselves and thus a phenomenological (or primary) language (*primäre Sprache*), rather than an analysis of forms encountered in our ordinary or secondary language (*sekundäre Sparche*). In 'Some Remarks on Logical Form', Wittgenstein maintained the view, which he had earlier expressed in the *Tractatus*, that it was possible to represent reality adequately, but he remodelled the way of achieving this goal. The account of the logical structure of reality was no longer produced on the basis of a priori enquiries, but on the basis of immediate experience and in relation to phenomena themselves, which were described in a phenomenological language. This analysis gave precedence to the *content* of propositions and foregrounded the fact that if the logical value of some propositions determined the logical value of other propositions or, which was basically one and the same thing, that it depended on the content of the proposition, this meant that the elementary propositions rather belonged to a certain *propositional system*, which was to be compared with reality as a whole.

It can thus be posited at this point that the idea of phenomenological language, albeit not the notion of it as such, germinated when Wittgenstein attempted to solve the colour exclusion problem in 'Some Remarks on Logical Form'. Engelmann approaches this issue in a similar manner[15] and argues that, in 1929, Wittgenstein still believed that it was possible to give the limits of language by means of new rules defining in what combinations words had sense and thus preventing the formulation of nonsensical propositions. However, these rules could not be established through a logical analysis of language, as the colour exclusion problem made clear; rather, this required 'the logical investigation of the phenomena themselves, *i.e.*, in a certain sense *a posteriori*, and not by conjecturing about *a priori* possibilities' (SLF, 30). Like in the *Tractatus*, the aim thus was to replace a wrong symbolism with a right one. In Wittgenstein's view, this could be accomplished by exploring phenomena and striving to understand their logical multiplicity. In Engelmann's interpretation, which basically seems sound to me, this was the goal Wittgenstein pursued in 1929. The idea of constructing a phenomenological language represented an endeavour to attain this goal, that is, to create such a lucid symbolism.

Initially, Wittgenstein did not define this language explicitly; instead, he contrasted it with ordinary language. His phenomenological language was supposed to be primary language differing from everyday, physical language, which was sometimes referred to as secondary language,[16] in that phenomenological language concerned immediate sense perceptions and was formed by phenomena themselves. Such a language would help avoid contradictions and ambiguities of ordinary language, which had sprawled into a complex and intricate structure barring us from things themselves as a result of, among other reasons, assimilating scientific concepts and categories. Phenomenological language was envisaged as logically correct and thus adequately reflecting the logical structure of phenomena.[17] Briefly, phenomenological language was supposed to be a language of phenomena themselves, one describing our immediate sense perceptions without using notions proper to ordinary, physical language. In *The Big Typescript*, Wittgenstein succinctly defined phenomenological language as 'the description of immediate sense perception, without hypothetical addition' (BT, 491). According to Engelmann, this definition lends itself to two interpretations. First, 'description' may denote the description of states of affairs (external properties), which can be either true or false, for example, 'a red spot is situated left to a blue spot'. Second, 'description' may mean the description of forms (internal properties), that is, a depiction of rules concerning space, colour and time, which are implicitly contained in the phenomena, for example, 'visual space has absolute direction'. Both these meanings of 'description' appeared in the *Tractatus*, and this is where Engelmann derives them from. He suggests that the former meaning of 'description' (the description of external properties) refers to phenomenological language solely in the sense that the description of immediate sense perception should be performed in the phenomenological language which is verifiable, that is, which *indicates* what is possible and hints at what belongs to the latter kind of description, which *delimits* possibilities. In Wittgenstein's framework, phenomenological language was supposed to be the latter kind of description, that is to say, a presentation of rules concerning the forms of space, time and colour captured in the analysis of phenomena themselves. In Engelmann's view, Wittgenstein's phenomenological language would be a description in which the general form of propositions would be a description.[18] Such a description should *show* in its symbolism that colour exclusions are eliminated from language as nonsense and that 'A is not blue' results from 'A is red'. This showing should be understood in the same sense in which truth-tables show relations between propositions, propositions *fa* and *ga* show that they are both about the same object (TLP, 4.1211) and a map shows spatial relationships.[19] My interpretation is somewhat different. Phenomenological language, defined by Wittgenstein as the description of immediate experience, cannot possibly be a description of rules. To describe rules concerning visual space was the goal of phenomenology as grammar, of which phenomenological language – that is, the language of phenomena themselves – was a realization. Briefly, phenomenology was to set the limits within which talking of visual space had sense and to determine the coordinates of space, time and colour for such speech, while phenomenological language was this speech itself. The propositions of this language would not belong to grammar (phenomenology) but would be empirical because, as Wittgenstein emphasized, they were supposed to be verifiable. Thus, phenomenological language was not the language of phenomenology itself, but the language of phenomena as such.

To briefly recapitulate our insights, phenomenology was supposed to describe the conditions of possibility of talking with sense about visual space. As such, it would thus be the description of possible, rather than actual, sense perceptions. The *Tractatus* propounded the language of logic as a language of the description of reality, with the notions of function and argument providing the basic coordinates of this description. It turned out, however, that this language did not encompass certain propositions, which was made clear by the colour exclusion problem. Hence, Wittgenstein was searching for another language in

1929. He was committed to developing a phenomenological language whose coordinate system was made up of the notions of space, time and colour and which could establish the limits of talking about the world of phenomena with sense. For example, such talking with sense presupposed that absolute directions (i.e. directions independent of the observer) were external (logical) properties of the visual field, which meant that one could not imagine visual space devoid of directions. Given all this, Wittgenstein's phenomenological project was somewhat Kantian since phenomenology was supposed to investigate the conditions of possibility of using the expressions that described visual space with sense.

Phenomenological notes elude any univocal interpretation and represent mental explorations rather than conclusions. Descriptions of phenomena themselves intermingle with descriptions of the grammar of expressions referring to visual space in Wittgenstein's phenomenological discourse. To give one example (which will be revisited later), when Wittgenstein ponders the imprecision, or immeasurability, of our visual field, he states that we see a hundred-sided polygon as a circle and only on closer scrutiny, possibly using optical tools, do we perceive the sides of the figure. This can be said to be an empirical description of real perception rather than a description of expressions related to perception. However, Wittgenstein remarks at the same time that we cannot basically convey this 'imprecision' otherwise than by falling back on the appearance/reality distinction, which is specific to our ordinary (physical) language and goes beyond perception itself. A correct description would require a language in which 'imprecision is rendered by imprecision' (MS 107, 162). The proposition 'a hundred-sided polygon is seen as a circle' is a description of immediate sensory perception, one which a priori presupposes the division into appearance and reality.

3. Phenomenological language vs. ordinary language

In 1929, Wittgenstein devoted a considerable part of his notes to explicating the difference between phenomenological language and ordinary language in an effort to highlight how unsuitable our everyday language was to describe immediate experience:

> The worst philosophical errors always arise when we try to apply our ordinary – physical – language in the area of immediately given.
> If, for instance, you ask, 'Does the box still exist when I'm not looking at it?', the only right answer would be 'Of course, unless someone has taken it away or

destroyed it'. Naturally, a philosopher would be dissatisfied with this answer, but it would quite rightly reduce his way of formulating the question *ad absurdum*.

All our forms of speech are taken from ordinary, physical language and cannot be used in epistemology or phenomenology without casting a distorting light on their object.

The very expression 'I can perceive x' is itself taken from the idiom of physics, and x ought to be a physical object – e.g. a body – here. Things have already gone wrong if this expression is used in phenomenology, where x must refer to a datum. For then 'I' and 'perceive' also cannot have their previous senses.

(MS 107, 160–1; PR, 88)

Mach's depiction of the visual field included in his *The Analysis of Sensations* stood for Wittgenstein as an interesting case of blending physical language with phenomenological language:

What sense does it make to say: our visual field is less clear at the edges than towards the middle? That is, if we aren't here talking about the fact that we see *physical objects* more clearly in the middle of the visual filed. One of the clearest examples of the confusion between physical and phenomenological language is the picture Mach made of his visual field, in which the so-called blurredness of the figures near the edge of the visual field was reproduced by a blurredness (in a quite different sense) in the drawing. No, you can't make a visual picture of our visual image.

(MS 108, 40; PR, 267)

Wittgenstein points out that Mach committed a categorial error.[20] The vagueness of objects in one's visual field and the vagueness of objects represented in a picture are two entirely different things. The former is simply the way in which the real world is given to us, and this way cannot be any different, which means that one cannot see objects situated at the edge of one's visual field clearly and those at the centre as blurred. Yet the vagueness of the image in the picture can always be changed: hazy objects can be sketched as more clear-cut, and those sharply drawn as fading. Besides, our perception always takes place from a certain perspective within which other possible perspectives cannot be included.

Another categorial mistake recognized by Wittgenstein involves mingling the present of immediate experience with the 'present' of its description in physical language. Language unfolds in time, but our immediate experience of the world lies outside of time:

The present we are talking about here [the present of experience] is not a picture of the film strip that is right now placed in the lens of the lamp, as opposed to pictures before and after it, those that have not been there yet or those that have already been there, but a picture on the screen which is wrongly called present, because the word 'present' is used here not in relation to 'past' and 'future'. Consequently, it is an adjective without meaning.

(MS 107, 4)

Wittgenstein neither confirms nor negates the assertion that phenomena unfold in time, but he considers such a statement to be a piece of nonsense. This begs the question how language, which proceeds in time, can describe something that is beyond time, such as phenomena. Of course, Wittgenstein does not endorse the complete incommensurability of the world and its representation in language, but he doubts in the capacity of our ordinary language to adequately present immediate experience. We believe that we can describe such direct perceptions in this language, just like Mach thought he was drawing what he saw. Yet, in fact, this is where we arrive at the limits of language or even cross them: 'That which is immediate finds itself in constant flow. (It has indeed the form of a stream). It is quite clear that if one wants to say something ultimate here, one reaches the limit of language which expresses it' (MS 107, 159).

Wittgenstein's notes frequently rely on film metaphors and analogies. Wittgenstein likened the world of our everyday experience – the world of physics, as he called it – to the images on (or, rather, frames of) a film reel and immediate sense perceptions to images on the screen. Phenomenology was supposed to deal with the latter, while the former constituted the domain of physics: 'If I compare the facts of immediate experience with the pictures on the screen and the facts of physics with the film strip, on the film strip there is a present picture and past and future pictures. But on the screen, there is only the present' (MS 105, 85; PR, 83). When discussing visual space and attempts at rendering it in our ordinary language, Wittgenstein also observed that this language imposed references to the subject on us, whereas, in his view, space was not anyone's possession:

Visual space has essentially no owner.

Let's assume that, with all others, I can always see one particular object in visual space – viz my nose. Someone else naturally doesn't see this object in the same way. Doesn't that mean, then, that the visual space I'm talking about belongs to me? And so is subjective? No. It has only been construed subjectively here, and an objective space opposed to it, which is, however, only a construction with visual space as its basis. In the – secondary – language of 'objective' – physical – space, visual space is called subjective, or rather, whatever in this language corresponded directly with visual space is called subjective. ...

> The essential thing is that the representation of visual space is the representation of an object and contains no suggestion of a subject.
>
> (MS 106, 124–6; PR, 100)

To Wittgenstein, phenomenological language and ordinary (physical) language were two manners of expression concerning visual space. In phenomenological language, the subject is, so to speak, bracketed off in order to show what is visible without referencing the seeing subject. Wittgenstein was interested in visual space as such, rather than in solipsistically, or privately, understood visual space.

> Visual space, the way it is, has a reality of its own.
> It does not contain any subject. It is autonomous.
> It can be directly described (but we are far from knowing the way of expression to describe it). Ordinary, physical language refers to it in a *very* complicated manner which is instinctively known to us. ...
> Or it is like this: Our ordinary language is also phenomenological, only that it does not make it possible to intelligibly separate sensory fields with all their multiplicity, which is its multiplicity.
> Its space is a space comprising sight, gustatory and tactile impressions, and hence I can 'turn' in this space and look at 'what is going on with me,' etc.
> Even the word 'visual space' is unsuitable for our purposes, since it contains an allusion to a sense organ .... If, now, phenomenological language isolates visual space and what goes on in it from everything else, how does it treat time? Is the time of 'visual' phenomena the time of our ordinary idioms of physics?
>
> (MS 107, 1–4; PR, 103)

Wittgenstein's subject-less point of view is entirely justified if phenomenological language was supposed to concern phenomena alone. In this respect, it was not a psychological language. Since Wittgenstein was not in the least interested in sensory perception as an internal, consciousness-related process, he discarded all references to the subject and his/her sensations. His phenomenology was designed to give the limits of talking about visual space with sense and to describe the grammar of expressions referring to immediate sense perceptions.

3.1. A farewell to phenomenological language

When discussing the difference between phenomenological and ordinary language, it must have been felt how difficult it would be to create a system of representation (a notation) capable of conveying the atemporality, imprecision and fluidity of sense perceptions. This indeed proved challenging to the utmost, and it eventually turned out impossible to construct a phenomenological language. The coordinate system defining this language did not guarantee a proper presentation of phenomena for at least two fundamental reasons.[21] First, Wittgenstein assumed that distance was an internal (logical) property of visual space (i.e. that it was part of its essence or was intrinsic to the very notion of it) and that it could be presented by means of numbers in a perspicuous notation. He concluded, however, that the so-called visual field could not be measured, meaning that it was inherently imprecise and that, secondly, this imprecision could not be expressed in a lucid symbolism. For example, we see a 100-sided polygon as a circle and cannot change that. The same holds for what is known as the Müller-Lyer illusion:

It is only on closer inspection or, better even, by using a measuring instrument that we realize that lines A and B are of the same length. In immediate perception, the two are not equal, with A being longer than B. Saying 'being' rather than 'appearing' longer is deliberate at this point since there is no distinction between appearance and reality here. This distinction arises only if an objective measure is applied, but, as Wittgenstein stressed, sense perception is not measurable. Two lines may look the same on paper, but after measuring them it may transpire that one of them is 24- and the other 25-length-units long. Nevertheless, the eye is unable to descry this difference, and additionally we cannot express it in phenomenological language. We would have to state that $n = n + 1$, and this would be not so much far from clear as rather entirely incorrect. We cannot simply say that n in visual space is the same as $n + 1$.[22]

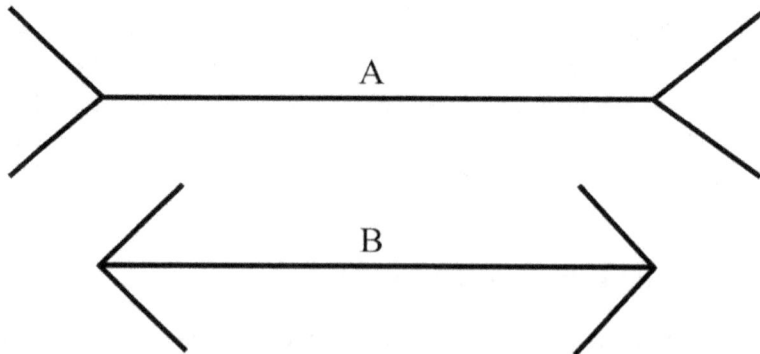

Figure 1 Müller-Lyer illusion.

The division into appearance and reality is not applicable to visual space; it only holds for Euclidean, physical space.[23] Such a division presupposes a hypothetical element, because in order to state that something appears to be one way or another, we must posit something, that is, adopt some external standards, for example, in the form of a defined measure that will settle what really is the case. However, the basic idea of phenomenological language was for it to be the description of immediate sense perception with no hypothetical admixture. The problem is serious indeed. On the one hand, the division into what *appears* to be one way or another and what *is* so cannot be applied to the description of visual space, but on the other we feel prompted to employ this division because, as Engelmann aptly emphasizes (Engelmann 2013: 37), words necessary to describe visual space only have meanings if such a division is presupposed. This is also true, let me add, about the imprecision (and thus immeasurability) of visual space. Attempts at describing it as a space to which the *appearance* vs. *reality* distinction is inapplicable by necessity presuppose such a division. For example, if one says 'this is an inexact circle', one must already have an image (an idea, a concept) of an exact circle. In our ordinary (physical, secondary) language, this division justifies the application of geometry to measuring length and makes a coherent description of the perceived possible. However, to negate the application of this division in this description entails a fundamental change in the meanings of some words and the need to look for new concepts, a new language or new rules for the already existing concepts. Since we do not have such new concepts, Wittgenstein observes, we fall back on the old ones:

> We would need new concepts, and we continually resort to those of the language of physical objects. The word 'precision' is one of these dubious expressions. In ordinary language it refers to a *comparison* and then it is quite intelligible. Where a certain degree of imprecision is present, perfect precision is also *possible*. But what is it supposed to mean when I say I can never see a precise circle, and am now using this word not relatively, but absolutely?
>
> (MS 107, 163; PR, 266)

If we were to institute new rules for the use of old words, we could not, for example, classify distance in our visual field. Moreover, we could not translate this new usage into ordinary, physical language, and hence we would have no tools for verifying the propositions of this language.

Ultimately, Wittgenstein concluded that the idea of developing phenomenology and phenomenological language would stumble on insurmountable difficulties and abandoned this project. This dismissal is registered in a note dated on 22

October 1929: 'The idea that it would be possible to construct a phenomenological language which would properly say what we have (want) to express in philosophy is, I believe, absurd. We have to manage with our ordinary language and only understand it correctly. This means that we must not let this language lead us to talk nonsense' (MS 107, 176). One month later, he wrote:

> I do not now have phenomenological language, or 'primary language' as I used to call it, in mind as my goal. I no longer hold it to be necessary. All that is possible and necessary is to separate what is essential from what is inessential in our language. ... A recognition of what is essential and what is inessential in our language ..., a recognition of which parts of our language are wheels turning idly, amounts to the construction of a phenomenological language.
>
> (MS 107, 205–6; PR, 51)

Wittgenstein came to the conclusion that we did not have suitable concepts to develop phenomenological language. As observed by Engelmann (Engelmann 2013: 43), by rejecting phenomenological language, Wittgenstein also rejected the idea that symbolism (a perspicuous notation) was fundamentally significant to philosophy. This marked a very important step on the path of his philosophical development. His new goal was to avoid linguistic confusion without having to construct a lucid symbolism. As early as in December 1929, Wittgenstein stated: 'I think that essentially we have only one language, and that is our everyday language. We need not invent a new language or construct a new symbolism, but our everyday language already is *the* language, provided we rid it of the obscurities that lie hidden in it' (WVC, 45). Phenomenal reality, phenomena themselves, cannot determine sense because they are ambiguous, imprecise, non-measurable and fluid.

There is one more vital aspect to Wittgenstein's eschewal of the idea of phenomenological language. This aspect is related to the notion of time. Specifically, if one wanted to say something positive about immediate experience, it would come down to stating that it found itself in constant flux: 'Rather this general indefiniteness, intangibility, this swimming of sense impressions is what has been referred to by the expression "Everything is in flux"' (BT, 448). Every language halts this constant flow, as it were. When one utters 'now', now is in fact already gone – it is the past. Language unfolds in time, and our immediate perception is outside of time. When describing immediate sensations, we must use personal pronouns, while, according to Wittgenstein, visual space has no owner and is autonomous. In his view, language as such belongs to the physical world rather than to the phenomenal one, in the sense that language consists of physical entities – signs – and progresses in time. Propositions are also understood in time. As already mentioned, Wittgenstein compared immediate perception to a film picture on the screen, while likening the physical world and our sensations to pictures (frames) on the film reel, which follow one upon another. This movement is not seen on the screen, where there are no clear boundaries between the pictures. Additionally, as the colour exclusion problem showed, understanding some propositions presupposes understanding other ones. By rejecting phenomenological language, Wittgenstein repudiated the idea that the symbols of this language could refer to the objects of immediate experience as different from physical objects of which our ordinary language speaks.

3.2. Wittgenstein, Sellars and the myth of the given

Evoking Wilfrid Sellars, we could add that by dismissing phenomenological language, Wittgenstein also dismissed the myth of the given – the myth of something primary and unmediated. Wittgenstein's reasoning would overlap with Sellars's argument against direct knowledge in his seminal 'Empiricism and the Philosophy of Mind'. According to Sellars (Sellars 1997), the given as an epistemological concept is supposed to make clear that empirical knowledge is founded on the non-inferential and the direct, on the knowledge of facts. This is exactly what Sellars considers impossible. Thinkers who hold on to the myth of the given confuse two different things when they refer to the immediate. The proposition 'S knows *p* directly' is ambiguous, as it may mean either that S knows *p* without inferring p from anything else, with no causal intermediary between S and *p*, or that S knows *p* and *p* is justified for S independently of anything else that S knows. To state that *p* is directly known or that *p* is directly justified amounts to saying that it does not require any other premises to be derived from. Sensory data can be said to be known directly in the former sense, but not in the latter one. These two meanings of immediate knowledge – the causal and the justificatory – tend to be confused. There is nothing problematic in saying that the experience of certain sensations is the *cause* of the subject's knowledge of a given physical object or phenomenon. This may be the reason why some philosophers have contended that these sensations are evidence which serves as an intermediary that justifies this knowledge as well.

In the *Philosophical Investigations*, Wittgenstein assessed our inclination 'to assume a pure intermediary between the propositional *sign* and the facts' (PI, §94) in a similar vein. What he meant was that because we rely on certain analogies between forms of expression in various areas of language, we separate the sense of propositions from propositions themselves. In this way, propositions come to be interpreted in the Platonic spirit as possessing a purely transcendental being, reminiscent of *ideas*, and this is called *sense*. In this model, sense is, as it were, a material objectivization of thought. In other words, a 'pure intermediary' is akin to the Platonic ideas which form a non-linguistic reality, to Kant's 'categories/pure concepts of the understanding' and to sensory 'data' or sensory 'images' arising in the mind, 'sensations', 'intuitions', etc. To use Sellars's terminology, they all add up to a general scheme of the given. It is founded on assuming that there are simple, primary epistemic entities which are non-referential, conceptually simple and epistemically independent, and that they make up the foundation of the rest of our knowledge. Yet, if these 'intermediaries', that is, sense data in Sellars's critique, are to be evidence justifying our knowledge, we must realize that such evidence is indeed evidence and can secure justification if, and only if, it is *known*. However, what is the direct cause of knowledge does not necessarily have to be known itself. Sensory experience may be a prerequisite for acquiring perceptual knowledge, but in and of itself it is not a simple and primary kind of knowledge.

When rejecting the possibility of phenomenological language, Wittgenstein realized that there was no way to construct, side by side with our ordinary language, a language capable of directly grasping the non-propositional and non-inferential. With the latter, we deal solely with various forms of mediation. In the chapter entitled 'Idealism, etc.' in *The Big Typescript*, composed after dropping the idea of phenomenological language, Wittgenstein revisited the problem of representing the immediate:

> Phenomenological language: the description of immediate sense perception without any hypothetical addition. If anything, then surely a portrayal in a painted picture or the like must be such a description of immediate experience. Such as when we look through a telescope, for instance, and draw or paint the constellation we see. Let's even imagine that our sense perception is reproduced by creating a model for describing it, a model that, seen from a certain point, produces these perceptions; this machine could be set into proper motion with a crank drive, and by turning the crank, we could read off the description. (An approximation to this would be a representation in film.)
>
> If *that* isn't a representation of the immediate – then what *can* be? – Anything that claimed to be even more immediate would have to forego being a description. Instead of a description, what results in that case is that inarticulate sound with which some authors would like to begin philosophy. ('Knowing of my knowing, I consciously possess something' – Driech.)
>
> (BT, 492, italics original)

If a painted picture or a drawing were to be a model of immediate perception, we find ourselves beset by the difficulties that Wittgenstein rehearsed responding to Mach's drawing. Additionally, Wittgenstein pointed out that the description of immediate experience was again nothing other than signs. In this sense, a phenomenological description would represent an attempt at going beyond language by means of the language:

> 'The flower had a reddish-yellow colour, but one that I can't describe more accurately (or more accurately in words).' What does that mean?
> I see it in front of me and could paint it.
> If we say that we can't describe this colour more accurately in words, then we're (always) thinking of a possibility of such a description (of course – otherwise the expression 'accurate description' would make no sense), and we have in mind the case of a measurement that wasn't carried out because of inadequate means.
> (BT, 490)

Consequently, we are left with a sole means of expression, that is, with our ordinary (physical, secondary) language. What remains for us to do is closely scrutinize the grammar of its expressions referring to immediate perception so as to avoid false analogies and categorial errors:

> How strange if logic were concerned with an 'ideal' language and not with *ours*. For what would this ideal language express? Presumably what we now express in our ordinary language; in that case, this is the language logic must investigate. Or something else: but in that case how would I have an idea what that would be. Logical analysis is the analysis of something we have, not of something we don't have. Therefore, it is the analysis of propositions *as they stand*.
> (MS 108, 51, italics original; PR, 52)

As already mentioned, a certain ambiguity *prima facie* inhered in Wittgenstein's phenomenology in 1929. On the one hand, his phenomenology could be construed as the grammar of expressions concerning perception, seeing, visual space or, more broadly, expressions describing direct experience. On the other, it was supposed to afford access to the directly perceived, that is, to objects themselves given in experience – to phenomena as such. This ambiguity can be succinctly encapsulated by asking whether Wittgenstein pursued phenomena themselves or a language referring to these phenomena and its grammar. Although this question rather crosses one's mind time and again as one reads through Wittgenstein's notes, it is defectively posed in a way. The problem is that it is premised on the idea of there being a non-linguistic reality of the phenomenal world on the one hand and a language that aspires to represent this reality on the other. From the very beginning, that is, from the *Tractatus* on, Wittgenstein was interested in how our language operated, and he pondered why some configurations of words fulfilled their role while others did not. He also wondered what this role actually was and whether there were perhaps many of them. Reality and language are interwoven, and their relation is internal, to use the Tractarian terminology. The description of phenomena themselves and the description of expressions referring to them fall within the limits of this relation. They are in fact one description rather than two although the logic of discourse may produce an impression of ontological difference. Wittgenstein did not develop two phenomenologies concerning phenomena and words, respectively.

4. Phenomenology as grammar

As ascertained in the account above, the phenomenological period proper was rather brief in the development of Wittgenstein's philosophy, stretching between February and the autumn of 1929. This makes one wonder why the draft of his planned book, known as *The Big Typescript*, contains a chapter entitled 'Phenomenology'. This query is basically tantamount to asking whether the rejection of phenomenological language meant the rejection of entire phenomenology as well.

For one, Jaakko Hintikka (1996: 71–2) claims that even though Wittgenstein negated the possibility of phenomenological language as a primary language or as the foundation of language as such, he never really stopped being a phenomenologist. This insight is corroborated by an observation noted by Desmond Lee: 'The world we live in is the world of sense-data, but the world we talk about is the world of physical objects' (Wittgenstein 1980: 82). Hintikka argues that Wittgenstein remained a phenomenologist insofar as the reality which we strive to represent in language is a phenomenal reality.[24] However, this reality cannot be directly grasped by means of phenomenological language. The only language we have at our disposal is our ordinary language, which always provides us with mediated representations of reality. Hintikka's interpretation is consistent and equates phenomenology with logic in the *Tractatus* or, to be more precise, identifies phenomenological language with logically ordered language. Abandoning the former amounted to abandoning the Tractarian stance and opened the path to a new conception, one fully embraced in the *Philosophical Investigations*. This reading is not a novelty in Hintikka's scholarship, and he argued this point in an earlier study co-authored with Merrill B. Hintikka, where the major turn in Wittgenstein's philosophy was interpreted as having been propelled by his growing awareness of the language–world relationship rather than as having been caused by the shift of attention from the language–world relation to the use of language. In their view (Hintikka and Hintikka 1986: 138*pass*), Wittgenstein abided by the idea that the elementary propositions must be directly comparable with the facts they present. Because our language belongs to the physical world, this comparison with facts takes place in the physical world rather than in the phenomenological one, that is, rather than in the world of our sense data. It is only the physical world that is representable in language, and for this reason phenomenological language had to be rejected for the sake of physical (i.e. ordinary) language.

Hintikka and Hintikka's notion that a major turn in the evolution of Wittgenstein's ideas took place in the autumn of 1929, that is, after relinquishing the project of phenomenological language, is basically on the mark. From that moment on, Wittgenstein's thought indeed took a new course. His notes more and more frequently delved into the use of language expressions, referenced examples of particular usages of these expressions, addressed grammar and compared language to a calculus or a game. However, the interpretation proposed by the Hintikkas does not explain why the concept of phenomenology as grammar appeared in *The Big Typescript*.

Some suggestions regarding this issue have been offered by Spiegelberg (1968: 251), who argued that answering the question about Wittgenstein's withdrawal from phenomenology hinged on establishing to what degree his concept of philosophical grammar had been a continuation of his phenomenology from 1929. Spiegelberg foregrounded the difficulty of ascertaining whether grammar in this case was the grammar of language referring to sense data or the grammar of phenomena. If the latter option were assumed and the grammar of phenomena stood for analysing phenomena as such and not only words, this grammar, Spiegelberg averred, would take over the role of phenomenology. In this case, Wittgenstein arguably never abandoned phenomenology but just relinquished the term itself to espouse a more conventional appellation of grammar.[25]

For his part, Ray Monk (2014: 325–6) claims that Wittgenstein was affiliated with phenomenology for a relatively short time of about nine months from spring to late autumn in 1929, whereby in 'Phenomenology is Grammar', chapter ninety-four of *The Big Typescript*, he recognized that the problems that phenomenology was devised to solve were better solvable by means of grammatical analyses. Monk believes at the same time that in this first short phenomenological phase Wittgenstein was at his closest to Husserl's position.[26] Having failed to construct a contradiction-free phenomenological language, Wittgenstein defined another goal for himself, and this involved explorations of the grammar of ordinary language. It is not the 'in a certain sense *a posteriori*' investigation or the investigation of phenomena themselves, which he envisaged in 'Some Remarks'. Analysing phenomena is not what we need in order to show that something cannot be simultaneously red and green; rather, this requires understanding how language functions, which entails understanding the rules and conventions that prevent defective constructions, such as 'it is red and it is green'. These rules and conventions determine which utterances make sense and which do not. However, they (i.e. rules and conventions) cannot be described in propositions, because every description of this kind must a priori presuppose a grammar. According to Monk, Wittgenstein did not look for propositions which were rules excluding some expressions as nonsensical; rather, he looked for ways of obtaining a clear insight into the grammar of our language. There are multiple ways of this kind and, though they vary widely, they share a common feature in that they enable us to realize that some expressions are nonsense. Briefly, realizing that what Wittgenstein was looking for was hidden in the grammar of ordinary language is key to understanding his rejection of phenomenology defined as a 'logical investigation of the phenomena themselves'.

Monk's interpretation seems to be corroborated by the very first sentence of the 'Phenomenology is Grammar' chapter in *The Big Typescript*, which reads:

> The investigation of the rules of the use of our language, the recognition of these rules, and their clearly surveyable representation amounts to, i.e. accomplishes the same thing as, what one often wants to achieve in constructing a phenomenological language. Each time we recognize that such and such a mode of representation can be replaced by another one, we take a step toward that goal.
>
> (BT, 437)

Yet, the further passages offer ample grounding for the doubts listed by Spiegelberg. Wittgenstein often smoothly passes from analysing phenomena to the grammar of language expressions concerning these phenomena. This may be why an effect of something missing is generated. The excerpt cited above is immediately followed by: 'Say my visual image were of two red circles of equal size on a blue background: what is there here in two's and what once? (And what does this question mean, anyway?) – One could say: Here we have one colour, but two locations' (BT, 437). Putting things in this way may suggest that the person who utters these words is about to investigate a real visual image but directly answers his/her own questions by adding that '[w]hat disturbs us is the lack of clarity about the grammar of the sentence "I see two red circles on a blue background" – in particular its relation to the grammar of sentences such as "Two red balls are lying on the table" and "I see two colours in this picture"' (BT, 438). Wittgenstein will continue to point out the faulty applications of our physical (i.e. ordinary) way of talking to sense data, but he will no longer seek to replace it with a contradiction-free language of phenomenology. His considerations will shift to surveying linguistic representations of visual space, and when busy with this, he will every now and then reveal the language traps into which we fall when attempting to describe the field of vision. For example, does it hold 'objects' in the same manner that the space of a room holds physical bodies?: 'The linguistic form "I perceive x" originally refers to a phenomenon (as an argument) in physical space (here I mean "in space" in the ordinary way of speaking). Therefore I can't automatically apply this form to what is called "sense data," say to an optical after-image' (BT, 438–39). If it is sometimes said that one cannot see brightness if one has not seen darkness, this does not amount to a description of one's visual experience, because one can perfectly imagine seeing entirely white surfaces without dark ones being there; what this means is that 'bright' is used in our language as part of the 'bright-dark' opposition, and that the very 'representation of completely white surfaces' presupposes this distinction. Thus grammar, as it were, determines the essence of our perception as a whole:

> If one were asked: 'What is the difference between a sound and a colour?', and the answer were 'We hear sounds, but we see colours', then this is only a hypothesis that is justified through experience, if saying this makes any sense in the first place. And to that extent it is conceivable that one day I shall perceive sounds with my eyes, i.e. see them, and shall hear colours. What is essential to sounds and colours is obviously shown in the grammar of the words for sounds and colours.
>
> (BT, 463)

Further investigating the grammar of language describing visual space, Wittgenstein analyses notions such as blurredness, indeterminacy, divisibility and infinite divisibility. For example, in saying 'we never see a true circle', one has simply chosen the form of representation in which the term 'true circle' is understood as an accurately measured round plate of very hard steel, which is more exact than a wooden plate, which is more exact than a paper one (see BT,

448). Wittgenstein highlights differences between visual space and Euclidean (physical) space. In visual space, equalness – such as in saying that two lines are equal – has a different multiplicity than equalness in Euclidean space. In the latter, this multiplicity can be numerically expressed, while in the former, as already mentioned, two lines of numerically different lengths often appear to be equally long. In BT, Wittgenstein implements the idea of phenomenological language, which was previously envisioned as an easily surveyable notation, in the investigation of the rules of language and in the form of a perspicuous representation of grammar. He states:

> When we speak about visual space we are easily seduced into imagining that it is a kind of peep-show box that everyone carries around in front of himself. That is to say, in doing this we are using the word 'space' in a way similar to when we call a room a space. But in reality the word 'visual space' only refers to a geometry, I mean to a section of the grammar of our language.
>
> (BT, 463)

Spiegelberg's hesitations whether all this concerns the grammar of language expressions for sense data or the grammar (analysis?) of phenomena themselves result from a certain misunderstanding, as already suggested. For Wittgenstein, the grammar of the description of phenomena is at the same time the grammar of the phenomena themselves, because they are not accessible in any other way than through language. As Sellars observes, in order to be phenomena, they must be known. Wittgenstein's considerations indicate that the division into visual space and language by which this space can be more or less adequately described is wrong. The very paying of attention, the act of intention, the turning to consider our field of vision are all intrinsically linguistic. Consequently, the grammar of the phenomena themselves cannot be severed from the grammar of language expressions for these phenomena. Language in a sense gives us access to them. The very notion of 'phenomena themselves' is a grammatical expression because it presupposes that there is something besides them and that we wish to focus exclusively on the 'phenomena themselves'.

Given all this, we would be hard-pressed to identify a transition from phenomenology understood as the description of the phenomena themselves to phenomenology conceived as grammar. A certain unity is at work here, meaning that the grammar of expressions concerning visual space is at once the description of this space. As Wittgenstein will state later: 'Grammar tells what kind of object anything is (Theology as grammar)' (PI, §373).

To conclude, shortly before and after his return to philosophy in 1929, Wittgenstein took part in a series of discussions with members of the Vienna

Circle. In all probability, he came across Mach's species of phenomenology on this occasion. He harnessed it to his own purposes, which were connected to the problems spawned by the *Tractatus*, primarily to the colour exclusion problem and by the same token to the postulated independence of the elementary propositions. Wittgenstein still stood by the idea that the limits of language could be determined by establishing in which combinations words made sense and in which they did not. The colour exclusion problem, which he addressed in 'Some Remarks on Logical Form', compelled him to realize that this could not be accomplished through a logical analysis of language; if anything, the goal could be attained by means of a logical analysis of the phenomena themselves. This was how the idea of phenomenological language was engendered. This conjectured phenomenological language resembled the T-F notation of the *Tractatus* in that it represented an attempt at constructing a clear symbolism. However, such a phenomenological language capable of describing immediate experience and avoiding the ambiguities of ordinary language soon proved impossible to construct. As a result, Wittgenstein abandoned the idea of developing phenomenological language, which was tantamount to rejecting the belief that a perspicuous notation was fundamental to philosophy. Instead, language confusion was envisaged as dispersible without recourse to any newly fashioned symbolism. How this was to be achieved took Wittgenstein several years to answer, but in the period in which he was committed to developing phenomenology, he unmistakably referred to grammar as a survey of the rules of the use of language. Phenomenology was grammar, that is, a system of rules that determined the sense of utterances about visual space, and phenomenological language was a language the use of which adhered to these rules. Admittedly, there was a certain ambiguity to Wittgenstein's version of phenomenology from 1929. Specifically, phenomenology was supposed to refer to the phenomena as such and simultaneously to the language describing these phenomena, and in this sense it was identical with grammar. As argued above, however, this ambiguity was only ostensible and resulted from Wittgenstein's tendency to fluidly alternate between the analysis of phenomena and the grammar of their description. Indeed, he never offered a point or a situation in which, for instance, visual space was pitted against language in which this space was represented. The grammar of spatial expressions was simultaneously the grammar of space itself. Consequently, it is basically impossible to pinpoint any transition from phenomenology understood as the investigation of the phenomena as such to phenomenology envisaged as grammar.

2

Verification: 1929–31

In the early 1930s, Ludwig Wittgenstein's philosophical thought went through fairly abrupt changes. These dynamic fluctuations are emphatically exemplified by his notion of verification and what it stood for. The term 'verification' started to appear on a regular basis in the notes Wittgenstein produced between 1929 and 1931. As a matter of fact, members of the Vienna Circle considered Wittgenstein the founder of the principle of verification, therein citing the authority of Friedrich Waismann (1930: 228) and Moritz Schlick (1969: 340). The principle was directly attributed to Wittgenstein by Rudolf Carnap, who explained in his *Intellectual Autobiography*:

> The view that these sentences and questions [the sentences and questions of metaphysics] are non-cognitive was based on Wittgenstein's principle of verifiability. This principle says first, that the meaning of a sentence is given by the conditions of its verification and, second, that a sentence is meaningful if and only if it is in principle verifiable, that is, if there are possible, not necessarily actual, circumstances which, if they did occur, would definitely establish the truth of the sentence. This principle of verifiability was later replaced by the more liberal principle of confirmability.
>
> (Carnap 1963: 44)

Some scholars[1] identify a verificationist period in Wittgenstein's philosophy and even aver that, around 1929, he 'was whole-heartedly committed to a verificationism of the most extreme kind' (Wrigley 1989: 265). This issue is salient not only in view of the relation between Wittgenstein's position in the *Tractatus Logico-Philosophicus* and the Vienna Circle, whose members made the principle of verification the axis of their entire philosophy. What is also noteworthy is the relevance of verification to the internal development of Wittgenstein's philosophy itself. Hence, it is pertinent to identify the sources and look into the meaning of Wittgenstein's verificationism between 1929 and 1931.

1. Sources

1.1. The Vienna Circle

To understand which of Wittgenstein's assertions were specifically cited by the Vienna Circle philosophers as they attributed the founding of the verifiability principle to Wittgenstein, one would be well advised to inspect writings by Waismann, who first articulated this principle in his paper 'A Logical Analysis of the Concept of Probability' ('Logische Analyse des Wahrscheinlichkeitsbegriffs', 1930):

> A statement describes a state of affairs. The state of affairs exists or it does not exist. There is no third thing, and hence also no intermediary between true and false. If there is no way of telling when a proposition is true, then the proposition has no sense whatever; for the sense of a proposition is the method of its verification. In fact, whoever utters a proposition must know under what conditions he will call the proposition true or false.
>
> (Waismann 1977: 5)

Similar formulations are to be found in Waismann's *Thesen*, written in late 1930 or early 1931, in which he attempted to interpret the major points of the *Tractatus Logico-Philosophicus* in the light of the new ideas hatched by the Circle. In *Thesen*, Waismann claimed, among other things, that:

> To understand a proposition means to know how things stand if the proposition is true.
> A proposition cannot say more than is established by means of the method of its verification.
> *The sense of a proposition is the way it is verified*
> A statement has sense, not because it is constructed in a legitimate way, but because it can be verified. Hence every verifiable statement is constructed in a legitimate way. If I specify a method of verification, I thereby lay down the form of the proposition in question, the meaning of its words, the rules of syntax, etc.
>
> (WVC, 244–5; italics original)

Waismann could not directly reference the *Tractatus* because it did not mention verification. Verification was addressed for the first time in his conversation with Wittgenstein in December 1929. However, like his Circle colleagues, Waismann could regard his views (as conveyed in the passage quoted above) as elaborating on the ideas implicitly entertained in the *Tractatus*. Actually, Waismann quoted a part of Tractarian thesis 4.024 – 'To understand a proposition means to know what is the case if it is true' – almost verbatim and combined it with verification, affirming that to understand a statement meant to know how it was verified. These two wordings appear to state the same thing. Such a reading presupposed a general interpretation of what Peter M. S. Hacker (Hacker 1981: 89) has labelled as 'the doctrine of isomorphism', which holds that language and reality have the same logical form. Names represent simple objects, and propositions describe states of affairs, which for their part refer to possible experiences. Members of the Vienna Circle understood a name to be linked to an object through ostensive definitions, and a proposition, which Wittgenstein said was 'laid against reality like a ruler' (TLP, 2.1512), to be connected with an object through verification. This means that in order to understand a proposition one must know what is the case when it is true, that is, what experience verifies it. Such an approach can also be construed as stemming from Wittgenstein's inherently Fregean thesis of the bipolarity of the proposition: a proposition has sense when it is either true or false because to know when it can be true or false means to know what verifies it.

Given this, it appears legitimate to conclude, as Hacker does (1996: 53), that the *Tractatus* to a degree allows regarding verifiability as a criterion of the empirical sense of the elementary propositions although it does not *define* the sense of a proposition as the method of verification.[2] Other researchers also trace inspirations of the Vienna Circle philosophers. According to Michael Wrigley (1989: 284), what Schlick and his colleagues found in the *Tractatus* was an insightful crystallization of the fundamental tenets of the position they had independently developed. Crucially, Wittgenstein's views did not undergo any radical change between the completion of the *Tractatus* and his first meeting with the Vienna Circle in 1927. This indicates that Schlick's (and his collaborators') interpretation of the *Tractatus* clashed with Wittgenstein's own understanding of it. Clash, though, may sound too harsh since the Vienna Circle's reading of the *Tractatus* was not entirely at odds with Wittgenstein's authorial intention; otherwise, he would not have found it worthwhile – let alone rewarding – to continue meeting up with people who completely misunderstood his ideas. In Wrigley's view, Wittgenstein perceived discourse on verification, protocol sentences, sense data, physicalism, etc., as an expression of a similar mindset. He may even have accepted that the issues of sense and meaning were not explainable without taking the epistemological context into account. Therefore, Wrigley concludes that the *Tractatus* itself was the source of verificationism, which remained implicit in it to be explicitly articulated in the 1930s.

1.2. The propositional system

Some other scholars have suggested that the short period of verification between 1929 and 1930 rather resulted from the internal dynamic of the development of Wittgenstein's standpoint. For example, Hacker (1986: 139), who basically does not rule out the verificationist interpretation of the *Tractatus* as proposed by the Vienna Circle, claims at the same time that Wittgenstein did not accept this interpretation and that he took a different path towards his verificationist stance of 1929. This path purportedly led through the acknowledgement of the challenges the *Tractatus* would encounter because of the colour exclusion problem and the untenability of the thesis of the independence of the elementary propositions, which are discussed in the previous chapter. Consequently, Wittgenstein began to refer to the *propositional system* (*Satzsystem*) as the basic unit of sense, because the sense of some propositions had been shown to depend on other sentences, instead of on their logical properties, such as bipolarity, alone.

As the thesis of the independence of the elementary propositions collapsed, the ontology of the *Tractatus* was wrecked along with the doctrine of the language/world isomorphism. Wittgenstein no longer averred that the world consisted of facts and that facts consisted of objects which were the meanings of names. Likewise, he did not claim that a proposition was a description of a possible state of affairs. For example, the indication of an object in the ostensive definition of colour ('It is red') should not be perceived, unlike Waismann and Schlick did, as a combination of word and thing, but as a pattern within a method of representation. Whether a given object is a pattern (of colour red) or whether it is described as read does not follow from the internal (logical) properties of the expression 'it is red' but depends on the way it is used. In other words, as the Tractarian idea of the independence of the elementary propositions was abandoned and the concept of *propositional system* was forged, the manner of actualizing the sense of a proposition changed. It did not involve comparing the proposition and reality anymore; in order to know the sense of a proposition, one had to relate it to other propositions, which meant, among other things, knowing how this proposition was verified and whether the proposition (e.g. 'It is red') was used as a pattern or as a description. Hacker claims that, in 1929, Wittgenstein's interest recognizably shifted towards the propositional system.[3]

Stuart Shanker (1987: 40–2) is another scholar to make Wittgenstein's discourse on verification dependent on the crafting of the conception of the propositional system. In his view, Wittgenstein differed from the Vienna Circle in that he was not interested in verification as a tool for limiting knowledge to sensory experience and thus as a criterion for separating science from non-science. Even if Wittgenstein's verification principle dated back to his 'positivist interlude',[4] it was only applied to distil the techniques for explaining the logical syntax of propositions. As the conception of the propositional system began to take shape, Wittgenstein started to emphasize the diversity of propositional forms. From his new *Satzsystem* perspective, whether a proposition makes sense is determined by the rules of logical syntax, that is, of the propositional system. But what if a proposition does not belong to any of such systems? To put it differently: Does it at all make sense to speak of propositions which do not belong to any system whatsoever? The key to Wittgenstein's answer was provided by the particular role of the verification principle. For Wittgenstein, the fact that the sense of a proposition is given by virtue of the method of its verification specifically means that this method shows to which propositional system the proposition belongs. According to Shanker, Wittgenstein later applied verification as a method for establishing the sense of propositions in the philosophy of mathematics in his *Philosophical Remarks*.

1.3. Brouwer's intuitionism

No investigation of the genesis of Wittgenstein's verificationism of 1929 should pass over the possibilities suggested by Michael Dummett (1978: 379), who locates the concept of verification in the contemporaneous dispute between realism and anti-realism. Dummett believes that, against the views of the Vienna Circle philosophers, the verificationist theory of meaning radically differs from the framework which defines meaning in terms of truth conditions, one that is explicitly expounded in the *Tractatus*. While, in the latter, to know the meaning of a proposition means to know under what conditions it is true, verificationism holds that one knows the meaning of a proposition if one is able to recognize this proposition as ultimately verified or falsified. In anti-realist semantics, meaning bound to truth conditions is replaced by meaning understood in terms of justifiable assertability conditions.[5] Wittgenstein's journey to this position led through Luitzen Brouwer's intuitionism. Wittgenstein is known to have attended Brouwer's lecture on 'Mathematik, Wissenschaft und Sprache' in Vienna in March 1928. By Herbert Feigl's report, he was excited by the lecture, though his vehement response to and lively discussions following the talk, which Feigl relates, were probably triggered by opposition rather than by approval, as the metaphysics of Brouwer's intuitionism – or, more precisely speaking, his psychologism – was likely to quite effectively antagonize Wittgenstein. However, if Brouwer's approach is examined the way Dummett has done it, psychologism may be found irrelevant, if not downright incompatible, with the essence of mathematical intuitionism. In Dummett's interpretation, intuitionism holds that instead of defining the meaning of mathematical propositions in relation to their truth conditions, it should be assumed that this meaning is always determined by *proof*-conditions.[6] Wittgenstein is likely to have construed Brouwer's intentions in a similar fashion and discerned a possibility of separating intuitionist semantics from its psychologist background. Subsequently, it only took applying the concept of meaning based on *proof*-conditions to all propositions, rather than exclusively to those of mathematics, to obtain the concept of meaning related to *verification* conditions. In this new approach, understanding a proposition meant knowing how it was verified.

Nevertheless, this interpretation breeds some doubts and reservations. The gist of Dummett's reading is that Brouwer's intuitionism supplied Wittgenstein with a model for a new approach to the meaning of mathematical propositions. If that had indeed been the case, verificationism would have resulted from generalizing this new approach and applying it to language as a whole. However, neither of these claims seems to be on point.[7] Except for some similarities, intuitionism and Wittgenstein's views on the foundations of mathematics between 1929 and 1930 were considerably divergent. Intuitionism, like other contemporaneous mathematical positions, assumed that the propositions of mathematics described a certain domain of facts and thus bore descriptive content, that is, were about something. Meanwhile, Wittgenstein fundamentally believed that mathematical propositions had prescriptive, that is, normative, and not descriptive content. For example, he asserted in *The Big Typescript* that '[w]hen we talk about the sense of mathematical propositions, or what they are about, we are using a false picture. For here too it's as if there were inessential, arbitrary signs that had something essential in common, namely their sense' (BT, 531). Wittgenstein rejected the idea that mathematical propositions had sense that called for explication or could be applied to language as a whole. Consequently, it is unwarranted to trace the source of Wittgenstein's verificationism to the extension of the proof-based model of meaning beyond mathematical propositions – onto the rest of language. There is simply nothing to generalize and to extend onto entire language. For this reason, although Brouwer's influence on Wittgenstein in an array of other issues, such as the mathematical infinite, must not be overlooked, the origin of Wittgenstein's verificationism should not be sought in the theories proposed by the founder of mathematical intuitionism.

2. Wittgenstein's verificationism in the notes from 1929 to 1931 and in conversations with Schlick and Waismann

2.1. The propositional system vs. verification

Another interpretation of Wittgenstein's verificationism – including both its core and its genesis – can be gleaned from his notes from 1929 to 1931 and his conversations with Schlick and his colleagues. The term 'verification' appears for the first time in the remarks Wittgenstein noted down amidst his considerations on mathematics at the beginning of 1929. In these remarks, verification is identified with mathematical proof. For example, at the end of 1929, he observed: 'Every proposition is the instruction for its verification' (MS 106, 16); tellingly, he crossed out 'proof' and put in 'verification' in this note. A few pages further, he wrote:

> What is the purely technical verification of
> $(x): x^2 = 2x \supset x = 0 \vee x = 2$
> I calculate x from the equation, put in the value everywhere, and then I must obtain a true proposition ...
> But what is the verification of $(\exists x) \, x^2 = 2x$? I mean the concrete verification of *this* proposition as opposed to the verification of '$(x): x^2 = 2x \vee x = 0$.' Oughtn't another proposition (i.e. another sense) to be *differently* verified? For example, a general proposition – more generally.
>
> (MS 106, 40–2)

This passage and other similar ones could imply that Wittgenstein did not originally use the term 'verification' in an empirical sense, for example, as referring to immediate sensory experience. Below, this notion will be proven wrong. I believe that the problem of verification should be viewed as directly linked to the project of phenomenology and so-called phenomenological (or primary) language, which is discussed in the previous chapter. As shown there, this project was closely associated with the colour exclusion problem, which, as argued below, was fundamental to Wittgenstein's idea of verification. To restate, a phenomenological investigation should make us realize that the structure of the elementary propositions cannot be foreseen, which we are anyway seduced into doing by our ordinary language, which relies on subject–predicate forms. The fact that these forms exist should not encourage us to infer anything about the real logical forms of the facts being described. Quite disparate propositions, such as 'This book is boring', 'God exists', 'It's going to rain tomorrow', and '2 + 2 = 4', etc., which have nothing in common with each other, are all subject–predicate propositions, apparently sharing the same form, yet we in fact project many different logical forms in various ways into our language. Describing these forms adequately takes a logical analysis of the phenomena themselves – that is, phenomenological (primary) language – rather than an analysis of forms encountered in ordinary (secondary) language. In 'Some Remarks on Logical Form', Wittgenstein argued that it was possible to adequately represent reality, but this required relying on immediate experience, on the phenomena themselves, described in phenomenological language. The colour exclusion problem demonstrated that the logical value of some propositions could determine the value of other propositions, or, which is one and the same thing, that it hinged on the *content* of propositions. This means that elementary propositions belong to a *propositional system*, which is compared with reality as a certain whole.[8] A *propositional system* arises as a result of inferential relations; in other words, propositions are combined into a system by their internal relations. Importantly, these relations are no longer formal, but material and based on the content of propositions.

This inferentialist view marked the middle Wittgenstein's clear departure from the formalism of the *Tractatus*.[9] Logic was shown to be incapable of expressing symbolically all the real ways of using language. Consequently, in this period, Wittgenstein began to explain the operations of language on the basis of its inferential relations and not of its logical structure. This had serious implications for the way of conceptualizing the sense of a proposition. Specifically, instead of being tied to the formal bipolarity of a proposition, the sense of a proposition was conceived as bound up with its belonging to a particular propositional system, which was premised on the content rather than on the form of the proposition. Verification was supposed to serve the purpose of establishing the content of propositions, what they were about and, consequently, of classifying them in respective propositional systems. This is a key aspect for grasping the problem under examination in this chapter.

2.2. Verification in conversations with Schlick and Waismann

From that moment (i.e. late 1929) on, Wittgenstein increasingly often referred to the verification method. Conversations with Schlick were one of the sites of his striving to clarify what it properly meant. In one of such meetings, Wittgenstein stated that '[i]n order to determine the sense of a proposition, I should have to know a very specific procedure for when to count the proposition as verified'

(WVC 47).[10] If one says, for instance: 'There's a book lying up there on the cupboard', when can such a proposition be regarded as verified? Is it when the book is spotted lying on the cupboard? Or is it when the book is examined from various sides? Or is it perhaps when the book is held in the hands and leafed through? Two interpretations are possible in this case. One is that such a verification will never be completed because whatever one should do, one can never be certain that one is not wrong. The other is that if a proposition can never be fully verified, one did not mean anything when uttering it, and consequently the proposition does not signify anything. The latter option was embraced by Wittgenstein himself. However, this is where ordinary language reveals its weakness, one more serious than that of the language of science, since symbols in ordinary language elude any unambiguous definition, words oscillate between various meanings, and hence one can never know when a proposition is fully verified and thus what sense it ultimately has. As a vivid example, Wittgenstein cites a sentence the verification of which is difficult to the utmost: 'Seitz has been elected mayor.'[11] How can this proposition be verified? Does watching the event count as its verification? Or is asking the witnesses of the election enough? If so, which witnesses: those who sat at the front or at the back of the hall? Or should one perhaps read a newspaper report of the proceedings? In Wittgenstein's view, one constantly stumbles upon the difference between appearance and reality in ordinary language. The proposition 'This is yellow' can be verified in a variety of ways, and depending on the method of verification it will have different senses. For example, if a certain chemical reaction were the means of verification, it would make sense to say: 'This looks *grey*, but in reality it is *yellow*' (WVC, 97). But if the verification lies in what one can see, to say 'This looks yellow, but in reality it is grey' does not make sense. In this case, one must not look for a sign of the thing being yellow because (one's seeing) this is a fact. One's seeing a yellow object is the ultimate point beyond which one cannot reach: 'I must not produce any hypotheses concerning what is immediately given' (WVC, 97). When discussing the notion of time, Wittgenstein observes that the difficulty bound up with physical discourse on time stems from confusing the rules of grammar, or more precisely speaking, from the dual meaning of the word 'time': as memory and as a physical unit. These two meanings result from two different ways of verifying propositions which contain temporal expressions. For example, if one says that something happened earlier, the proposition can only be verified based on memory; in this case, 'time' will mean something else than in propositions including the word 'time' which are verified by documents or knowledge confirmed by others. Sometimes, memories are called images of the past, but this metaphor is faulty, because memories, unlike images, cannot be confronted with reality. In any case, memories of the past do not exist in the way that objects in a room exist; even if one cannot see these objects at a given moment, one can always walk into the room and have a look at them. The past, however, cannot be walked into. Therefore, Wittgenstein asserts: 'Where there are different verifications there are also different meanings' (WVC, 53).

The issue of verification was again addressed in a conversation with Schlick in January 1931 (see WVC, 158). Schlick enquired about how the statement that the sense of a proposition was the method of its verification was to be understood. Could it at all be said that *one* proposition was verified in various ways? In Schlick's opinion, the laws of nature were what connected various ways of verification. He explained: 'We can take a very simple example: at one time I measure a length by laying a measuring-rod against it, at another time by means of gauging-instruments. In and of itself it would not be necessary that the two results coincide. But if they do, then this is the manifestation of a natural law' (WVC, 158). Wittgenstein replied that such a situation is the case not only in science but also in everyday life.

> For instance, I hear piano-playing in the next room and say, 'My brother is in that room.' If I were now asked how I knew, I would answer, 'He told me that he would be in the next room at that time.' Or 'I hear the piano being played and I recognize his way of playing.' Or, 'Just now I heard steps that sounded just like his,' etc. Now it seems as if I had verified the same sentence in ways that were different every time. But this is not so. What I have verified are different 'symptoms' of something else. ... The playing of the piano, the steps, etc. are symptoms of my brother's presence.
>
> (WVC, 158–9)

These and similar assertions offered by Wittgenstein indicate that what he had in mind was not a new concept of meaning but the problem of various uses of language expressions. Diverse ways of verifying a proposition served to classify it into one of propositional systems.

At the time, Wittgenstein distinguished three main propositional systems, that is, three kinds of propositions: genuine propositions (*eigentliche Sätze*) or primary propositions (*primäre Sätze*), hypotheses and mathematical propositions. The first group comprised propositions that could be effectively verified or falsified by comparing them with reality, because they expressed the content of sensory experience. In this sense, they corresponded to propositions of so-called phenomenological language describing the directly given, even though Wittgenstein had already concluded that such a language was impossible. The second type encompassed hypotheses, which Wittgenstein conceived rather broadly and, admittedly, not always described with any accuracy. Side by side with scientific hypotheses, for example, the hypotheses of physics, he listed propositions of our ordinary language as hypotheses: 'Every proposition we say in ordinary language appears to have the character of a hypothesis' (MS 108, 249). Most generally speaking, hypotheses were, to him, propositions which evaded any definite verification in experience: 'By hypothesis I mean every sentence that is not definitively verifiable. If an hypothesis can't be definitively verified, it can't be verified at all, and there's no truth or falsity for it' (MS 108, 284; PR, 283). One of the chapters in *The Big Typescript* is entitled 'The Nature of Hypotheses' and consists of passages from manuscript MS 108, which Wittgenstein selected while omitting others. This was not a random choice as shall be seen. In *The Big Typescript*, Wittgenstein claimed that '[a] hypothesis is law for forming propositions. One could also say: A hypothesis is law for forming expectations. A proposition is, so to speak, a section of a hypothesis at a certain point' (BT, 118). This wording refers to conversations with Schlick about the verification of the propositions of physics. In one of these exchanges, Wittgenstein claimed that physical equations were not propositions but *hypotheses*. What we observe are only pieces or cross-sections through hypotheses (*die Schnitte durch die Hypothesen*), which not only are made at a particular place and time but also have a particular logical form. These cross-sections are thus actually various facts. What can be verified is one such cross-section, piece or side of a given hypothesis, which is, in this sense, like a three-dimensional solid projected in various ways. According to Wittgenstein, a hypothesis combines all these disparate pieces the way a curve connects various points or a solid various projections. A thus-conceived hypothesis refers not only to physical equations but also to propositions of our ordinary language. Examples of colloquial hypotheses marshalled by Wittgenstein include 'A book is lying here', 'My brother is in the next room', etc. These propositions can be verified in various ways that form these pieces, cross-sections, sides or aspects, which Wittgenstein sometimes called 'symptoms'.

The third of Wittgenstein's propositional systems includes mathematical propositions. In mathematics, verification amounts to the *proof* method. In his notes, Wittgenstein often juxtaposed verification and proof, sometimes even using them interchangeably. However, this analogy is deceptive, and Wittgenstein was far from identifying proof with verification, since equating them would have indicated a certain similarity between empirical and mathematical propositions while Wittgenstein rather sought to bring out differences between the two. His point was that mathematical proof did not prove any truth about the world of mathematical objects but was a grammatical construction, a rule of representation. For example, he insisted that '[n]othing is more fatal to philosophical understanding than the notion of proof and experience as two different but comparable methods of verification' (MS 108, 295; PG, 361).

This tripartite division of propositions did not hold ground for long. It was already entirely absent in *the Blue and Brown Books*. In 1932–33, Wittgenstein began to pay more attention to the diversification of propositions concerning immediate sense perception, which he disparately compared with reality. This can be seen by examining propositions such as 'I have a headache' and 'I see a red apple' in this regard. The notions of 'hypothesis' and 'symptom' disappear from Wittgenstein's lexicon equally fast.[12]

3. Verification as grammar

Wittgenstein's statements and observations about verification suggest that he formed the idea of verification as having a grammatical sense – that is, as being a manner of establishing the sense of a proposition – practically as soon as he broached the subject. He remarked for example: 'The verification is not *one* token of the truth, it is *the* sense of the proposition (Einstein: How a magnitude is measured is what it is' (MS 107, 143; PR 200, italics original) and 'Asking about verification is just another form of asking *how do you mean?*' (MS 112, 97). Originally, Wittgenstein used the term 'verification' in relation to mathematical propositions and tended to equate it with proof, which was questioned when he began to recognize that language operated in various ways and to perceive that propositions of mathematics were of a specific kind. More often than not, verification appeared in the context of phenomenology and so-called phenomenological language, where it referred to immediate experience. This empirical sense of verification may have been picked up by Wittgenstein during his discussions with the philosophers of the Vienna Circle. Wittgenstein would meet the Circle members at Schlick's seminars from 1927 on, and the theme of verification is highly likely to have been discussed on these occasions. Importantly, in 1929, Wittgenstein still upheld many of the theses propounded in the *Tractatus*.[13] Though he never explicitly resorted to the notion of verification in this work, thesis 4.024 says: 'To understand a proposition means to know what is the case if it is true.' Wittgenstein basically reiterated this insight in a note of 10 June 1929: 'My central thought (*Hauptgedanke*) is that one *compares* the proposition with reality' (MS 107, 155). Now his object was to establish how such a comparison was made, bearing in mind the principle of the determinacy of sense, that is, remembering that 'A proposition must restrict reality to two alternatives: yes or no' (TLP, 4.023). Wittgenstein made the comparison of the proposition with reality dependent on the method of its verification, which represented a considerable change in relation to his position in the *Tractatus*. As the concept of the system of propositions appeared, in which '[i]t isn't a proposition which I put against reality as a yardstick, it's a system of propositions [*System von Sätzen*]', a new problem arose as well. Specifically, one was no longer supposed to compare a proposition with reality and have a proposition limit it to the either-yes-or-no option; rather, one was to grammatically determine to what system of propositions this proposition belonged. To accomplish this, one first of all had to define the sense of the proposition by availing oneself of the method of verification that indicated how and in what context it was used. Wittgenstein himself later admitted: 'I used at one time to say that, in order to get clear how a sentence is used, it was a good idea to ask oneself the question: "How would one try to verify such an assertion?" But that's just one way among others of getting clear about the use of a word or sentence' (qtd. in Monk 1991: 294).

I believe that this observation offers some useful hints for settling the problem captured by Michael Hymers in his paper 'Going Around the Vienna Circle: Wittgenstein and Verification' (Hymers 2005: 226). Hymers argues that while the colour exclusion problem prompted Wittgenstein to renounce the conception of logical atomism, he continued to cling to the idea of the conclusive verification of elementary propositions. In Hymers's view, however, it is a sheer impossibility to coherently claim that there are no elementary propositions and, at the same time, that there is a defined set of propositions which are effectively verifiable in empirical experience, because these propositions are linked to the facts that verify them.[14] On realizing this discrepancy, which admittedly took him quite a while, Wittgenstein relinquished verificationism. However, our analysis implies that the version of verificationism that Wittgenstein espoused in 1929 swayed towards the grammatical interpretation from the very beginning. For some time, he may not have objected to the interpretation endorsed by the Vienna Circle members, who connected verification with the empiricist theory of meaning, demarcation, protocol sentences, etc., but he was not really interested in epistemological questions. Feigl recalls that Wittgenstein was altogether not interested in philosophy: 'He felt that he had said all he could in the *Tractatus*. Moreover, only on relatively rare occasions could we get him to clarify one or another of the puzzling or obscure passages in his work. He seemed himself rather unclear on the ideas he had developed during the First World War' (Feigl 1980: 63). However, when Wittgenstein resumed his systematic philosophical practice and re-engaged with Tractarian problems, his thoughts took a different course than the ideas proposed by Schlick and his colleagues. Therefore, despite dropping logical atomism, Wittgenstein could still insist that the sense of the proposition was the method of is verification, because it was less associated with the empiricist theory of meaning and more with grammar.

To single out a distinct verificationist period in the development of Wittgenstein's philosophy does not make much sense, either. Rather, the years 1929–30 and the following period embody Wittgenstein's gradual shift away from the Tractarian notions and the budding of his new concepts about the workings of language. In this period of trying out an array of ideas, the empirical interpretation of some crucial problems and notions coexisted and interpenetrated with the grammatical interpretation. This was also the case for verification, which, given this ambiguity, may be recognized as a transitional-period notion and a conceptual harbinger of the new position. It is not without reason that Brian McGuinness has identified Wittgenstein's discourse on verification as the dismissal of his abstract, Tractarian approach to language and the commencement of his focus on concrete language phenomena.[15] The notion of verification itself was still used by Wittgenstein in the *Philosophical Investigations*, where it acquired a clearly grammatical character: 'Asking whether and how a proposition can be verified is only a special form of the question "How do you mean?" The answer is a contribution to the grammar of the proposition' (PI, §353).

3

Wittgenstein's critique of Frege in the notes from 1929 to 1932

Having returned to Cambridge in January 1929, Ludwig Wittgenstein plunged himself into work and, after a break of ten years, recorded his insights in a diary again. The themes of his notes varied widely, ranging from phenomenology, to spatial vision, numbers, propositions, mathematical infinity, colours, the grammar of commands and the expression 'I've a toothache', to polemics with Russell, Frege and Ramsey. Out of this wealth of ideas, I will focus below on Wittgenstein's comments on Frege's critique of formalism. Several Wittgenstein scholars (Baker and Hacker 2005: 46–7; Kienzler 1997: 200) insist that these remarks actually form a very important source which stands at the origin of the language-games conception and, consequently, of the entire discourse on meaning and language which we know from the *Philosophical Investigations*. Still, I believe that whether Felix Mühlhölzer (2008: 116) is right to contend that Wittgenstein's reflections on mathematics were a decisive impulse for his later use-oriented philosophy is still an open question that calls for further examination. In this chapter, however, my main aim is different, as I seek to analyse Wittgenstein's remarks about the Fregean critique of formalism in more detail and to define their relevance to the transitional period in which they were formulated. Specifically, my point is that they not only herald Wittgenstein's future position but also re-state some of the insights from the *Tractatus Logico-Philosophicus*. I argue that these remarks are not so much a critique of Frege as rather a defence of the formalist standpoint in this dispute, especially of the formalist anti-metaphysical investment.

This chapter is a slightly revised version of my article 'The Middle Wittgenstein's Critique of Frege', *International Journal of Philosophical Studies*, vol. 28/2020, 75–95.

1. Frege's critique of formalism

Frege included his critique of formalism in §86–§137 of the second volume of his *Grundgesetze der Arithmetik* (*The Basic Laws of Arithmetic*). Frege's direct adversaries were his Jena colleagues: Johannes Thomae and Eduard Heine, who were upholders of what came to be referred to as older – or radical – formalism in the philosophy of mathematics. At the beginning of §88, Frege quotes Thomae from *Elementare Theorie der analytischen Functionen einer complexen Veränderlichen* (*Elementary Theory of Analytical Functions of a Complex Variable*) (1898):

> The formal conception of the numbers works within more modest limits than the logical. It asks not, what are numbers and what do they demand, but rather it asks, what do we require of numbers in arithmetic. Now, for the formal conception, arithmetic is a game with signs, which one may well call empty, thereby conveying that (in the calculating game) they do not have any content except that which is attributed to them with respect to their behaviour under certain combinatorial rules (game rules). A chess player makes use of his pieces in a similar fashion: he attributes certain properties to them that constrain their behaviour in the game, and the pieces are only external signs for this behaviour. There is, of course, a significant difference between chess and arithmetic. The rules of chess are arbitrary; the system of the rules of arithmetic is such that, by means of simple axioms, the numbers can be related to intuitive manifolds and as a consequence perform essential service for us in the knowledge of nature.
>
> (Frege 2013: 97–8)

According to Frege, formalism treats numbers as written or printed signs which possess properties of material figures, such as chess pieces. In this model, numerical sequences are envisaged just as arrangements of such figures. What matters in chess pieces is not what they represent but what rules govern their behaviour on the board. If we misplace, say, a rook, we can pick any random object to replace the missing piece without losing anything, perhaps except some aesthetic appeal. The same holds for arithmetic, where numbers are treated as signs or figures, in which their meaning/reference (*Bedeutung*), as Frege understands it, does not matter. In the calculation game (*Rechenspiel*), the signs-game (*Zeichenspiel*) or the numbers-game (*Spiel mit den Zahlen*),[1] the rules are important. Frege calls this concept *formale Arithmetik* (formal arithmetic) and contrasts it with *inhaltliche Arithmetik* (variously translated into English as 'arithmetic with content', 'meaningful arithmetic', 'contentual arithmetic', 'contentful arithmetic', etc.). While the question of what numbers are is just a redundant metaphysical problem in formal arithmetic, in contentual arithmetic, numbers are regarded as objects representing meanings of numerals, and mathematical equations are considered to be thought-expressing propositions. The numeral sign '0' does not have the property of making the sign '1' when it is added to the sign '1'. At the same time, written signs have properties that cannot be ascribed to numbers. For instance, circularity is not the property of the number signed by '0'.

Mathematics is a science to Frege, not a numbers-game; and, for its part, science is a quest for truth.[2] At this point, Frege advances his first objection to formalism: one associated with what he called 'applicability' (*Anwendbarkeit*). According to Thomae, while arithmetic is indeed similar to chess, the chess rules are arbitrary, but the rules of arithmetic are not and, as such, can be applied to the study of nature. To Frege, such an account is insufficient since the difference between the game of chess and the game of numbers lies beyond arithmetic itself – in other sciences which use it. As a system of rules, arithmetic is located exactly on the same level as chess, and as such it is arbitrary and resembles art or a game, rather than science. According to Frege, arithmetic can be regarded as an aid in the study of nature only if numerals do mean something. The numbers are not the numerals without reference to the independently existing objects that are their meanings (*Bedeutungen*). In meaningful arithmetic, equations and inequations are sentences which convey thoughts and, as such, are not arbitrary, while in formal arithmetic equations and inequations can be likened to the positions of chess pieces on the board, which can be changed according to certain rules, irrespective of the meanings of the pieces. Frege writes:

> Why should a group like '3 = 4' not be allowed? In contentual arithmetic, of course, it cannot occur with any claim to validity, since what matters there are references of the number-signs. The reason lapses here. Writing down a figure-group like '3 = 4' has not been prohibited at least this far. It is only when such a prohibition is decreed that a contradiction arises, or better a conflict within the rules, which are partly prohibitive, partly permissive.
>
> (2013: 123, §117)

Arguing against the arbitrariness of arithmetic, Frege first points to meaning and sense. It is also on them that he predicates the applications of arithmetic: numbers and numerical relations are applicable in physics, astronomy, geology and the like, because they represent and express something; they are meaningful statements which can be either true or false. Applicability, which Frege addresses in §91,[3] is also a paramount feature of science for him, though he understands applicability as an internal (logical) property of arithmetic rather than an external (empirical) one.[4] Moreover, he imperatively binds the scientific nature of arithmetic to applicability, which he understands as an example of deductive reasoning. Deduction is possible only if it starts from true thoughts, that is, from facts.[5]

Another objection mounted by Frege against formalism is that it fails to differentiate between a game as such and its theory.[6] The moves of chess pieces follow the particular rules of the game of chess, but the rules themselves are the basis and the theory of the game, rather than its object. Neither the pieces on the chessboard nor any moves express the rules, for they do not express anything altogether – not any thought which could be either true or false. A general mathematical formula, such as '$a + b = b + a$' renders a certain rule of 'the calculation game', without being itself an object of the game, something that is played and is comparable to the placement of pieces on the chessboard. It can rather be compared to a linguistic expression of a particular chess rule. As such, it belongs to the theory of this game, which consists of meaningful propositions about the moves of the pieces, chess positions and play systems, which can be demonstrated like mathematical theorems. According to Frege, there are thus two kinds of rules: rules regarding the manipulation of pieces in the game itself (these rules can be established in a purely arbitrary way without taking any meaning into account) and rules based on which the same pieces are viewed as signs in the theory of the game. Crucially, the rules of the game theory, rather than arbitrary, must be sense-oriented, with the sense expressed by particular configurations of the signs (pieces) in the game theory. In relation to mathematical theories, it would mean that if we could imagine a formal system – a calculation game – there would be nothing to stop us from constructing a metatheory of this calculation game consisting of meaningful propositions derived from deductive evidence. According to Frege, the formalist point of view cannot prevent a metatheory from emerging but, at the same time, does not want to have it in the philosophy of mathematics. The reason is that such a metatheory would have to include some content, which contravenes the formalist tenets. Unable to forestall the forming of a metatheory, the formalists could only formalize it anew. Yet, they would be thwarted by another difficulty, which is pointed out by Frege: how can we know that the formalized set of metatheoretical rules is complete and no contradiction will appear as we go on? After all, there are countless figure-number groups on the chessboard of arithmetic. Until the full list of rules is established, formalization thus remains incomplete and inapplicable, because it does not preclude contradictions. Here, the charge of not differentiating between the game and the theory of the game ties in with the critique of the formalist account of the applicability of mathematics. The formalists are unable to consistently empty mathematics of meaning and sense; at most, they are only capable of removing content from mathematical propositions through the meta-statement of their derivability. But the statement 'that a given formula is derivable', as Michael Dummett notices, 'is still a meaningful a priori statement in a language'.[7] The formalists fail to eliminate the principle of meaningful a priori statements from mathematics; more than that, they articulate such statements themselves, which reveals and makes us aware of the key distinction between the game of chess and chess theory – theory and metatheory.[8]

Frege's third objection, presented in §121– §136, concerns the inability of formalism to explain coherently the notion of infinite sequences and irrational numbers. The only infinity allowed by the upholders of formalism is potential and not actual infinity. 'Thomae believes that it is possible to advance from a number to ever greater and greater numbers since nothing places a boundary on new formation by addition', notes Frege (2013: 127, §123), and he dismisses this approach entirely, claiming that the formation of new numbers is constrained just as the expansion of a city is. He observes: 'We have neither an infinite blackboard, nor infinitely much chalk at our disposal' (2013: 127, §123). This empirical argument may seem completely out of place as physical infinity is not Thomae's point. Still, Frege is by no means being inconsistent since, on the formalist model, numbers are interpreted the way material products are; that is as numeric figures 'made of' chalk and ink. Of course, Thomae's imaginable rejoinder could be that the sequence currently written on a surface always has a finite number of terms, but the possibility of expanding it is actually unlimited. Nonetheless, possible numerical signs are not numerical signs at all, just like possible houses are not houses as such. A given numerical sequence cannot consist of numbers that are written down, numbers that are not but can be written down and numbers that are not and cannot be written down, just like a sequence of houses is not composed of houses already built, houses yet to be built and houses never to be built. In Frege's view, formalism is unable to provide a satisfying explanation of infinite sequences; in particular, it cannot account for the irrational numbers since '[t]o introduce the irrationals, we require infinitely many numbers, and formal arithmetic only has a finite collection of number-figures' (Frege 2013: 134, §131). In order to introduce the irrational numbers, formal arithmetic, as Frege sees it, must again become content-arithmetic and speak of actual infinity. If we did not know the concept, we could not put the word 'infinite' to any meaningful use. For why should we need a word if the thing it means is missing?

2. Wittgenstein's defence

Before addressing the central issue of this chapter, an outline of Wittgenstein's early philosophy of mathematics is in order. The *Tractatus* does not directly evoke formalism. The Tractarian point of reference is provided by logicism as developed by Bertrand Russell and Frege, which was basically preoccupied with defining the number in terms of set theory and with transforming induction into definition. Wittgenstein took a slightly different approach to the construction of the natural numbers; also, he somewhat differently conceived of the unity of logic and mathematics: 'Mathematics is a logical method' (TLP, 6.2). First and foremost, Wittgenstein dismissed the theory of classes as redundant in mathematics and, at best, secondary to the concepts of operation and the series of forms in logic. Briefly, unlike in 'former logic', the search for general forms, including the definition of number, did not involve defining and deducing, but rather focused on the possibility of effectively generating some forms from other forms. The position that Wittgenstein espoused in the *Tractatus* tends to be described as a variety of logicism (Black 1964: 340; Frascolla 1994: 37, 1998: 133; Marion 1998: 26).[9] Nevertheless, the *Tractatus* is also said to exude 'the formalistic flavor' (Frascolla 2017: 310). The point is that, according to Wittgenstein, mathematical propositions do not describe any mathematical entities and hold no assertoric content ('A proposition of mathematics does not express a thought', TLP, 6.21); instead, they are expressions of the rules of syntax, that is, rules for the use of signs grounded in their formal properties. Wittgenstein's early anti-realistic stance in the philosophy of mathematics is exemplified by his treatment of mathematical propositions as equations, which express the substitutability of two expressions (cf. TLP, 6.24). Yet what would this substitutability (conveyed by the '=' sign) be should the assertion and reference to objects of the mathematical notions be discarded? Unlike Frege, Wittgenstein does not ground the substitutability of the two expressions of an equation in the identity of their meaning, understood as the identity of their denotations, but rather in the structural (formal) properties of the expressions themselves. For example, the correctness of $2 + 2 = 4$ consists in the formal possibility of obtaining both parts of the equation from one: $(1 + 1) + (1 + 1) = (1 + 1 + 1 + 1)$ (cf. TLP, 6.231, 6.232). Substitutability can be seen in the signs themselves, and, to realize this, one does not need to go beyond the signs. Wittgenstein relied on the same reasoning in his later defence of formalism against Frege's critique, in which the concept of game played the crucial role.

Addressing this defence as such, we should begin from the fact that Wittgenstein concluded that the formalist comparison of mathematics to a game was apt and useful in describing mathematics. In his discussion with Schlick and Waismann on 19 June 1930, Wittgenstein said:

> Part of formalism is right and part is wrong.
>
> The truth of formalism is that every syntax can be conceived of as a system of rules of a game. I have been thinking about what Weyl may mean when he says that the formalist conceives of the axioms of mathematics as like chess-rules. I want to say that not only the axioms of mathematics but all syntax is arbitrary.
>
> In Cambridge I have been asked whether I believe that mathematics is about strokes of ink on paper. To this I reply that it is so in just the sense in which chess is about wooden figures. For chess does not consist in pushing wooden figures on wood. ... It does not matter what a pawn looks like. It is rather the totality of rules of a game that yields the logical position of a pawn. A pawn is a variable just like 'x' in logic.
>
> (WVC, 103–4)

Basically, Wittgenstein reiterates the formalist concepts of sign and meaning and deploys them to advance his own ideas. The meaning of chess pieces resides in the rules that determine their behaviour in the game, and the sign, likewise, means for him the totality of the rules that govern its use in language. Importantly, Wittgenstein also relies on such reasoning when investigating geometry, whose signs appear to be directly linked to the experience of space and which for this reason was neither logicized by Frege nor formalized by Thomae. So even in this most scopic of mathematical disciplines, meaning is determined not so much by the geometric properties of objects as rather by the way in which expressions are used in the game that goes by the name of geometry. In the note of 20 May 1930, Wittgenstein wrote:

> Different chess-pieces: bishops, knights, etc., correspond to different words.
>
> I have hit here upon that method of explaining signs which Frege ridiculed so much.
>
> One could, that is to say, explain words like 'knight', 'bishop', and so on, by giving the rules relating to these pieces.
>
> Exactly the same holds for the expressions 'point' and 'straight line', etc. in geometry. One sees what a point is and what a straight line is only by the position each occupies in a system of rules.
>
> (MS 108, 169)

Wittgenstein proceeds to consider the situation where two different rules yield two different kinds of words. Because each word is underpinned by its own rule of use, wherever there are two different words there must also be two different rules. If the difference between two kinds of words were not bound to the difference between two kinds of rules, differentiating these words would not make any sense. This was also underscored by Frege himself in §111 of *Grundgesetze*, where he insisted that if all rules related to two figures were also related to a third one, it was pointless to differentiate them. However, the essence of Frege's position was 'that the rules find grounding in the reference of the signs' (2013: 101). For Wittgenstein, rules are logically prior to figures or signs. Given this, the objection Frege made to formalism by citing the materiality of the sign was misconceived. This shift from the meaning (*Bedeutung*) of expressions to the rules of using them had far-ranging consequences. Admittedly, the idea had already been articulated in the *Tractatus*, where Wittgenstein had claimed that 'we cannot give a sign the wrong sense' (TLP, 5.4732), but now, in the transitional period between 1929 and 1932, Wittgenstein overthrew the entire paradigm generated by the notions of the sign and its signified. The three relationships – of the sign to the rule, of the sign to sense (*Sinn*) and of the sign to meaning (*Bedeutung*) – were brought in stark contrast. (Of course, the relation between meaning and sense was more complex in Frege, given that he comprehended the sense of an expression as a way in which its meaning was given to us.)

Another factor to be taken into account is the so-called context principle, which Wittgenstein himself consistently endorsed and which can be understood as stating that the sense of a part of a proposition depends on how it is placed and used in this proposition. Therefore, one does not capture the point fully by simply opposing the rules of use to Frege's concept of sense and meaning.[10] Wittgenstein's critique, which bypasses some aspects of Frege's distinction between *Sinn* and *Bedeutung*, can be justified by the fact that Frege did not explicitly refer either to the context principle or to the complex relationship between sense and meaning in his polemics against formalism in the *Grundgesetze*. Frege simply pursued another goal; specifically, he endeavoured to preserve mathematics from being reduced to a 'mere game' (*müßiges Spiel*) that disregarded the meanings of signs, which he considered to be the core idea of formalism and which made him adamant in pitting meaning against the rules of use, for '[i]t is striving for truth that drives us always to advance from the sense to the thing meant' (1984: 163). Rather than criticizing Frege, Wittgenstein's intention was actually to defend the formalist notion that one did not need to reach beyond signs to understand their meaning. Crucially, understanding takes place on the level of the signs themselves and the way they are used.[11] Wittgenstein agreed with Frege that numbers were not marks on paper, but he did not accept the view that they had meanings (*Bedeutungen*) conceived as objects. According to Wittgenstein, the meaning of numeral signs in mathematics was derived from the rules of their use. Defending formalism required making a lucid point, even at the price of passing over certain nuances of Frege's argument. In his conversation with Schlick and Waismann on 19 June 1930, Wittgenstein reportedly said:

> *Frege* was right in objecting to the conception that the numbers of arithmetic are signs. The sign '0', after all, does not have the property of yielding the sign '1' when it is added to the sign '1'. Frege was right in this criticism. Only he did not see the other, justified side of formalism, that the symbols of mathematics, although they are not signs, lack a meaning. For Frege, the alternative was this: either we deal with strokes of ink on paper or these strokes of ink are signs *of something* and their meaning is what they go proxy for [*vertreten*]. The game of chess itself shows that these alternatives are wrongly conceived – although it is not the wooden chessmen we are dealing with, these figures do not go proxy for anything, they have no meaning [*Bedeutung*] in Frege's sense. There is still a third possibility, the signs can be used the way they are in the game.
>
> (WVC, 105, italics original)

Notably, Wittgenstein is not entirely fair here, because Frege was perfectly aware of the third option pointed out by Thomae. In Frege's view, to say that signs were empty but acquired content via the rules for their use in the game was to produce just an appearance of content. One cannot say, for example, that the black knight denotes something because of the rules the way the name Sirius denotes a particular fixed star. Clearly, Frege knew very well that the material sign and the sign as an object of a rule-governed action were two different things, but this distinction basically did not change anything about formalism as it did not fill arithmetic with content.[12] Therefore, in the cited passage from the conversation at Schlick's home, Wittgenstein not so much develops a third possibility competing with Frege's alternatives as rather carries on the idea that Frege discarded and does so in order to grasp the relationship between the sense of a sign and the rule of its use. According to Frege, content is not conferred on signs by drawing on their rules of use; or, in other words, use cannot be the content of signs. They continue to be empty.[13]

Wittgenstein's enquiry into the essence of the formalist framework in mathematics and into Frege's critique of it led him to conclude that Frege had failed to recognize the gist of Thomae's and Heine's position. This is at least what Waismann suggested to Wittgenstein, and he accepted this view (WVC, 150).

Yet, as we have seen, this was not exactly an apt conclusion as Frege had indeed grasped that gist – that is, he had accurately explained the comparison of mathematics to the game of chess though he had not considered it correct, first and foremost because of the formalist rejection of semantics. Unlike Frege, Wittgenstein viewed the comparison of mathematics to the game of chess as seminal and relevant to explaining the question of meaning as well. First of all, the formalists foregrounded the notion of rules, which Wittgenstein picked up and developed throughout his later philosophy. At the core of formalism, as he saw it, was the insight that the meaning of chess pieces and of the game of chess as such was constituted by its rules, just like the meaning of signs in mathematics and of words in our language was determined by their rules of use and not the other way round, as claimed by Frege, who insisted that rules ensued from the meanings of figures, signs and words. The two positions generated different approaches to the problem of understanding, which is particularly relevant to my argument, because Wittgenstein's response to Frege's critique of formalism is usually analysed in the context of the philosophy of mathematics, which may be why the 'pedagogical' aspect of understanding and learning the rules tends to be overlooked. Admittedly, in his notes, Wittgenstein himself located this critique amidst his considerations on mathematics; however, later, for example when compiling *The Big Typescript*, he re-arranged his argument to tie it with the question of understanding,[14] as exemplified in the following passage:

> When Frege argues against a formal conception of arithmetic he is saying, as it were: These pedantic explanations of symbols are idle if we understand the symbols. And understanding is like seeing a picture from which all the rules follow (and by means of which they become understandable). But Frege doesn't see that this picture is in turn nothing but a sign, or a calculus, that explains the written calculus to us. And in general, what we call 'understanding a language' is like the understanding we get of a calculus when we come to know the reasons for its existence or its practical application. In that case too, we merely come to know a more surveyable symbolism in place of the strange one. [Here 'understanding' means something like 'having an overview.']
>
> (BT, 3)

This comparison of the Fregean understanding to seeing a picture may suggest an entirely misguided idea that knowing, for example, what numbers are is direct and unmediated by language and the rules of arithmetic. The definition of number as a class of classes has nothing in common with the immediate knowledge of ideal beings or with seeing a picture.[15] For Frege, understanding symbols always entails understanding them in language. This does not mean, of course, that his logicism is not informed by certain metaphysical tenets, such as that mathematics and logic are sciences of immaterial objects existing independently of their subjective representations and that the meanings and senses of language expressions by means of which we render these objects are objective and communicable. Yet, again, Wittgenstein's target is not Frege himself, whose outlook he radically simplifies, not to say distorts. What Wittgenstein is after is a vivid background against which to show his own form, that is, the relation of understanding to overview, to the perspicuity of symbolism within which we operate and use numbers. Understanding would thus be an ability to navigate, which is possible only when one attains a clear overview. Hence, Wittgenstein insists that understanding means having an overview. Learning the rules, learning how to navigate in calculation means, at the same time, learning the meanings of signs. The sign $\sqrt{-1}$ is possible only if we can navigate the complex numbers calculus, if we have a clear overview of the rules of this calculus. Still, the rules do not result from the meaning of the sign $\sqrt{-1}$ as some supra-sensory correlate, a spiritual object or an image we associate with it. Behind the sign is just a rule stating how it is used in a given system of signs. Wittgenstein's entire later philosophy is permeated with a critique of Frege's idea that the rules of language are underpinned by the meanings of symbols.[16] Meanwhile, for Wittgenstein, it is always a calculus, an ability to navigate numbers, that stands at the origin. Certainly, this ability is more difficult to master for the complex numbers than for the natural numbers, but its essence is the same. Both formalism and logicism are only interpretations and philosophies of the pre-existing practice of calculation. After all, we would not be able to learn how to count from the writings of Frege, Thomae or David Hilbert. If unacquainted with numbers, one would find their works entirely incomprehensible. In Wittgenstein's view, the difference between the formalists and Frege lies in that Frege, as it were, appropriates the practice of calculating we know from school and claims that formalism produces a new one. By the same token, he presupposes his own judgements to be correct. Therefore, it is not so much that Frege's theory of numbers (conceived as non-sensory meanings of numerical signs) gives grounding to arithmetic as rather that the existing practice of adding, subtracting, multiplying, etc., is the object of this theory's philosophical interpretation. The same, however, can be said about formalism, which, for its part, interprets arithmetic in the framework of the rules governing numerical calculations. Denying the need to 'ground' mathematics in something else, Wittgenstein rejected both logicism and formalism as grounding discourses. Nonetheless, he considered the latter to be founded on the apt notions of game and rules, which better accounted for our practice of numerical operations, without calling for a metaphysical enquiry into the nature of these peculiar beings. The anti-metaphysical and anti-essentialist investment of formalism must have appealed to Wittgenstein far more powerfully than Frege's logicism.

Of particular importance in this context was the concept of game applied by the formalists to mathematics and, later, extended by Wittgenstein onto the whole of language. Consequently, the notions of *Zeichenspiel* or *Rechenspiel* can be said to have served as a model for the concept of language games. In his notes, Wittgenstein was to repeatedly revisit the chess analogy, Frege's critique and the concept, understanding and application of rules. He did so, for example, in the autumn of 1931, when he once again engaged in a polemic with *Grundgesetze der Arithmetik*. On 5 October 1931, Wittgenstein wrote at the very beginning of MS 112, entitled *Bemerkungen zur philosophischen Grammatik* (*Remarks towards Philosophical Grammar*):

> Arithmetic is no game … There isn't any winning or losing.
> But one could imagine … an arithmetical game. …
> What do we deny mathematics when we say it is only a game (or: it is a game)?
> A game in contrast to what? What do we award mathematics when we say (it isn't a game), its propositions make sense?
>
> (MS 112, 1)

These observations were included in Chapter 108 of *The Big Typescript*, entitled 'Mathematics Compared to a Game', in which Wittgenstein also addressed the limitations of such a comparison. Besides winning not being a purpose in mathematics (unlike, for example, in chess), there is no room in a game for affirming and negating.[17] Supposing, we did the multiplication 21 x 8 = 148 in the calculation game, which were a false move, but ~ (21 x 8 = 148) were a correct arithmetical proposition which had no application in our game: 'So one ought to say: No, the word "arithmetic" is not the name of a game. (Of course once again this is trivial.) – But the meaning of the word "arithmetic" can be explained by the relationship of arithmetic to an arithmetical game, or also by the relationship of a chess problem to the game of chess' (BT, 373).

Discussing the sense of mathematical propositions, Wittgenstein cites Frege: 'But a mathematical proposition does express a thought.' Any answer to the question what thought is expressed by a mathematical proposition must be a proposition itself. Thus, can the thought of a mathematical proposition be expressed by any other proposition or only by this very proposition? Or, perhaps, it cannot be expressed at all? Wittgenstein agrees with Frege's critique of psychologism: '[I]f you say that the mental processes accompanying the use of mathematical symbols are different from those accompanying chess, I don't know what to say about that' (MS 112, 3; PG, 289). Still, he rejects the notion of a 'pure thought', one that is independent of its expression and dissociated from the proposition. Of course, in Frege, the problem is more complex. On the one hand, because a thought cannot be grasped (*fassen*) independently of the sentence which is its structural model, the grasping of thoughts (i.e. thinking) is mediated by language.[18] On the other, Wittgenstein is right insofar that Frege emphatically claimed that a thought was 'timeless and unchangeable' (1984: 370) and in this sense independent of language expressions.[19] Emphatically, in Wittgenstein, the rejection of a 'pure thought' is grounded in the link between meaning and the rules of use. When Wittgenstein says that mathematics is like a game, he does not mean that one can win or lose something by playing it, or that there is a winner and a loser in it, but that when one manipulates numbers in mathematics, one follows certain defined rules. In order to perform these manipulations, one needs neither to know the meaning of numerals nor to boast expertise in the mental processes that accompany the use of mathematical symbols. In any case, at school we do not learn to manipulate supra-sensory beings or logical objects which, though different from plants, animals and minerals, are anyway objects, just ones of another kind. This argument by Wittgenstein treats Frege's logical objects as though they were comparable to physical things and played a similar role, which would be an abuse.

In his emphasis on the link between the meaning of expressions and the rules for their use, Wittgenstein sides with formalism against Frege's assertion that 'a mathematical proposition does express a thought [*der Gedanke*]', because if it did not, it would be just a game (*Spiel*).[20] As already mentioned, Frege's first argument against formalism was the argument from applicability. Arithmetic has its applications, while the game of chess does not. Wittgenstein, however, sees the difference between mathematics and the game in rather different terms:

> But one could say that the real distinction [between mathematics and the game] lay in the fact that in the game there is no room for affirmation and negation ...
>
> (Here we may remind ourselves that in elementary school they never work with inequations. The children are only asked to carry out multiplications correctly and never – or hardly ever – asked to prove an inequation.)
>
> (MS 112, 27; PG, 292)

> Calling arithmetic a game is no more no less wrong than calling the moving chessmen according to chess-rules a game; for that can be a calculation too.
>
> So we should say: No, the word 'arithmetic' is not the name of a game. ... But the meaning of the word 'arithmetic' can be explained by bringing out the relationship between arithmetic and an arithmetical game or between a chess problem and the game of chess.
>
> (MS 112, 29; PG, 292)

Subsequently, Wittgenstein directly addresses Frege's division into 'formal arithmetic' and 'contenual arithmetic':

> In the debate between 'formalism' and 'contentful mathematics' what does each side assert? This dispute is so like the one between realism and idealism in that it will soon have become obsolete, for example, and in that both parties make unjust assertions at variance with their day-to-day practice.
>
> (MS 112, 29; PG, 293)

Revisiting the problem of applicability, Wittgenstein observes that the problem of the applicability of arithmetic is something else than the problem of arithmetic as such.

> They [people] think ... that if you make definition out to be a mere substitution rule for signs you take away its significance and importance. Whereas the *significance* of a definition lies in its application, in its importance for life. The same thing is happening today in the dispute between formalism and intuitionism, etc. People cannot separate the importance, the consequence, the application, of a fact from the fact itself; they can't separate the description of a thing from the description of its importance.
>
> (MS 112, 35, italics original; PG, 294)

Wittgenstein would thus not subscribe to Frege's belief that the applicability of arithmetic he discusses is not, unlike in formalism, external applicability but rather internal, that is, logical applicability. The scientific nature of logic does not result from the fact that it is used in arithmetic. In Frege's view, logic deals with the objective laws of thought, just as physics deals with the laws of nature, and the scientific nature of physics is not founded on that, say, a bridge can be built based on its laws. The same is true for logic: although, as the most general of sciences, it is applicable in an array of fields, its essence and its scientific character are independent of all its applications. Wittgenstein emphasizes inconsistencies in Frege's standpoint since, on the one hand, Frege insists on the 'immense intellectual effort' put into arriving at 'a concept in its pure form' (e.g. in his Introduction to *Die Grundlagen der Arithmetik*) (Frege 1953: xix), but on the other he underscores the applicability of arithmetic. The fact that what he means is internal applicability does not make any difference altogether, because it is based on the general tenets of logicism, which Wittgenstein repudiated. To assert, for example, that numbers are logical entities is a metaphysical gesture and not an application. Yet it can be and, in fact, was used by Frege to justify mathematics just as mathematical theorems are justified by their application in physics, geodesy, navigation, etc. For his part, as we remember, Wittgenstein argues that mathematics does not need justifications, because it simply involves operations on numbers – calculations we know from school.

In his defence of formalism, Wittgenstein also addressed Frege's second objection to formalism, in which Frege claimed that formalism conflated the game with the theory of the game. When asked by Waismann whether there could be a theory of chess – and thus a theory of the game of arithmetic – Wittgenstein answered that what was called the theory of chess was not a theory that described anything, but a calculus or, to use Hilbert's expression, a 'technique of our thinking'. To Wittgenstein, there was no difference between saying 'I can get there in eight moves' and saying 'I've proved through theory that I can get there in eight moves'. In symbolism, indeed, one does by means of signs what one does on the chess board by moving pieces. Every step in the calculation corresponds to a step in the game, and the only difference lies in the mechanical movements of wooden pieces. Wittgenstein found it vital to underline that it was unsound to say: this is a pawn and there are such and such rules for this figure: 'It is the rules that *define* this piece: a pawn *is* the sum of rules for its move (a square is a piece too), just as in the case of language the rules define the logic of the word' (WVC, 134, italics original).

Frege's objection to Thomae's formal approach regarding the possibility of having a theory of a game was, nevertheless, quite serious, which Waismann appears to have acknowledged as he cited passages of §107 and §108 of the *Grundgesetze* and asked Wittgenstein to comment on them. In §108, Frege attributed a double role to arithmetic equations: one in the game in which they do not refer to anything (like the arrangements of chess pieces on the chess board do not refer to anything) and the other in the theory of the game, where they refer to rules and consequences of the rules. If it held for chess as well, the rules of the game would be conveyed in the corresponding configurations of the pieces on the chess board, which appear in the game itself too. For example, the equation $31 = 5^2 + 2^2 + 1^2 + 1^2$ can appear in the calculating game and at the same time can express a rule of this game, that is, a sense (specifically, Lagrange's theorem, which states that every natural number can be represented as the sum of four integer squares). However, this would mean having to formulate a general proposition to define how we should understand the configurations of chess pieces as theoretical rules or theorems; in other words, when configurations were the game and when they were its theory. This would entail treating the arrangements of pieces in a dual way: firstly, as part of the game in which they would not refer to anything, having simply emerged from a previous arrangement as a result of a move of a piece and being ready to change again into a new arrangement through the next move; and, secondly, as part of the theory of the game, where they would be theorems and, as such, convey a *sense*.

Wittgenstein's commentary is very astute and does not directly abolish Frege's objection. Supposing, we passed from:

$4 = 2 + 2$[21]

$2 = 1 + 1$

to:

$4 = (1 + 1) + (1 + 1)$.

We could ask whether we passed from the former two equations to the third one, or rather whether we passed from the first *via* the second to arrive at the third. In other words, the question would be whether the former two equations were configurations from which we inferred the third, or whether the second equation represented a *rule* by which we transformed the first equation into the third one. In Wittgenstein's view, we mean exactly the same thing in both cases. To him, this question is in fact altogether irrelevant to the problem of the foundations of arithmetic. One can say, for example, that one makes the conjunction $(4 = 2 + 2) \wedge (2 = 1 + 1)$, and now one needs a rule to formulate the equation

$4 = (1 + 1) + (1 + 1)$.

This rule cannot be represented by $2 = 1 + 1$, just as in the modus ponens

p

p → q

―――――

q

»p → q« does not represent the inference rule. According to Wittgenstein, the rule of inference cannot be represented by a proposition at all. He believes thus that the rule of replacement cannot be expressed by the equation $2 = 1 + 1$, either. However, as he insists, 'the rule and the equation have something in common, their logical multiplicity, and *for this reason*, we can as it were *project the rule onto the equation*' (WVC, 152, italics original; cf. also TLP, 6.1264). The question how one arrives from the equation $4 = 2 + 2$ to the equation $4 = (1 + 1) + (1 + 1)$ should be answered as follows: by means of the rule, which allows one to replace 2 with $1 + 1$. The verbalized rule and the equation $2 = 1 + 1$ correspond to each other, but they are not identical. In conclusion, Wittgenstein states that the rule is actually an internal relation which obtains between the equations $2 + 2 = 4$, $1 + 1 = 2$ and the equation $(1 + 1) + (1 + 1) = 4$; and, being an internal relation, it cannot be represented by a configuration in the game (cf. WVC, 157). This way of thinking was already discernible in the *Tractatus*, as mentioned above.

Let us take another example that Wittgenstein offers and imagine a series of numbers written down in two rows:

1 2 3 4 5

1 4 9 16 25

If we understand the rule for the formation of this series, we can continue writing down numbers in it, but we can also express this rule as:

$x\,()$

$x^2\,()^2$

and say that the rule consists in forming a series of the natural numbers and always providing the squares of these numbers underneath. However, according to Wittgenstein, letters do not express generality as generality cannot be conveyed in symbols at all; it can only be rendered in induction. The algebraic formula corresponds to induction, but cannot express it. By writing:

x

x^2,

I do not convey a general rule; I only put together a particular combination of letters, which are just signs in the same way as 1, 2, 3, 4 are signs. As Wittgenstein insists, a rule cannot be expressed by a singular, specific configuration, because 'the essential thing about it [a rule], its generality, is inexpressible. Generality shows itself in application. I have to *read* this generality *into* the configuration' (WVC, 154, italics original). It does not matter in the least whether this is a configuration of letters or a configuration of numbers since in either case generality must be read into it. It is also not the case that the rule expressed by x and x^2 is simply *applied* to particular numbers, because in order to do so, one would need another rule that stated how one passed from an arrangement of letters to the formation of a series of numbers. However, such a rule would again have to consist of signs (letters), and those would themselves require a new rule explaining how these signs were used, and so on. Wittgenstein emphatically concludes: '*A rule is not like the mortar between two bricks*. We cannot lie down a rule for the application of another rule. We cannot apply one rule "by means of" another rule' (WVC, 155, italics original). That two things are connected by means of a third one is deemed by Wittgenstein as a peculiar logical mistake since we can imagine two things that are connected directly – without any mortar in the form of a rule – for example, like links in a chain are.

In his reasoning, Wittgenstein reduces the difference between a game and its theory, a difference that was pointed out by Frege. Rather than performing two different functions (one in a game and another in its theory), configurations of signs do *the same thing* in different ways. An equation and a rule have the same logical multiplicity, and that is why we can say that they are somehow connected, that they have something in common. This something is generality, albeit variously expressed. Implicit, but quite clear, in Wittgenstein's argumentation is the theory about what cannot be *said* but can be *shown*. Included in the *Tractatus*, the theory helped Wittgenstein advance his critiques of Russel's 'theory of types' and of Frege's *Begriffsschrift*. Basically, the theory held that the logical properties of language were inexpressible, a position typical of the *Tractatus*, just like the concept of internal relations.[22]

To conclude, the defence of formalism against Frege's critique that Wittgenstein developed in his notes from 1929 to 1932 paved the way to the concept of language as a family of 'language games', which we know from the *Philosophical Investigations*. While this defence did not always do justice to Frege's theory, its aim was not to determine who was right or wrong, but rather to bring forth the idea that served to convey the prescriptive (normative) character of mathematical propositions. It did not entail the complete acceptance of the view advocated by Thomae, Heine and Hilbert, either. Wittgenstein could not endorse any mathematical position, which is directly communicated in *The Big Typescript*, where he wrote, for example, that '[a] calculus cannot give us fundamental insights into mathematics' and 'calculus is not a chess piece that belongs to mathematics'. We do not say anything about mathematics if we define it as the calculation game. The word 'calculus' (alternately, 'calculation games' or 'number-games') does not have to appear in mathematics: 'And if it is used in a calculus nonetheless, that doesn't make the calculus into a metacalculus; in such a case the word "calculus" is itself just a chess piece, like all the others'

(BT, 376). In his defence of formalism against the objections launched by Frege, Wittgenstein built on some formalist ideas of the *Tractatus*, first and foremost on the general insistence that when talking about mathematical proposition, one should not abandon the level of signs and their use. In the notes from 1929 to 1932, this insistence is asserted and developed in the formalist comparison of mathematics to a game, in which the notions of rules and use are foregrounded, a concept Wittgenstein continued to elaborate throughout his later philosophy. It is in this foregrounding of rules that the difference between Wittgenstein and Frege lies as the latter considered rules to have a justification in the meaning of expressions. Frege admitted that the understanding of these expressions occurred in language, and language itself merely helped us grasp an abstract entity which was referred to as meaning. As for the middle Wittgenstein, it was gradually becoming clear to him that the understanding of expressions was not a matter of grasping any abstract entity, but a matter of using these expressions according to the rules which were given to us through the explanation of meaning. Hence, these rules were not hidden, unlike the logical syntax of language, which the *Tractatus* set out to discover by analytical means. Of course, Wittgenstein did not unreservedly accept all the formalist presuppositions. For example, similarly to Frege, he did not believe that numbers were only 'strokes of ink on paper', but neither did he claim that 'these strokes of ink are signs of *something*'. Rather, he asserted that the meaning of signs in mathematics and the meaning of words in our language were determined by the rules that governed their use. Whereas Frege insisted that these rules needed a metaphysical foundation in the form of meaning, Wittgenstein underscored the role of human creativity in their formation.

The formalistic game analogy had one more important aspect, namely, the problem of understanding and learning the rules for the use of words which we learn the way we learn chess moves, that is, simply by playing. In doing this, we do not need a theory to provide any further explanation of the moves. This aspect tends to be overlooked by scholars, especially when the defence of formalism against Frege's critique is approached as part of Wittgenstein's philosophy of mathematics. Still, Wittgenstein's reflections do not really seem to be meta-mathematical; rather, they seek to illuminate notions such as meaning, sense, use and rule from within language through comparisons, examples and paraphrases, instead of by creating a metatheory or a metalanguage, which Wittgenstein always vocally opposed.

In his middle work, Wittgenstein did not revisit the detailed issues associated with Frege's (and Russell's) logicism which he addressed in the *Tractatus*. He concluded that the Tractarian position on sense and meaning, logical constants, definitions of number and proposition, etc., which he had developed in polemics with his masters, was correct. Now, that is, after 1929, he regarded Frege as one of the participants, alongside Luitzen Brouwer and Hilbert, in the dispute on the foundations of mathematics. Wittgenstein's entanglement in Frege's polemics with formalism is relevant not only to the former's view of mathematics but also (first of all perhaps) to the whole of his later philosophy. It is also representative of the critique of Frege in the transitional phase between the *Tractatus* and the *Philosophical Investigations*.

4

'A clever man got caught in this net of language!'

Wittgenstein's attack on set theory

In the 1930s, Ludwig Wittgenstein was very much committed to the philosophy of mathematics. His engagement was undoubtedly fuelled by exchanges with Frank Ramsey, which also expanded the intellectual horizon of the issues addressed by Wittgenstein. While in the *Tractatus* period, the logicism of Bertrand Russell and Gottlob Frege provided the major point of reference for Wittgenstein's philosophy of logic and mathematics, his notes from the transitional period feature names such as Thoralf Skolem, David Hilbert, Hermann Weyl, Luitzen Brouwer, Richard Dedekind and Georg Cantor. When inspecting these notes, one is struck by Wittgenstein's unambiguous, implacable and scathing criticism of the two latter mathematicians and set theory as a whole. Wittgenstein denounces it as 'wrong' (*falsch*) (MS 106, 155; PR, §145), bewailing that '[m]athematics is ridden through and through with the pernicious idioms of set theory' (MS 106, 251; PR, 211) and dismissively calling it 'empty chatter' (PG, 467) or 'blather' (*Geschwätz*) (BT, 747). This harsh appraisal remained unmitigated in the *Remarks on the Foundations of Mathematics* (written between 1937 and 1944), which teems with even more deprecating expressions, for example 'I believe, and hope, that a future generation will laugh at this hocus pocus' (RFM II, 22) and 'Imagine set theory's having been invented by a satirist as a kind of parody on mathematics. – Later a reasonable meaning was seen in it and it was incorporated into mathematics. (For if one person can see it as a paradise of mathematicians, why should not another see it as a joke?)' (RFM V, 7). In his last articulation on set theory in the *Remarks on the Foundations of Mathematics*, Wittgenstein depicts it with some rhetorical flourish as resembling 'a cancerous growth, seeming to have grown out of the normal body aimlessly and senselessly' (RFM VII, 11).

Such formulations may easily come across as surprising, if not downright astonishing, especially that today set theory is one of the basic mathematical theories applicable to nearly all fields of mathematics.[1] Some mathematician even claim that set theory has revolutionized mathematics to a degree unprecedented since Newton and Leibniz.[2] At the same time, it is also true that when set theory was founded by Cantor towards the end of the nineteenth century, the new framework indeed provoked varying responses from mathematicians, including very negative reactions, such as Leopold Kronecker's veritable hostility. However, when Wittgenstein levelled his most blistering criticism at set theory, it was already a well-entrenched and robustly developing branch of mathematics. Crucially, Wittgenstein's criticism is one of its kind, and I mean this not in terms of his views on logic and mathematics from the *Tractatus* period. In fact, if those are taken into consideration (especially, his critique of logicism as exercised by Russell and Frege, which will shortly be discussed), Wittgenstein's negative attitude to set theory appears to some extent consistent. What one may find eyebrow-raising, though, is the categorical, even impertinent, undertone of his discussion and the attitude that it bespeaks. The point is that Wittgenstein treated set theory not simply as a mathematical concept but as a worldview of sorts – or, rather, an expression of a certain worldview – that permeated the culture and the spirit of his time. Wittgenstein deemed this worldview the harmful and dangerous 'sickness of a time' that needed to be cured, which could only be achieved 'through a changed mode of thought and life, not through a medicine invented by an individual' (RFM II, 23).[3]

This chapter depicts and analyses Wittgenstein's arguments against set theory, with a special focus on his writings from the transitional period and somewhat later works since he never revised his negative assessment of Cantor's work, other than making it even harsher. Before doing this, a brief outline of Wittgenstein's general views on logic and mathematics is in order.

1. The critique of class theory in the *Tractatus Logico-Philosophicus*

In the *Tractatus*, Wittgenstein criticized the idea of reducing mathematics to logic and rejected logicism as practised by Russell and Frege, at the same time describing his own view on the unity of logic and mathematics, which made no room for the notion of class. In 6.031, he was quite straightforward about this: 'The theory of classes is completely superfluous in mathematics.

This is connected with the fact that the generality required in mathematics is not *accidental* generality.' When evoking 'accidentality', Wittgenstein meant that Russell's attempt at defining the basic notions of mathematics, such as number, in logical terms – and, in particular, in set-theoretical terms – was founded on two 'non-logical' axioms: infinity and reducibility. Discarding these axioms was essentially tantamount to dismissing the theory of classes. Wittgenstein is known to have harboured objections to this theory even before producing the *Tractatus*. Specifically, in his *Notebooks, 1914–1916*, he insisted that '[i]n the class-theory it is not yet evident why the proposition needs its counter-proposition. Why it is a part of logical space which is *separated* from the remaining part of logical space' (NB, 56, italics original). In other words, the theory of classes does not show the connection between the proposition and its negation clearly enough. The theory of classes proposes that negation (~p) is a class of propositions contradicting p; however, this means that if p and ~p are regarded as two separate classes of propositions, there is no connection between p and ~p. Wittgenstein institutes this connection by defining negation as a logical operation that produces classes and, as such, pre-exists them. Wittgenstein also argues that p and ~p share 'a common boundary', as a result of which the negative of a proposition can only be established by means of this very proposition. Briefly, instead of relying on set-theoretical categories, Wittgenstein proposes explaining negation as an operation in which one proposition is constructed on the basis of another one.

These reflections were later developed in theses 5.2–5.23 of the *Tractatus*, where Wittgenstein linked the notion of operation to the notion of internal relations and defined operation as a principle transforming one proposition into another, that is, as a rule that constructs one form out of another. Having defined the general form of the proposition, from which it followed that every sentence was the outcome of successive applications of the negation operation to the elementary propositions, and having provided the general form of operation, that is, how a proposition could be produced from another one, Wittgenstein could define 'number' as a particular case of a series of forms,[4] which is ordered by an internal relation and results from repeating a certain operation: x, $\Omega'x$, $\Omega'\Omega'x$, $\Omega'\Omega'\Omega'x$, and so on. Having introduced the natural numbers through the definition: $1 = 0 + 1$; $2 = 0 + 1 + 1$; $3 = 0 + 1 + 1 + 1$; and so on, Wittgenstein arrived at $(0, \xi, \xi + 1)$ as the general form of the natural number, which was derived from the general form of the proposition.[5] This corresponded to performing the +1 operation upon the basis, that is, 0.

In this framework, the concept of 'number' was pivotal, because various mathematical disciplines could be axiomatized on the basis of the axiomatization of arithmetic. In this sense, the project of logicism principally boiled down to defining the natural number in set-theoretical terms and to turning induction into definition. Wittgenstein accepted neither. First, an element in a series of forms is something entirely different from an element in a set, just as a series of forms is not a set in set-theoretical terms. Thus, Wittgenstein rejected Russell's (and Frege's) definition of number as a class of classes with the same number of members. In order to avoid a vicious circle, Russell (1993: 15) defined numerical equivalence between two classes in terms of one-to-one correlations. Wittgenstein regarded the theory of classes as redundant in mathematics and, at best, derivative in logic. He thus replaced it with the notion of operation (a series of forms), which represented a possibility of the effective generation of symbols constituting a given domain. Wittgenstein's thought always demanded deriving some forms from others, that is, a certain *action* which made it possible for the world of propositions or numbers to emerge, to be properly constructed. Importantly, for my later argument, his notion of 'operation' was intensional, meaning that it denoted the generation of symbols in conformity with certain rules. Wittgenstein explicitly put it in his *Notebooks*: 'The concept of operation is quite generally that according to which signs can be constructed according to a rule' (NB, 90). When, propped by this notion of operation, he finally arrived at his general form in TLP, 6.03, the natural numbers were reduced to the notion of successive applications of an operation. The very definition of number as 'the exponent of an operation' (cf. TLP, 6.021) indicates that 'number' is also an intensional concept in Wittgenstein.

The concepts of operation and series comprise the notion of induction expressed as 'and so on' or as three dots placed at the end of logical operations and indicating that these operations can be applied to their own results into infinity. In this sense, as Wittgenstein states, '[t]he concept of successive application of an operation is equivalent to the concept "and so on"' (TLP, 5.2523). Induction makes it possible not only to generate infinite series of forms but also to institute certain relations between their elements. In this way, induction guarantees a 'not accidental generality', to evoke thesis 6.031.

The concepts of induction and operations themselves encompass the notion of infinity, which is basically equivalent to induction.[6] One property shared by all series of forms is that they can be constructed into infinity. But what does 'infinity' actually mean? Did Wittgenstein have in mind actual or potential infinity in the *Tractatus*? This is actually far from obvious. For example, when commenting on Russell's infinity axiom in thesis 5.535, Wittgenstein states: 'What the axiom of infinity is intended to say would express itself in language through the existence of infinitely many names with different meanings.' The infinity of names implies the infinity of objects. Wittgenstein explains: 'Objects make up the substance of the world. That is why they cannot be composite' (TPL, 2.021); objects are stable and enduring, and they form an infinite whole. In 4.2211, Wittgenstein observes that: 'Even if the world is infinitely complex, so that every fact consists of infinitely many states of affairs and every state of affairs is composed of infinitely many objects, there would still have to be objects and states of affairs.' These assertions may be taken to evince that Wittgenstein does not rule out the existence of actual infinity in the *Tractatus*. Such a possibility also inheres in the concept of 'logical space', understood as the infinite whole of all possible propositions. As a proposition only demarcates a certain – one – place in logical space, this space must already be given (see TLP, 3.42) as an infinite and determined whole.[7]

However, these theses, which appear to endorse actual infinity, are on a collision course with thesis 4.1272, in which Wittgenstein claims: 'So one cannot say, for example, "There are objects," as one might say, "There are books." And it is just as impossible to say, "There are 100 objects," or, "There are $\aleph_0$ objects." And it is nonsensical to speak of the *total number of objects*' (italics original). Thus in terms of the Tractarian framework of formal concepts, the proposition 'There are infinitely many objects' is a pseudo-proposition. Wittgenstein introduced the term 'formal concepts' for no other purpose than revealing how formal concepts were confused with genuine (material) concepts. In Wittgenstein's view, formal concepts, such as 'fact', 'function', 'proposition', 'number', 'object', etc., cannot be correctly expressed in language, either by means of the notion of function, as Frege would have it, nor by means of the notion of class, as Russell proposed. In Wittgenstein's model, the formal concept is represented by the propositional variable, and its values are represented by the objects that fall under this concepts. As every variable signifies a constant form characteristic of all its values, it can be regarded as a formal property. If formal concepts are used as genuine concepts rather than as propositional variables, nonsensical pseudo-sentences are produced. In other words, in the *Tractatus* period, Wittgenstein considered 'etc.' or ' … ' to be an adequate expression of infinity, so infinity could only be 'seen' in these symbols and rendered in a certain scheme, pattern or template, which was replicated in repeated applications to successive outcomes of an operation (i.e. to members of a series of forms).

2. *Horror Infiniti:* Wittgenstein's discussions with Ramsey on infinity and quantification

The dismissal of the theory of classes as redundant in mathematics and, at best, secondary in logic, combined with supplanting it with the concepts of operation and series of forms, can undoubtedly be regarded as prolegomena to Wittgenstein's critique of set theory in the transitional period. However, it was only his exchange on infinity and quantification with Frank Ramsey in 1929 that indeed pushed the door wide open for this criticism. Discussions with Ramsey steered Wittgenstein towards finitism, which was the major thread of his polemics with Cantor's and Dedekind's theories.[8]

In the *Tractatus*, it was not a problem for Wittgenstein to follow Russell and Frege in defining universal quantification as the logical product: $\forall x.f(x) = fa \land fb \land fc\ldots$ and existential quantification as the logical sum: $\exists x.fx = fa \lor fb \lor fc\ldots$ (TLP, 5.521). The role of quantification was thus to generate propositions – conjunctions or disjunctions. At the time, it did not really matter to Wittgenstein whether the number of elements in a conjunction or a disjunction was finite or not. However, his discussions with Ramsey prompted him to change his mind on this issue. Ramsey insisted in his 'General Proposition and Causality' that solely quantifications over a finite domain could be regarded as propositions, that is, as conjunctions or disjunctions.[9] Meanwhile, quantifications over an infinite domain, which he called variable hypotheticals, were rules for the generation of propositions rather than propositions as such.[10] If $\forall x.f(x)$ replaces the infinite logical product, one can infer every sentence in the form of *fa*, provided that one knows what '$\land$' means and that this product is true. However, since this cannot be known for infinite conjunction, our inferences are highly uncertain and, more importantly, indeterminate. We cannot know whether at one point or another we will not come across an instance of '$\sim fa$' that is inconsistent with $\forall x f(x)$, because this expression means that the propositional *fx* is true in all cases. Consequently, as Hilbert highlighted,[11] we cannot infallibly infer that $(\exists x)\,fx$ from the proof $\sim \forall x \sim f(x)$.

At the turn of the 1920s, Wittgenstein came to the conclusion that universal quantification could be written as the conjunction $fa \land fb \land fc\ldots$ only if the three dots ' … ' were treated as 'the dots of laziness',[12] used to substitute a finite number of propositions that are arguments of the truth function. This is analogous to listing the letters of the alphabet: *a, b, c*, …, but does not correspond to writing a series of the natural numbers: 1, 2, 3 …. It is exclusively when a conjunction is finite – that is when ' … ' equals 'the dots of laziness' – that we can construct a proposition with sense to replace $fa \wedge fb \wedge fc$ .... Yet this is impossible if the variable is not limited to the finite domain and can take infinitely many values. Such a proposition is devoid of sense in the light of the Tractarian claim of the determinacy of sense (TLP, 4.023) and of the basic impossibility to ascertain the truth conditions of all the elements of an infinitely long conjunction.[13] The point is that a proposition has sense when we know under which circumstances it is true and under which it is false. One can only know this if the variable takes on a finite number of values. (For this reason, the infinite logical sum is nonsense as well.) Given this, in order for the proposition $\forall x.f(x) = fa \wedge fb \wedge fc \ldots$ to have sense, the infinite logical product must be made finite: $\forall x.f(x) = fa \wedge fb \wedge fc \ldots fn$. This, however, is only possible if one adopts what Hans-Johann Glock[14] calls an 'axiom of finitude', which holds that the number of objects in the world is finite. The problem is that the number of objects in the world is an empirical question and not a logical one. Therefore, such an axiom would be a non-logical foundation of logic, and its truth and necessity would be fundamentally dubious, like the 'axiom of infinity' in Russell's 'theory of types', which Wittgenstein decisively criticized and rejected.

3. Set theory: Between the calculus and prose

Discussions with Ramsey made Wittgenstein realize how deeply difficult it was to talk about infinity and that the complications related to the infinite could be avoided in logic and mathematics if we only adhered to finite domains. Such an approach was nothing exceptional, given that mathematics of the day was predominantly finitist. Therefore, Cantor's set theory was a significant event, which Hilbert compared to the emergence of a mathematical paradise. Wittgenstein did not share the optimism expressed by the founder of formalism and, if anything, viewed set theory as a hell. However, Hilbert was a mathematician, and Wittgenstein was a philosopher. More precisely speaking, Wittgenstein's assessment of Cantor's theory was not a mathematician's assessment; rather, it was an assessment by a philosopher of mathematics. To say that much would certainly be true and quite uncontroversial. Moreover, Wittgenstein sought to rigorously differentiate the *calculus* (i.e. algorithm or proof) from everything that was *words* or *prose*. Wittgenstein observed:

> In mathematics *everything* is algorithm, *nothing* meaning; even when it seems there's meaning, because we appear to be speaking *about* mathematical things in

> *words*. ... In set theory what is calculus ought to be separated from what claims to be (and of course cannot be) *theory*. The rules of the game have thus to be separated from inessential statements about the chessmen
>
> (MS 108, 179, italics original).[15]

On another occasion, Wittgenstein evoked *prose* and the calculus:

> It is a strange mistake of some mathematicians to believe that something *inside* mathematics might be dropped because of a critique of the foundations. Some mathematicians have the right instinct: once we have calculated something it cannot drop out and disappear! And in fact, what is caused to disappear by such a critique are names and allusions that occur in the calculus, hence what I wish to call *prose*. It is very important to distinguish as strictly as possible between the calculus and this kind of prose. Once people have become clear about this distinction, all these questions, such as those about consistency, independence, etc., will be removed.
>
> (WVC, 149, italics original)

However, it is a steep challenge to distinguish *prose* from the calculus in Wittgenstein's discourse itself, regarding the grounds for his incisive criticism of Cantor's diagonal method and Dedekind's cuts along with his definition of infinite set. This criticism may suggest that Wittgenstein altogether denied that set theory had mathematical sense. Hilary Putnam, for one, would say it did.[16] Despite Wittgenstein's reiterated assertions that one must not posit anything in philosophy, Putnam believes that Wittgenstein did just that with respect to set theory. More than that, in Putnam's view, what Wittgenstein posited was thoroughly wrong, and his philosophical explorations of conceptual issues, encountered also in science, demanded a considerably greater scientific knowledge and far more respect for science. Below, I seek to show that Putnam's evaluation is too harsh and his interpretations sometimes fail to do justice to Wittgenstein's observations.

3.1. Confounding intensional and extensional contexts

Upon realizing problems bound up with quantification over infinite domains, Wittgenstein looked more carefully into the meanings of and the categorial difference between the words 'finite' and 'infinite'. One of Wittgenstein's first notes after his return to Cambridge refers to his discussions on the infinite with Ramsey:

> I once said there was no extensional infinity. Ramsey replied: 'Can't we imagine a man living for ever, that is simply, never dying, and isn't that extensional

> infinity?' I can surely imagine a wheel spinning and *never* coming to rest. There is a peculiar difficulty in it; it seems to me something in a way accidental (a nonsensical expression) that there are infinitely many objects in the room. But I can *intensionally* think of an INFINITE LAW (or an *infinite rule*) by virtue of which something new is constantly produced – ad infinitum – but naturally only that which a rule can produce, that is, constructions.
>
> It seems thus that infinite rotations of the wheel may be constructions, while I cannot construct new objects. ...
>
> I believe the merely negative description of not stopping cannot yield a positive infinity.
>
> (MS 105, 23–7, italics original; see PR, 304–5)

This implies that at the beginning of 1929 Wittgenstein concluded that there was a fundamental difference between an extensional and intensional take on infinity. He did not see this difference clearly in the *Tractatus* and tended to zigzag from the one context to the other, just like Cantor, Dedekind and Frege did.[17] However, Wittgenstein insisted that an extensionally constructed set essentially differed from an intensionally constructed one. The former way simply involved enumerating the elements of this set, that is, listing its components ('The symbol for a class is a list' [BT, 740]). The latter way entailed defining the rule for the generation of the elements of the set or providing an overall description of its elements.

> To be sure, it is true that all classes that allow a one-one mapping have the same number of members. But the specification of those classes is not the specification of a number. Either we construe classes intentionally, as properties (propositional functions), in which case a specification of equivalent classes does not tell us how many objects fall under them. Or we construe classes extensionally, as extensions, in which case the description of such a classes already contains a picture of the number in question and it is again wrong to wish to define a number through such classes.
>
> *To specify a number is to specify How Many and not to specify equinumerosity.*
>
> (WVC, 221–2, italics original)

In Wittgenstein's view, one of the errors of set theory was to claim that the meaning of a set could be understood without knowing whether this set was finite or infinite and that this could be established only later.[18] This was a wrong assumption, because the term 'set' denoted an entirely different thing in either of these instances. 'Set' was not one and the same concept that was simply more specifically depicted by means of the modifiers 'finite' or 'infinite'. The difference between finite and infinite sets was *a categorial difference*, so what could make sense if said about the former would not make sense when said about the latter. In order to provide grounds for this difference, Wittgenstein referred to the above-mentioned distinction between extensionally and intensionally understood sets. For example, the finite set of all the even numbers smaller than 10 can simply be itemized by enumerating all its elements or, to use Wittgenstein's terminology, we can make its list or provide its extension. Such a list cannot be supplied for infinite sets. An infinite set can be generated exclusively by intension. The only way to list its elements is to define the rule behind it or to come up with a general depiction of these elements. At the same time, Wittgenstein claimed that a correct symbolism should represent infinite sets differently than finite ones. Finiteness and infinity must be visible in the very syntax of a given set. First of all, Wittgenstein emphatically argues that *'Infinite" is not a quantity*. The word "infinite" has a different syntax from a number word' (WVC, 228, italics original). Similarly, 'infinity' does not mean 'an immense number of' though it is used in this way in the sentence 'there are infinitely many stars' as if this word indeed represented reality: 'We wrongly use the word "infinite" like a number word because in everyday speech both are given as answers to the question "How many ... ?"' (BT, 742). In his notes, Wittgenstein observed that '[i]nfinity is not a quantity, but it appears like a quantity. This is our difficulty' (MS 111, 190). These and similar statements indicate that Wittgenstein regarded 'finiteness' as a number, which is to say that one could use this word as a numeral or a reply to the question 'how many?'

According to Wittgenstein, when one says that something is 'infinite', the word is always used as a closer specification of the word 'possible'. For example, when one says that a distance is infinitely divisible, one talks about possibility rather than reality, because what one has in mind is the infinite possibility of repeating the operation of dividing and not that this infinite possibility means the possibility of infinity. The proposition 'a distance is infinitely divisible' can serve as the basis for constructing a series of sentences: 'a distance is divisible into two parts; a distance is divisible into three parts; a distance is divisible into four parts; etc.' This series is generated in compliance with a certain law, that is, through an operation which is performed on one propositional form to produce another form and then repeated on the latter to produce a third one, and so on. We know a priori – which is to say, on the basis of the logical structure of the propositions themselves – that such an operation is viable, meaning that every successive proposition will have sense. Thus, when stating that 'the possibility of division is infinite', one actually states that 'the possibility of constructing propositional forms that describe that division is infinite'. Therefore, an infinite possibility itself appears as an *infinite possibility* in language (WVC, 229) or in symbolism: 'The infinite possibility in the symbol relates – i.e. refers – only to the essence of a finite extension, and this is its way of leaving its size open' (PR, §144). The signs themselves contain merely the possibility, and not the actuality, of repetition. Infinity is thus, in Wittgenstein's view, a property of our language, rather than of reality ('property of a law, not of an extension' [Wittgenstein 1980: 13]).

Wittgenstein understood infinity in terms of potentiality, and in this he continued a long tradition dating back to Aristotle himself.[19] Infinity is a possibility of infinitely applying a rule that generates successive elements of a given sequence. Crucially, Wittgenstein conceived of this infinite possibility of rule application in negative terms as something that never comes to an end[20]: 'The infinite number series is only the infinite possibility of finite series of numbers. It is senseless to speak of the *whole* infinite number series, as if it, too, were an extension' (PR, §144). In this sense, Wittgenstein eschewed actual infinity in all its manifestations, as opposed to Cantor,[21] who regarded potential infinity as an indefinite variable finite quantity that increases or decreases beyond any finite limits. As such, it is essentially no infinity, which is why he called it improper infinity in his *Grundlagen einer allgemeinen Mannigfältigkeitslehre*. Cantor contrasted potential infinity, which he dubbed as a 'agreeable illusion', with actual infinity, which is constant in all its part and at the same time goes above any finite numerical quantity of the same kind. This is well exemplified by the totality of all finite positive integers that form a set as a definite numerical quantity – a thing for itself – independently of the natural sequence of numbers that belong to it. Potential infinity constantly points to actual infinity, which is its condition and makes it real. The point is that if infinity is defined as the infinite application of a rule, actual infinity must be presupposed as the condition of possibility of this infinite application.[22] For his part, Wittgenstein argues that actual infinity would be acceptable if we could know infinite extension, but such knowledge is regrettably unattainable. As a result, it is senseless to introduce the concept of the infinite sets of natural, rational or real numbers. Wittgenstein embraced the finitist position and limited the concept of set to finite extensions.[23] As already mentioned, this outlook was by no means unusual since the overriding model of mathematics was definitely finitist at the time and tended to keep away from the dangerous dimensions of actual infinity.

According to Wittgenstein, one could not talk about that which was possible in the same way as about that which was real, and, similarly, there was an essential categorial difference between finite and infinite sets. Inopportunely, set theory failed to recognize this categorial difference. For example, Cantor's premise was that, in categorial respect, the cardinality of an infinite set was the same thing as the cardinality of a finite set. Furthermore, Wittgenstein insisted that set theory not only failed to distinguish between extensional and intensional contexts but also confounded them to bring forth objects – such as 'infinite sets' and 'infinite numbers' as 'infinite wholes' – that simply did not exist. In *The Big Typescript* (1933), he directly denounced set theory:

> After the many things I have already said about this, it may sound trivial if I now say that the mistake in the set-theoretical approach consists time and again in viewing laws and enumerations (lists) as essentially the same kind of thing and placing them on a line next to each other, the one filling in the gaps left by the other.
>
> (BT, 739–40)

To Wittgenstein, the concept 'set' was a symbol signifying a list (extension), as he insisted it in *The Big Typescript*, but he claimed that sets were in fact generated intensionally, that is, by virtue of a rule or a technique. Therefore the problem of set theory, as he saw it, was that it presented infinite sets as extensions whereas such sets were actually intensional concepts, meaning that they must be interpreted as a *rule*, a *law* or a *technique* for generating extensions. For example, the set of the even numbers is constructed by applying the recursive rule +2. Its list – or enumeration – has the form of {2, 4, 6, 8 ... }, but it does not present actual infinity. What it does present is the infinite possibility of applying the +2 rule. Thus, if Wittgenstein stated that a set was the symbol for a list, he suggested in this way that there were only finite sets, in the same way as a list first and foremost connoted something that had a first element and a last element. An infinite list was in fact not a list or a set of things that could be enumerated or catalogued.

3.2. Dedekind and the real numbers

Entitled 'On Set Theory', Chapter 138 of *The Big Typescript* is Wittgenstein's longest piece of writing on set theory. It is basically devoted to Dedekind's theory, his definition of infinite set and his construction of the real numbers. These considerations are continued through to Chapter 140. Wittgenstein vehemently disparages Dedekind's definition of infinite set and his concept of the real numbers as cuts of the rational numbers. As far as the former issue is concerned, Dedekind's definition of infinite set held that a set was infinite if it was equinumerous to a proper subset of itself. In Wittgenstein's interpretation,

Dedekind's definition of infinite set says that whether a class is infinite or not follows from the success or failure of an attempt at mapping a proper subclass onto the entire class. However, Wittgenstein claims, such a conclusive attempt does not exist. 'Infinite class' and 'finite class' are distinct logical categories, and what holds for one of them does not hold for the other. For a finite class, the proposition saying that it is equal to its subclass is but a tautology. Grammar rules for the general implication in the proposition 'k is a subclass of K' comprise what is said in the proposition 'K is an infinite class'. The proposition 'There is no last natural number' simply violates common – and proper – sense. One is right to feel that where one can talk about something/somebody that is last (e.g. the last person in a queue), it is nonsensical to state 'there is no last one' (e.g. 'there is no last person in the queue'). Wittgenstein explains: 'But of course that means: The proposition "There is no last cardinal number" should read, correctly: "It makes no sense to speak of a "last cardinal number"'" – that expression has been unlawfully formed' (BT, 744).[24] At the same time, 'the last person in the queue' is a correct expression. According to Wittgenstein, to say that 'm = 2n correlates a class with one of its proper subclasses' takes on a banal sense as a result of a false analogy clad in a paradoxical form:

> Thus one first confuses the word 'number' with a concept word like 'apples.' Then one talks about a 'number of numbers' and doesn't see that in this expression one shouldn't use the same word 'number' both times; and finally one deems it a discovery that the number of ten even numbers is equal to the number of the even and odd numbers.
>
> (BT, 745)

In Wittgenstein's view, it would be more correct to say that m = 2n permits a *possibility* of correlating each number of one class with a number in the other class. In this case, grammar again must determine the meaning of the expression 'possibility of correlation'. The generality of the expression m = 2n is, as Wittgenstein phrases it, an arrow that points to a certain series which is generated by applying an operation. Admittedly, an arrow could be said to point to infinity, but this does not mean that something like infinity exists and that the arrow points at it as at a thing. The 'possibility of correlation' is not a possibility which should become reality. One rather thinks of a process unfolding in time and concludes that if mathematics has nothing to do with time, a possibility is reality in mathematics.

> The 'infinite series of cardinal numbers' or 'the concept of cardinal number' is a possibility only in this way – as emerges clearly from the $[0, \xi, \xi +1]$. This symbol

is itself an arrow, with the '0' as its tail and the 'ξ+1' as its tip. It's possible to speak of things which lie in the direction of the arrow, but it's misleading or absurd to speak of all possible positions for things lying in the direction of the arrow as an equivalent for the arrow itself. If a searchlight sends light out into infinite space it does indeed illuminate everything lying in the direction of its rays, but you can't say it illuminates infinity.

(BT, 746)

Wittgenstein's objection to Dedekind is analogous to the objection he advances against Cantor; namely, that Dedekind takes an infinite whole (or an infinite extension) as his *object* of study: 'Dedekind's definition of an infinite set is another example of an attempt to describe the infinite without *presenting it*' (MS 106, 48; PR, 208, italics original). Interestingly, Wittgenstein refers here in positive terms to the definition of number from the *Tractatus* (TLP, 6.03). This may be taken as a hint that his criticism of set theory was grounded in his prior ideas (as recounted above), primarily in the intensional concept of number. Nevertheless, Wittgenstein's chief argument against Dedekind's definition of infinite set stemmed from Wittgenstein's constructivist notion that it was impossible to determine effectively whether a set was equinumerous with its subset.

Dedekind's construction of the irrational numbers was another major target of Wittgenstein's critique. Dedekind defined irrational numbers as cuts of rational numbers (A, B) not brought about by any rational number (so-called Dedekind cuts). Dedekind founded his theory on a certain intuition known as the principle of continuity, which holds that '[i]f all points of the straight line fall into two classes such that every point of the first class lies to the left of every point of the second class, there exists one and only one point which produces this division of all points into two classes, this severing of the straight line into two portions' (Dedekind 1909: 11). Dedekind relied on this principle in order to develop his construction of the irrational numbers. What he calls 'cut' is the division of all rational numbers $\mathbf{Q}$ into two classes A and B such that every number a in class A is smaller than every number b in class B. This is symbolically expressed as:

1. $A \neq \emptyset, B \neq \emptyset$
2. $A \cup B = \mathbf{Q}$
3. $\forall a \in A, b \in B: a < b$

Every rational number produces a cut if there is a largest number in A or there is a smallest number in B. According to Dedekind, one can easily see that there are infinitely many cuts that are not produced by any rational number. This happens when there is not a largest number in A, and there is not a smallest number in B. The example cited by Dedekind is a cut made by means of the natural number D which is not a square of any integer. If every positive rational number b whose square is > D is assigned to class B, and all the remaining rational numbers a are assigned to class A, then this division forms a cut, meaning that every number a is smaller than every number b. However, this cut does not comprise either the greatest rational number in A nor the smallest rational number in B. Thus, it follows that the cut is produced by an irrational number since it can easily be proven that there exists no rational number whose square = D. When addressing Dedekind's method in *The Big Typescript*, Wittgenstein vocally protested that:

> The explanation of the Dedekind cut pretends to be clear when it says: There are three cases: either the class R has a first member and L no last member, etc. In fact two of these three cases cannot even be imagined, unless the words 'class', 'first member', 'last member', completely change the everyday meanings they supposedly have retained. For if we're dumbfounded by someone's talk of a class of points that lies to the right of a given point and has no beginning, and we say: Do give us an example of such a class – then he trots out the example of the rational numbers! But here there is no class of points, in the original sense!
>
> The point of intersection of two curves isn't the common member of two classes of points; it's the intersection of two laws. Unless, quite misleadingly, we use the second form of expression to define the first.
>
> (BT, 739)

Wittgenstein's objection to Dedekind's theory was that a cut was not an arithmetical operation and that numbers representing cuts were not outcomes of a law: 'If, according to Dedekind, the rational numbers fall into two classes, how can this division be indeed made without some law? I can't enumerate the rational numbers on either side. Though it is easily done geometrically' (MS 106, 76). Then, in one of his notes from late 1931, Wittgenstein observed that the confusion about actual infinity ensued from an unclear notion of irrational number. We have an illusion of this concept which is rooted in the belief that signs, such as *0, abcd … ad inf.*, convey a certain standard to which the irrational numbers must correspond, while the name of 'irrational numbers' is given to an array of sundry logical constructs.[25] In Wittgenstein's view, it is only due to the wrong understanding of the word 'infinite' and of the role of 'infinite expansion' in the arithmetic of the real numbers that we are tempted to believe that there is a uniform notation for the rational numbers as the infinite extension, for example, infinite decimal fractions.[26] Let us assume that a length is cut where there is no rational point (no rational number). Can this be done in the first place? What length are we talking about? If one's measuring tools were accurate enough, could one approximate this point endlessly close? Not really, because one would never know whether one's point were this kind of point. Even if one had absolutely precise instruments of measure to construct the point $\sqrt{2}$ by approximating it, one would anyway *know* that the procedure would never reach the targeted point. In spite of successive approximations, the point would still remain indefinite. In Wittgenstein's view, this process of approximating in Dedekind's cut resembles demarcating a point by coin toss. In the last chapter of *The Big Typescript*, Wittgenstein proposes imagining that one tosses a coin and divides an AB line segment following the rule of bisecting the left half of the AB line segment if the toss ends up at 'heads' and bisecting its right half, if the result is 'tails'. In this way, is the position of the point adequately rendered by saying that this is the point one is approximating through repeated coin-tosses? It would be a point corresponding to the infinite decimal number determined without any rule whatsoever. Yet the depiction clearly stipulates that no such point can be determined, unless the expression 'point on a straight line' in and of itself 'determines the point'. Which is obviously not the case.

It is not enough to ever more accurately determine the point in every successive coin-toss, because, emphatically, this point must be *constructed*. Dedekind's cut could be endorsed as a method for establishing a real number only on condition that it were defined by an arithmetical law unambiguously classifying the real numbers into two sets and in this sense grounding the determination as to which of these two sets a given real number belonged.[27] In Wittgenstein's view, Dedekind's cuts are not such constructions, and in this sense they are not regulated by any arithmetical law. Rather, they represent an interminable process of approximation, which is bound to leave one endlessly far from the real number for which one is looking. For this reason, Wittgenstein enquires 'How does an infinitely complicated law differ from the absence of a law?' (BT, 767). To Wittgenstein, the irrational numbers are not extensions but rules, or laws, for constructing decimal expansions. We refer to these rules and numbers simply because we can use them to count, similarly to the rational numbers.[28] For example, 1/7 is another rule for forming a decimal expansion, one more direct than $\sqrt{2}$. Meanwhile, Dedekind's cuts are rather an extensive representation stemming from geometry.

The third point on which Wittgenstein's polemics with Dedekind pivoted was the theory of the real numbers as cuts of the rational numbers. In Wittgenstein's view, the very idea that there was a point corresponding to a complete approximation of $\sqrt{2}$ was specious. For its part, this idea ensued from the assumption that a straight line consisted of points and gaps between them, which the principle of continuity demanded to be filled; additionally, these points and gaps as if preceded our constructs:

> Mathematics is ridden through and through with the pernicious idioms of set theory. *One* example of this is the way people speak of a line as composed of points. A line is a law and isn't composed of anything at all. A line as a coloured length in visual space can be composed of shorter coloured lengths (but, of course not of points).
>
> (MS 106, 251; PR, 211, italics original)

Mathematicians would concoct incorrect analogies that projected a likeness between the real numbers and a geometrical line comprising points that corresponded to these numbers. Lured by such an image, Dedekind sought to fill the purported gaps for the sake of the inalienable idea of continuity.[29] As Wittgenstein put it: 'The comparison of a number to a point on the number line is valid only if we can say for every pair of numbers a and b whether a is to the right of b or b is to the right of a' (BT, 759). To Wittgenstein, however, a straight line was not a set of points, but 'the *law* for producing further' (RFM V, 36). The former would be an extensional representation, with the latter – that is, the intensional model – nevertheless being primary to it.

Wittgenstein's central objection to Dedekind's cuts was again the confounding of extensional and intensional approaches.[30] He starkly opposed the model in which points on a line were thought to correspond to numbers. If one assumed that by cutting a straight line at a random point one would chance upon either a rational number or an irrational one, one presupposed that these numbers already existed, independently of one's constructions. In other words, Wittgenstein rejected the extensional representation of the rational and irrational numbers by means a straight line and points, recognizing Dedekind's cuts as geometrically motivated.[31] In the *Remarks on the Foundations of Mathematics*, he even called the cuts a 'dangerous illustration' (RFM V, 29), one that made analysis seem redundant: 'The misleading thing about Dedekind's conception is the idea that the real numbers are there spread out in the number line. They may be known or not; that does not matter. And in this way all that one needs to do is to cut or divide into classes, and one has dealt with them all' (RFM V, 37). With his finitist and constructivist leanings in the philosophy of mathematics, Wittgenstein would opt for introducing cuts as laws (or rules) for sets rather than sets themselves. However, as elucidated by Paul Bernays (1959: 20), this would entail either using a very hazy notion of 'law' or, as observed by Weyl, plunging one's analytical foundations in a vicious circle of non-predicative definitions. In Bernays's view, Dedekind actually avoided this by espousing what Wittgenstein consistently incriminated as an extensional approach. In line with this approach, Dedekind adopted the concept of the set of natural numbers and, consequently, of the set of rational numbers as intuitively important and not requiring any further clarification.

Wittgenstein's criticism not always did justice to Dedekind's theory. In his *Stetigkeit und irrationale Zahlen* (*Continuity and Irrational Numbers*), Dedekind explicitly claimed that reliance on geometrical intuitions was useful as a didactic tool, but that his own express object was 'theorems established in a purely arithmetic manner' (Dedekind 1909: 1). Repudiating the hitherto manner of constructing irrational numbers as outcomes of measuring extensive magnitudes by means of another such magnitude, Dedekind explained: 'Instead of this, I demand that arithmetic shall be developed out of itself',[32] which among other things entailed defining 'irrational numbers by means of the rational numbers alone'.[33]

Putnam (2007: 244) illumines yet another aspect of the relation between points in space and numbers, which Wittgenstein arraigned with such fervour. Specifically, since Descartes' invention of analytic geometry, which also marked the beginning of mathematical physics, the concept of a point in space – today, in time-space – has been dependent on the concept of real number. This means that every point in space can be defined by three real numbers (three coordinates). If Wittgenstein were right to claim that the concept of real number was indefinite, the concept of a point in space would be equally indefinite. As will be shown shortly, Wittgenstein stated that 'there is no set of irrational numbers', but then one may also say that 'there are no points in space'. Equally importantly, the concept of particle has lost its primary role in contemporary physics, having been overtaken by the concept of field. The magnitude of a field, for example, the electromagnetic field or the gravitational field, can be measured by means of the rational numbers at any point in space. Given this, if the concept of 'a point in space' were indefinite as the concept of real number is indefinite, the concept of field would consequently also be indefinite.

3.3. Wittgenstein's criticism of Cantor's diagonal method

As already mentioned, Wittgenstein rejected the possibility of actual infinity and, consequently, the extensional concept of infinite set. His finitist and constructivist convictions precluded accepting the concepts for which we could not effectively construct their corresponding objects (such as, for example, infinite numbers). When tackling set theory, Wittgenstein threw in another demand – for mathematical generality to be anchored in reality, that is, to have a specific area of interest of its own. He did not uphold generality whose application to particular cases was unforeseeable. It was exactly this kind of what he dubbed 'suspect generality' (*verdächtige Allgemeinheit*)[34] that he deplored as surfacing time and again in set theory. It is exemplified in the results of employing Cantor's diagonal method in the proof for the uncountability of the set of the real numbers.

Cantor's preeminent achievements included proving that there are more real numbers than natural numbers, integers and rational numbers, whose sets are countable, which means that their elements can be put in a one–one correspondence. This is, however, not the case for the real numbers, which Cantor proved by what is known as the diagonal method. In his reasoning, Cantor relied on an indirect proof: suppose that the set of real numbers between 0 and 1 can be put in one-to-one correspondence with natural numbers, for example:

natural numbers		real numbers
0	↔	0,1**0**533789624...
1	↔	0,1**3**059123109...
2	↔	0,02**5**49876621...
3	↔	0,621**8**2055311...
4	↔	0,9328**1**510457...
5	↔	0,96219**8**41473...
6	↔	0,478201**1**9831...
7	↔	0,0812115**2**632...
8	↔	0,49001349**7**59...
9	↔	0,029438572**1**0...
10	↔	0,5872192110**6**...

The digits in bold along the diagonal make up the diagonal number:
0,13581812716.

Meanwhile, we want to construct a number between 0 and 1, in which the successive numbers following the decimal point differ from this number. For this purpose, we assume that the *nth* number of the expansion is 1 if the corresponding digit of the diagonal number is different from 1, and that it is 2 if the corresponding digit of the diagonal number = 1. The number we arrive at is thus:

0,21112121121 ...

This number cannot occur in our list because it differs from the first number in the first digit after the decimal point, from the second number in the second digit after the decimal point, from the third number in the third digit after the decimal point, etc. Consequently, our list does not contain all the numbers greater than 0 and smaller than 1; therefore, there is no one–one correlation between the natural numbers and the real numbers, which means that there is more of the latter than of the former and the set of the real numbers is uncountable.

The bulk of Wittgenstein's comments on the diagonal procedure are included in the second part of the *Remarks on the Foundation of Mathematics* (1938), but remarks on Cantor's method appear in Wittgenstein's notes as early as in 1930. Two of them, dated to June 1930, are particularly important in this context as they herald Wittgenstein's more comprehensive future critique. The remarks are made in conjunction with the insight that, 'the mistake in the set-theoretical approach consists time and again in treating laws and enumerations (lists) as essentially the same kind of thing and arranging them in parallel series so that one fills in gaps left by another ... ' (MS 108, 180; PG, 461). This remark is followed by two notes on the diagonal method:

> If we apply my considerations to Cantor's diagonal procedure, we'll see that the infinite set of decimal fractions can only represent a law for the generation of laws, that is, basically a function of two variables. The general form of these decimal fractions is $F(x, y)$. $F(x, n)$ is the nth of them, and $F(m, n)$ is its mth decimal place. A decimal fraction according to the diagonal is $F(x, x)$ and, transformed, it looks like, for example, $F(x, x) + 1$ (it should also be established that $0 + 1 = 1$, $1 + 1 = 2$, ... $q + 1 = 0$ etc.). But what the inductive proof shows is that $F(x, x) + 1$ has a different expansion than any $F(x, y)$. Where is a higher-order infinity here?
>
> (or simply 'proper infinity')
>
> Here again, the difficulty arises from the formation of mathematical pseudo-concepts. For instance, when we say that we can arrange the cardinal numbers, but not the rational numbers, in a series according to their size, we are unconsciously presupposing that the concept of an ordering by size does have a sense for *rational numbers*, and that it turned out on investigation that the ordering was impossible (which presupposes that the *attempt* is thinkable). – Thus one thinks that it is possible to arrange the *real numbers* (as if it were a concept of the same kind as 'apple on this table') in a series, and now it turned out to be impracticable.
>
> (MS 108, 181; PG, 461, italics original)

As can be seen, what Wittgenstein criticizes is not the diagonal argument itself, which is in fact constructive, but the way Cantor used it. Wittgenstein's primary point is that if this procedure was supposed to prove that the attempt at putting the real numbers in a series was doomed to failure, the very possibility of doing so must have been presupposed in advance. Wittgenstein develops this reasoning in the second part of RFM, where he identifies proving that it is impossible to order the irrational numbers in a series as the actual aim of the diagonal procedure. In his view, Cantor's major mistake was that his notion of infinite series was derived from the natural number series and other similar series. As a result, an infinite series 'stands for a certain analogy between cases, and it can e.g. be used to define provisionally a domain that one wants to talk about' (RFM II, 16). However, this is not enough to confer a clear sense on the question whether the set of the real numbers can be ordered in a series. At best, one can state that there are examples of arranging natural, rational and algebraic numbers, and that these represent certain analogous constructions which are called series. Yet, there is nothing to bridge these cases and the case of 'all real numbers'. There is no universal method for establishing whether a given set can be put in a series. Hence, Wittgenstein's answer to the question whether the set of the real numbers can be ordered in a series is 'I don't know ... what it is that *can't be done* here.' Wittgenstein claims that there is no sufficiently clear difference between the way that terms such as 'root', 'algebraic number', etc., are used and the notion of 'real number'. Finally, he points at an aspect which, though potentially befuddling, seems of little relevance to Cantor's method as a calculus, specifically, that talking about a series of all real numbers is nonsense if even the diagonal number of this series is referred to as a 'real number' in Cantor's procedure (RFM II, 16). Briefly, Wittgenstein considers Cantor's diagonal proof to be a method or a rule for the successive construction of numbers that differ from every following number in a given system (series).[35]

The other use of the diagonal method that Wittgenstein criticized involved employing it to prove the uncountability of the set of the real numbers: $\aleph_0 < c$. 'Where's a higher-order infinity here?!', he seemed to protest. If the diagonal procedure simply sought to show that the notion of 'real number' was less analogous to the notion of 'natural number' than we habitually believed, it would be a clear and straightforward thing. However, Wittgenstein avers that exactly the opposite is the case as 'one pretends to compare the "set" of real numbers in magnitude with that of cardinal numbers. The difference in kind between the two conceptions is represented, by a skew form of expression, as difference of extension. I believe, and hope, that a future generation will laugh at this hocus pocus' (RFM II, 22). The derisive 'hocus-pocus' is Wittgenstein's moniker for the diagonal argument-based proof that the infinite set **R** has a greater extension than other infinite sets. Such an approach is extensionalist, meaning that it is focused on the results of the diagonal procedure – the diagonal number D, which is supposed to prove that the set of the real numbers is uncountable. Therefore, if the diagonal method were regarded as evidence for there being a lesser or greater infinity, it would be, to use Wittgenstein's wording, 'a puffed-up proof', that is, one that showed more than the means it used permitted.[36] Wittgenstein claims that the difference between finite and infinite sets is a categorial difference rather than one of extent (or degree). What he objects to is then not uncountability as such but its prose interpretation. To say that Cantor's method shows that the set of the real numbers is greater than the set of the natural numbers is the 'hocus-pocus' Wittgenstein deplores.[37] What one should say, according to Wittgenstein, is that the method shows that the concept of 'real number' has less analogy to the concept of 'natural number' than is commonly believed. In other words, the diagonal argument is best depicted as a conceptual change and not as a method for discovering new mathematical facts.

In the context of Wittgenstein's intensional understanding of the infinite set, no proof for a greater of lesser infinity is by definition possible. More importantly, Cantor's theory treats $\aleph_0$ and **c** alike as numbers and compares them with other numbers, both finite and infinite, particularly with the set of the real numbers:

> The rational numbers cannot be *enumerated*, because they cannot be counted – but one can count with them, as with the cardinal numbers. That squint-eyed way of putting things goes with the whole system of pretence, namely that by using the new apparatus we deal with infinite sets with the same certainty as hitherto we had in dealing with finite ones.
>
> It should not have been called 'denumerable', but on the other hand it would have made sense to say 'numerable'. And this expression also informs us of an application of the concept. For one cannot set out to enumerate the rational numbers, but one can perfectly well set out to assign numbers to them.
>
> (RFM V, 15, italics original)

If Wittgenstein says that the rational numbers cannot be counted, he basically means that one cannot make a complete list of them, which is in fact rather little controversial. However, he suggests that the misconceived idea of an infinite whole pervades the calculus itself. If an infinite set is conceived extensionally, Cantor's diagonal method does not yield an irrational number different from an infinite number set, because it is never capable of presenting another infinite set (or infinite extension). What it can indeed do is constructing a real number through a different *rule* than the one through which other numbers in the system are generated: 'The diagonal method shows a kind of infinite possibility' (MS 106, 60). According to Wittgenstein, Cantor confers sense on an 'expansion which is different from all the expansions in a system' by proving that it differs diagonally from other expansions in this system:

> Cantor's diagonal procedure does not shew us an irrational number different from all in the system, but it gives sense to the mathematical proposition that the number so-and-so is different from all those of the system. Cantor could say: You can prove that a number is different from all the numbers in the system *by* proving that it differs in its first place from its first number and in its second place from its second number and so on.
>
> (RFM II, 29)

Yet Wittgenstein does not consider this sufficient, because the grammar of the word 'expansion' remains undetermined, which means that Cantor assumes that an infinite expansion is not subject to a rule. The concept of infinite series has been derived from other series, such as the series of natural numbers, roots, algebraic numbers, etc. What is missing is a clear and certain transition from these series to the series of the real numbers, because the 'infinite set' is a recursive rule rather than an extension; consequently, it does not make sense to talk about a 'set of all real numbers'. In any case, the diagonal number is a real number as well. In RFM, Wittgenstein states quite definitively: 'One might say: Besides the rational points there are diverse systems of irrational points on the number line. There is no system of irrational numbers – but also no super-system, no "set of irrational numbers" of higher-order infinity' (RFM II, 33). In his commentary on this passage, Putnam (2007: 239) observes that Wittgenstein is quite brash in rejecting the idea that there is a set of the irrational numbers and that this set is uncountable, which is as a matter of fact the central theorem not only of set theory but also of entire contemporary mathematics. *Pace* Putnam, Wittgenstein's words should be understood in the context of his non-extensionalist position, which holds that the real numbers do not exist as a homogeneous whole but are constructed in various, not predefined ways. In §33 cited above, Wittgenstein points out that the geometrical way in which Cantor expresses his ideas suggests that there is a 'super-system' of 'higher-order' (or actual) infinity, while Cantor's diagonal argument shows that there is no system of the real numbers – that is, a series of them – because one can always find a number which does not belong to the system. In this sense, there is no 'set of the irrational numbers' (the 'real' numbers precisely speaking) extensionalistically understood as a homogeneous domain of numbers, because sets, as Wittgenstein views them, are not defined by their members but by rules, laws and techniques for constructing these members. From this perspective, domains of numbers are not homogeneous entities and have no clear-cut boundaries. For example, the real numbers cannot be defined as cuts of the rational numbers (Dedekind) or by recourse to points on the number line, or through decimal expansions.[38] Wittgenstein would be inclined to accept that there can be various systems of the irrational numbers, but one cannot construct one entirely comprehensive system of such numbers. He already highlights this in his analysis of various kinds of real numbers, such as π and $\sqrt{2}$, in *The Big Typescript*, where he also observes: 'For we use the expression "prime numbers", and it sounds similar to "cardinal numbers", "square numbers", "even numbers", etc. So we think it can be used in a similar way, but forget that for the expression "prime number" we have given quite different rules – rules different in kind – and now we get into a strange conflict with ourselves' (BT, 764).

There is one more attention-worthy aspect. Wittgenstein's harsh criticism in §33 is driven by his insistence that the concept of 'infinite expansion' (or the concept of 'real number') is undetermined.[39] If there is no such thing as *a set of all irrational numbers*, it is erroneous, Wittgenstein points out, to assert, as set theory does, that the set of the irrational numbers is uncountable. Meanwhile, '[t]he dangerous, deceptive thing about the idea: "The real numbers cannot be arranged in a series", or again "The set … is not denumerable" is that it makes the determination of a concept – concept formation – look like a fact of nature' (RFM II, 19). That uncountability is a 'hocus-pocus' is shown by the fact that this concept has no practical application: 'What can the concept "non-denumerable" be used for?' Wittgenstein's answer is, blandly, nothing. Wittgenstein explains that the mathematical 'language game' employs concepts and signs which we use outside of mathematics – that is, in empirical propositions – passing from the former to the latter and back again:

> Indeed in real life a mathematical proposition is never what we want. Rather, we make use of mathematical propositions *only* in inferences from propositions that do not belong to mathematics to others that likewise do not belong to mathematics. (In philosophy the question, "What do we actually use this word or this proposition for?" repeatedly leads to valuable insights.)
>
> (TLP, 6.211)

Crucially, Wittgenstein's fundamental tenet was that a calculus – or a rule-governed sign game – only became mathematics if it had non-mathematical applications.[40] More than that, it was nothing else, in his view, than a non-mathematical utility that made signs meaningful: 'I want to say: it is essential to mathematics that its signs are also employed in *mufti*. It is the use outside mathematics, and so the meaning of the signs, that makes the sign-game into mathematics' (RFM V, 2).[41] Regarding set theory, Wittgenstein directly enquires about its applicability as a necessary condition to be met by a mathematical calculus.[42]

Strange though this may sound, Wittgenstein believes that there is a 'solid core' behind 'all these glistening concept-formations' (RFM V, 16) of set theory, and that this core makes them into productions of mathematics. Unfortunately, set theory cannot be said to be wholly a mathematical calculus or wholly a mathematical language game. Set theory generates concepts but is not clear on their applicability. It is satisfied with the mysteriousness, intellectual allures or charm[43] of theorems, such as the one holding that there are numbers greater than the infinite, and, instead of directly explaining them as effects of faulty reasoning, it bestows seriousness and respect on them.[44] Misunderstandings about the infinite engendered the calculus of set theory, which would never have come into being without them. What has come forth as a result of flawed understanding cannot possibly be engaging. The net of language in which Cantor got caught may appear interesting, but this is merely an illusion. An outcome of wrong understanding cannot be interesting, that is, applicable. Mysteriousness and charm are irrelevant since the only thing that matters in calculi is their practical implications, for example, their applications in physics.

> When set theory appeals to the human impossibility of a direct symbolization of the infinite it thereby introduces the crudest imaginable misinterpretation of its own calculus. To be sure, it is this very misinterpretation that is responsible for the invention of that calculus. But of course that doesn't show the calculus to be something inherently incorrect (at most it shows it to be something uninteresting), and it's odd to believe that this part of mathematics is imperilled by any kind of philosophical (or mathematical) investigations. ... What set theory has to lose is rather the atmosphere of thought-fog surrounding the bare calculus, that is to say, the references to a fictional symbolism underlying set theory, a symbolism that isn't employed in its calculus, and the apparent description of which is really nonsense. (In mathematics we're allowed to make up everything, except for a part of our calculus.)
>
> (BT, 750)

Wittgenstein's claim is that concepts such as 'infinite set', 'infinite series' and $\aleph_0$ owe their mathematical sense to the use of the word 'infinite' in ordinary language, in which it means unlimited, though it is often employed to answer the question 'How many?' – that is, as a numeral.[45] These concepts actually express an infinite possibility or an infinite operation. On this take, the extensional, if not downright Platonic, sense of the proposition 'there are infinitely many even numbers' vanishes. What this proposition means is simply that there is a mathematical rule for interminably generating even numbers. This is at the same time something entirely different from, for example, generating even numbers smaller than 100. In the latter case, the numbers can be enumerated and written down. One tends to do so because there is a certain resemblance between the method for one–one correlation of the elements of two infinite series and the method for mutual correlation of the members of finite classes. Yet, as Wittgenstein cautions,

> [f]rom the fact, however, that we have an employment for a *kind* of numeral which, as it were, gives the number of the members of an infinite series, it does not follow that it also makes some kind of sense to speak of the number of the concept "infinite series"; that we have here some kind of employment for something like a numeral.
>
> (RFM II, 38)

In Wittgenstein's view, the notion of the cardinality of infinite sets, which Cantor expressed by symbols $\aleph_0$ and **c**, has no application, which means that there is no mathematical technique showing us how such expressions can be used.

Therefore, Wittgenstein argues that '[c]ertain considerations may lead us to say that 10^{10} souls fit into a cubic centimetre. But why do we nevertheless not say it? Because it is of no use. Because, while it does conjure up a picture, the picture is one with which we cannot go on to do anything' (RFM II, 36). The image of infinity produced by Cantor's concept leaves one, so to speak, in a state of suspension as one does not know how it is related to the calculus, because it is certainly not the relation like that of | | | | | | | with number 7 (cf. RFM II, 35). Since, according to Wittgenstein, there is nothing infinite in the calculus, it would be best to remove the picture. Moreover, on closer inspection, an infinite extension simply vanishes as nonsense, and what remains is the calculus alone. Cantor's theory makes an impression of discovering facts of nature, that is, of being a *description* of actual infinity.

In terms of Wittgenstein's distinction between *prose* and the *calculus*, the proposition 'There are infinitely many even numbers' misleadingly comes across as a confirmed hypothesis similar to hypotheses of the empirical sciences.[46] In fact, however, it is simply the *prose* of set theory, the way that the proposition 'There are infinitely many prime numbers' is prose. Superficially, both propositions express a similar idea, but if one examines them on the level of the *calculus*, one will find that this is not the case. For the prime numbers, infinity means that for the finite set of these numbers $A = \{p_1, p_2, p_3 \ldots \ldots p_k\}$, there is number $n = p_1 \cdot p_2 \cdot p_3 \ldots.. p_k + 1$ such that in its reduction to prime factors there is at least one prime number p that is not a member of set A. In Wittgenstein's view, it is only the *calculus*, that is, the proof, that can adequately present what it means that there are infinitely many prime numbers. *Prose* may only distort the issue.

To Wittgenstein, the grammatical similarity of expressions such as $\aleph_0 < c$, $2\aleph_0 > \aleph_0$, etc., with the grammar of natural or rational numbers is too superficial to produce conditions of applicability for these expressions. They would embody the 'suspect generality', which is dissociated from any particular field of application, or 'a piece of mathematical architecture which hangs in the air' (RFM II, 35). General considerations make sense in mathematics on condition that one has a specific area of use in mind. But there is no generalization whose application to particular cases cannot be anticipated. This is the reason why, as Wittgenstein concludes, 'the general discussions of set theory (if they aren't viewed as calculi) always sound as empty chatter, and why we are always astounded when we are shown an application for them. We feel that what is going on isn't properly connected with real things' (MS 108, 180; PG, 467). Wittgenstein's point is that set theory treats the relations between the general and the particular in the manner that is proper for physical objects but not for mathematical structures[47]:

> Set theory attempts to grasp the infinite in a more general way than the investigation of the laws of the real numbers can. It says that you can't grasp the actual infinite through mathematical symbolism at all, and that therefore it can only be described and not represented. The description would encompass it in something like the way in which you carry with you a quantity of things too numerous to be held in your hand by packing them in a box. They're then invisible, but still we know that we're carrying them (so to speak). One could say of this theory that it buys a pig in a poke. Let the infinite accommodate itself in its box as it likes.
>
> (BT, 747–8)

4. Conclusion

As pointed out at the beginning, it is a steep challenge to separate what Wittgenstein counts as the mathematical *calculus* from what he deems mathematical *prose* in his critical discourse. This difficulty is exemplified by his criticism of Cantor's diagonal method though some of his interpreters admittedly offer rather different readings of this critique. For example, Ryan Dawson (2016: 323–6) argues that Wittgenstein's critique of the diagonal procedure is not a critique of the mathematical proof but of what is added to it in *prose*. This criticism targets Cantor as a *prose writer* or a metaphysician, rather than Cantor as a mathematician. In Dawson's view, what is prose in this case is the interpretation of Cantor's proof as a proof supposed to show that the set of the real numbers is 'greater' than the set of the natural numbers in the same sense as a set of five objects is greater than a set of four object. The prose (or metaphysical) addition to the diagonal proof consists of commentary claiming that what happens here is a seminal discovery of the pre-existing difference in the sizes of sets of the real numbers and the natural numbers or of the pre-existing different domains of infinity. This produces an impression of infinity being something real – an actual entity that can be studied as 'a fact of nature'. Meanwhile, according to Wittgenstein, Cantor only showed a manner of comparing our concept of natural number with our concept of real number and the fact that these concepts were less similar than we habitually believed. Yet showing this did not require adopting the Platonic notion of infinity, and it would be best to discard this deceptive picture as mere *prose*.

This interpretation invites some objections. First, it sounds really dismissive to refer to what has proven Cantor's greatest achievement – that is, his diagonal argument and theorem of the uncountability of the set of the real numbers – as prose. One can say that the set of the real numbers is greater than the set of the natural numbers, that $\aleph_0 < c$, or that the cardinality of **R** is greater than that of **N**, and this is neither interpretation nor prose, but a pure mathematical truth. Secondly, while Wittgenstein denounced prose, by means of which mathematicians, including Cantor, elucidated their formalizations, and called for eliminating it as a pernicious metaphysical surplus, he himself practised prose when interpreting Cantor's and Dedekind's work in a particular way. He did not criticize them as a mathematician, and his considerations, rather than being a *calculus*, replaced one instance of *prose* with another instance of it: a Platonic narrative was substituted with a finitist and constructivist narrative.

Wittgenstein's criticism can be depicted as a critique offered by a philosopher of mathematics and not by a mathematician, even though time and again (quite often, indeed) he pronounced firm mathematical judgements, which regrettably tended to be precipitate, as Putnam has pointed out. Indeed, the problem of infinite mathematical extension, a recurring theme in Wittgenstein's critical fugue, is a philosophical problem and not a mathematical one. It does not matter in the least to mathematics whether one is a Platonist or a Hegelian embracing actual infinity or a constructivist espousing potential infinity. When one says, for example, that a given numerical sequence is divergent to plus or minus infinity, or mentions the limit of the sequence a_n with n tending to infinity, or defines a numerical sequence as a function whose domain is the infinite subset of the set of the natural numbers, it is entirely irrelevant whether one conceives of infinity as actual or potential. To put it differently, a given numerical sequence is divergent to any infinity, no matter how it is understood. If mathematics is approached as a calculus, which Wittgenstein himself demanded, it does not in the least matter to the calculus whether, for example, the real numbers are regarded as infinite extensions or as rules. Similarly, Dedekind's definition of infinite set, which Wittgenstein criticized so scathingly in *The Big Typescript*, does not have to bother whether one speaks of the possibility or the actuality of one–one correlation of a subclass with the entire class.

Putnam explicitly dismisses Wittgenstein's anti-set-theoretical theses as overhasty though he appreciates the conceptual study of scientific (and not only scientific) knowledge as paramount and salient. Such exploration, however, require a far more extensive scientific knowledge and respect for science than Wittgenstein possessed. In Putnam's view (Putnam 2007: 245–6), if Wittgenstein had written *Remarks on the Foundations of Physics,* the volume would have attacked everything that mattered in science. This is probably an exaggerated view. Wittgenstein sufficiently respected science and the scientific knowledge of nature, but he was critical of attempts at imitating the scientific method in research on the human world. Wittgenstein's criticism can be partly explained as fuelled by his finitism, his refusal to accept Russell- and Frege-style logicism and his essentially intuitionist approach to mathematics. At the same time, it should be remembered that the mathematical community as such was far from unanimous in assessing Cantor's theory. Kronecker, for one, regarded Cantor as a 'scientific charlatan', renegade and corruptor of the young. For his part, Henri Poicaré labelled set theory as 'a perverse pathological illness' and prophesied that future generations would approach *Mengenlehre* as a disease from which they had already recovered.[48] Even Gösta Mittag-Leffler, a Swedish mathematician and the editor of *Acta Mathematica*, who drew on set theory in his own theory of analytic functions, refused to publish a paper by Cantor as irrelevant and incomprehensible. Against the backdrop of these detractive evaluations, Wittgenstein's critique should basically not come as a surprise. What may indeed be rather surprising is the timing of his criticism since, as already mentioned, Wittgenstein came up with it when set theory was already a recognized and dynamically developing part of mathematics in its own right.

Of course, Wittgenstein's critique was of a different kind. Whereas the frequently harsh appraisals of the mathematicians evoked above always revolved around a specific mathematical point or a calculation problem, Wittgenstein had something more in mind. Georg Henrik von Wright in his 'Wittgenstein in Relation to His Times' identified set theory and behaviourism as two unhealthy habits of thought that Wittgenstein considered devastating to the culture of his day: 'Had he lived to see the role which set-theory has since come to play in many or most countries as a basis for teaching mathematics to children he would no doubt have felt disgusted and perhaps have said that it signalled the end of what used to be known as mathematics' (von Wright 1982: 208). Wittgenstein followed Spengler in describing his own time in deeply censorious terms as civilization, that is, the twilight and decline of culture.[49] He believed that, unlike the spirit of the powerful current of European and American civilization, which 'expresses itself in an onwards movement, in building ever larger and more complicated structures' (PR, 8), the spirit in which he himself wrote expressed itself in striving for clarity and transparency. In his view, the collapse of culture and its mutation into civilization were caused by a drive to step beyond 'language games' and erect sophisticated thought-constructs, epitomized by Cantor's set theory, which were unrelated to any form of life. He seemed to ask: 'What use is there for Cantor's $\aleph_0$ infinity?' Crafting such bold visions entailed crossing the boundaries of sense and the limits of the ordinary use of language in a given 'language game' based on a set of shared rules and modes of life.

Set-theoretical concepts are, so to speak, outside, out of home, beyond what we usually do. They represent a discourse which guides one beyond the horizon of everydayness, of the ordinary, known and familiar. When following it, one must leave the field of social practices, abandon one's home and community, which means breaking bonds, losing one's bearings and sliding into loneliness. Philosophers of the infinite take us on a journey into the unknown and entice us to forsake the austere land of tradition or to stop heeding the commandment of the effective constructability of theorems in mathematics. The question is where one is supposed to head whence, what one's destination is. Wittgenstein's opposition to set theory was driven less by an anxiety of the unknown and more by his recognition of the consequences of abandoning one's home and everyday practices – of confusion and estrangement. However, our everydayness is dynamic and constantly pushing the limits, with new practices and new uses arising as we speak of them; this everydayness is different from what it was one hundred years ago. Today, Cantor's and Dedekind's world is no longer outside. And, I guess, children learn about sets as early as in kindergartens.

5

The Big Typescript as a middle-period work

1. The intent to write a new book

After his return to Cambridge in 1929, which was effectively also his return to philosophy, Ludwig Wittgenstein every now and then mentioned in his notes his desire and even his plan to write another book to follow the *Tractatus Logico-Philosophicus*. The earnestness of his intent is borne out by the fact that he went as far as to sketch out preliminary prefaces to this future work. Were typescript TS 208 and its revised and expanded version in TS 209, which Rush Rhees published as *Philosophische Bemerkungen* (*Philosophical Remarks*) in 1964, a draft of such a book? It does not seem to have been the case. Typescript TS 208, which Wittgenstein dictated building on manuscripts MS 105 to MS 108 (volumes I–IV), was rather intended as a report on his scholarly work up to that point. Wittgenstein was asked to submit such a document by Bertrand Russell, at George Moore's request, in order to have his fellowship at Cambridge prolonged. In response, Wittgenstein sent typescript TS 208 as a summa of his pursuits to Russell in April 1930. Subsequently, by relying on a collage method – cutting out and rearranging TS-208 passages and interspersing them with handwritten inserts – he compiled typescript TS 209. Regrettably, against the intentions of Wittgenstein himself, who had not treated TS 209 as a complete book to be published, Rhees made it look like the very thing by prefacing it with a peculiar 'Foreword' extracted from MS 109, a manuscript dated to 6–8 November 1930 and thus falling outside of the corpus of *Philosophische Bemerkungen*, which contained manuscripts MS 105 to MS 108.[1] This preface is thoroughly incompatible with the content of the *Remarks*; what is more, Rhees made quite an arbitrary choice in splicing it together from two short passages picked from a far more sizeable collection. Additionally, some researchers insist that TS 208, which served as the basis for TS 209, does not fully convey the content of its corresponding manuscripts.[2] From the perspective of a future book envisioned by Wittgenstein, TS 211, which was produced in the autumn, would certainly represent a far more relevant edited version of the manuscripts.³ Without a doubt, it more faithfully reproduces the original notes, that is, MS 109 to MS 114, which went into the making of it. The sequencing of the remarks was the sole alteration in that typescript.⁴

A genuine attempt at making the plan of a second book a reality can be recognized in what has come to be referred to as *The Big Typescript*, that is, typescript TS 213. It was dictated on the basis of TS 212, which Wittgenstein again developed by the collage method, using selected passages from manuscripts contained in volumes I–IV (i.e. TS 208 and TS 210) and excerpts from manuscript volumes V–X (i.e. typescript TS 211). This indicates that TS 213 is a collation of Wittgenstein's remarks that he himself selected from all the manuscripts produced between February 1929 and June 1932.⁵ Although *The Big Typescript* was undated, it is possible to deduce when it came into being by piecing together the dates of other typescripts and manuscripts. By common consensus, Wittgenstein started dictating TS 213 in Vienna in March 1933 and completed the dictation before 14 December 1933.⁶ Some features of TS 213 suggest that it could be an almost complete draft of the book Wittgenstein had in mind. For example, it is his only text to sport a table of contents (nineteen chapters and 140 subchapters, adding up to a total tally of 768 pages, though the number of pages is admittedly difficult to determine). At the same time, it has neither a title nor a preface nor an afterword, even though Wittgenstein's notes include drafts of introductions, titles and even epigrams. Most researchers of Wittgenstein's work actually believe that BT was nothing more or else than an assemblage of resources, and that its book format is only an illusion, a very misleading one, as claimed, for example, by Wolfgang Kienzler. Kienzler also argues that the major achievement of BT lies in imbuing the pre-existing texts with some order rather than in offering something new.⁷ Yet the truth is that Wittgenstein revised and corrected a considerable portion of his remarks as compared to both the manuscripts and the typescript sources of TS 213. What could be relevant to the idea of producing something more than just a *Big Typescript* (i.e. a typed version of the manuscripts) was the fact that, as Pichler points out, having read Rudolf Carnap's *Die physikalische Sprache als Universalsprache der Wissenschaft* (1931), Wittgenstein was afraid that a part of his own work would be regarded as plagiarizing Carnap and pressed for Friedrich Waismann's planned book, which presented his own position, to be published as soon as possible. This suggests that in BT, Wittgenstein was at least endeavouring to arrange his thoughts and give them a more intelligible form, in this way making them presentable to a broader public and limiting the random circulation of his ideas. In this sense, BT was certainly meant as something more than simply an ordinary typescript made for the technical purpose of better legibility than offered by manuscripts. Alois Pichler (Pichler 2004: 89) is also right to claim that BT should at least be appreciated as an indispensable contribution to the process of producing a book, if not as a draft copy of this book. Joachim Schulte expresses a similar view of BT *Umarbeitungen*, stating that 'they were attempts at transforming of unwieldy mass of remarks into something that might one day become the "natural and smooth" summary of his ideas that Wittgenstein was striving for' (Schulte 2013: 86).

On closer scrutiny of the content and style of BT, it appears to have indeed little to do with a traditionally conceived book, except its external format (a table of contents and the division into chapters and subchapters). Remarks included in it are often very loosely, if at all, connected to each other and not infrequently sound like incidental thoughts or aphorisms. Similarly to the manuscripts, its passages are separated from each other by blank spaces. At moments, the way they are assembled and distributed over respective chapters seems random as well. All in all, BT does not differ much from the manuscripts in terms of the internal structure. The title was not coined by Wittgenstein, who later (i.e. between 1934 and 1938) tended to refer to it as his *Maschineneschritf* or the 'old typescript' (*alte Maschinschritf*); *The Big Typescript* was named so by the heirs to his legacy.[8] In a letter to physicist William Heriot Watson, his friend from Cambridge, Wittgenstein wrote: 'in Vienna … I was busy dictating about 800 of my bl. Philosophy. They contain all I want to say but very badly said and I have now begun to rewrite the whole business. When that'll be done I'll have it printed (provided that I'm alive)' (McGuinness 2012: 156). This reveals that immediately after TS had been put together, or possibly even before its completion, Wittgenstein started to correct and revise it extensively. The outcomes of these efforts in all likelihood went into the making of the second half of MS 114, which Wittgenstein entitled 'Umarbeitung. Zweite Umarbeitung im großen Format', and of its continuation, that is, the first part of MS 115, entitled 'Philosophische Bemerkungen'. These two manuscripts were subsequently merged into MS 140, which is known as *Großes Format* (1934).

These materials were published by Rhees as *Philosophische Grammatik* (*Philosophical Grammar*) in 1969. The publication consisted of two parts, with the first containing eight revised BT chapters (from the 'Umarbeitung', i.e. MS 114) and the second including seven out of 19 BT chapters (TS 213). Rhees's editorial interventions provoked a considerable criticism. For example,

Jaakko Hintikka (1991: 183–201) complained that while TS 213, that is, *The Big Typescript*, was the only partly conventional book left by Wittgenstein and Rhees had just been supposed to publish it, he had done an entirely different thing by compiling a miscellany of materials from sundry sources, which Wittgenstein had never intended to combine into one whole and which had often been wrung from their important contexts. Though in some ways critical of Rhees's edition, Anthony Kenny (2005: 343–4), the English translator of *Philosophische Grammatik*, disagreed with Hintikka and argued that it was not certain at all that Wittgenstein had not wished to put together the passages selected by Rhees, but admitted that the Rhees-edited text was just one of the many possible ways of arranging Wittgenstein's writings. Kenny's (1976: 41–53) major objection to Rhees was that his edition of *Philosophische Grammatik* failed to explain his editorial strategy or to spell out the rationale behind removing some chapters, among them as important ones as 'Philosophy' and 'Phenomenology'.

As a matter of fact, Wittgenstein never completed his work on correcting and revising *The Big Typescript*. Instead, he abandoned it to start developing a new book project. This suggests that even if his letter to Watson mentions submitting the typescript to publication, TS 213 as we know it was certainly not the form Wittgenstein intended to see in print. His revisions did not produce the desired outcome. It is not a coincidence, either, that when he sent a sample of his work to Russell, it was not BT but *The Blue Book*, which he dictated at the turn of 1933.[9] This should not make one believe that BT did not represent an important contribution to Wittgenstein's work on a new book. That the opposite was the case will be discussed below, but at this point let us only stress that, at that particular moment, Wittgenstein was not entirely satisfied with the results of his work and that directly after dictating TS 213, he set out to revise it. Anyway, a copy of TS 213 was going to long remain his companion as a repository and an underpinning of his later work.

2. The middle Wittgenstein

The Big Typescript marks the middle or transitional period in the evolution of Wittgenstein's thought. The division of Wittgenstein's philosophy into the early period of the *Tractatus Logico-Philosophicus* and the late period of the *Philosophical Investigations* was conceptualized and gained currency at the time when these two works were, for the most part, the sole known texts by Wittgenstein. However, as Wittgenstein's writings from the years between the *Tractatus* and the *Investigations* were gradually being made available to researchers, the scholarly community incrementally recognized that these two philosophies of Wittgenstein were in fact not sharply distinguishable and that the transition period could not be reduced to Wittgenstein's rejection of the early position and his adoption of the late views. Additionally, if one realizes what a sizeable body of writings was produced by Wittgenstein in this period, one comes to understand that it makes sense to accept the 'middle Wittgenstein' label. If a brief outline of the middle period in the development of Wittgenstein's philosophy was offered in the 'Introduction', this chapter seeks to paint its more detailed picture. Before doing this, two caveats are in order. First, distinguishing the early, middle and late Wittgensteins should not suggest that these phases were relatively autonomous and clearly separable from each other. This would blur the continuity and dynamics of Wittgenstein's philosophy. Second, such a clear-cut division could suggest that we were faced with a philosophical theory or respective wholes that added up to such a theory. Meanwhile, Wittgenstein himself persistently stressed that philosophy was not about preaching any 'theories' and that it was an 'activity'.[10]

The middle period in the development of Wittgenstein's philosophy roughly covers the period from 1929, when he came back to Cambridge, and 1936/1937, when he drafted an early version of the *Philosophical Investigations*. This timeframe was predominantly marked by a gradual shift away from the ideas of the *Tractatus* and towards a new philosophical position. At the time, Wittgenstein was engrossed in two major pursuits: efforts to explain the problems and difficulties ensuing from the *Tractatus* and plans to write a new book. Wittgenstein embarked on the former venture as early as in the mid-1920s, when he began to meet with Moritz Schlick and his circle on a regular basis. As discussed in the previous chapters, the problem of colour exclusion, addressed by Frank Ramsey in his review of the *Tractatus*, was among the most pressing issues with which Wittgenstein busied himself at the time. The colour exclusion problem and attempts to solve it by redefining the rules of logical syntax through reliance on phenomenological language set a new horizon of Wittgenstein's explorations. The realization that the logical value of a proposition depended on logical values of other sentences indicated that the elementary propositions belonged to a propositional system (*Satzsystem*), which was to be compared with reality as a whole. In a conversation with Schlick in December 1929, Wittgenstein stated:

> Once I wrote, 'A proposition is laid against reality like a ruler. Only the endpoints of the graduating lines actually touch the object that is to be measured.'[11]

> I now prefer to say that a *system of propositions* is laid against reality like a ruler. What I mean by this is the following. If I lay a ruler against a spatial object, I lay *all the graduating lines* against it at the same time. It is not the individual graduating lines that are laid against it, but the entire scale. ... If I say, for example, that this or that point in the visual field is *blue*, then I know not merely that, but also that this point is not green, nor red, nor yellow, etc.
>
> (WVC, 63–4, italics original)

From this perspective, it is not a proposition but a *system of propositions* made of inferential relations among propositions that is the basic unit of sense. Crucially, these relations concern the content of propositions and not their formal properties since the colour exclusion problem has shown that logic cannot symbolically express all the real ways in which language expressions are used. Hence, in this period, Wittgenstein no longer relies on the logical structure of language to explain how it functions but vokes inferential relations for this purpose. His inferentialist approach to language is indubitably one of the signature features of his thought in the early 1930s. Although Wittgenstein continues to compare a proposition to a picture, he increasingly often likens language to a calculus (*Kalkül*) or a game (*Spiel*). This overlapping of the old – Tractarian – concepts with the new notions is also typical of his middle work. As already mentioned, another fundamental change takes place in this period as well, with Wittgenstein rejecting phenomenological language (one previously envisioned as free from the difficulties and obscurities of ordinary language) and thus ending up with everyday language use as the only object of investigations. What is done in these investigations does not involve a reconstruction of the logical structure, logical syntax or logical grammar of this language, which was what the *Tractatus* was dedicated to, but of its material grammar, so to speak. This means that there is a transition to describing the rules for using language which is compared to a calculus or a game. Consistently with this comparison, the sense of propositions and the meanings of words are determined by rules in the same way as propositions in a calculus or moves in a game are determined by the rules of this calculus or this game. Some Wittgenstein scholars emphasize that the language-calculus analogy was a distinctive feature of his thought between 1929 and 1933.[12]

A group of researchers outline the evolution of Wittgenstein's view in this middle period as a turn from the concept of language as a calculus to the concept of language as a game, which they date back to more or less the mid-1930s, with the notion of calculus being supplanted by the notion of language games starting from *The Blue and Brown Books*. As already pointed out in the 'Introduction', this view is not corroborated either by Wittgenstein's manuscripts from 1929 to 1932 or by his later writings. Wittgenstein likened language to a game as early as at the beginning of the 1930s and then used this comparison alternately with the notion of language as a calculus, depending on the context. Briefly, Wittgenstein employed the concepts of both calculus and game when he wanted to describe language through them. There is even a certain pattern to it; specifically, language as a calculus appears when Wittgenstein's remarks concerning mathematics (above all the number-concept) neighbour with his remarks about the proposition. Therefore, it is quite unfounded to claim that in the early 1930s Wittgenstein described the language as a calculus only to relinquish this term later and adopt the notion of game instead. Emphatically, the two terms alternated in Wittgenstein's writings, both in the period called the middle one and later, including in the *Philosophical Investigations* (PI, §81).

To briefly summarize, Wittgenstein's three major achievements pivotal to the middle period of his philosophical development include: a critical revision of his position in the *Tractatus Logico-Philosophicus* (first and foremost, discarding the idea of the independence of the elementary propositions, abandoning the formal approach to language analysis and proposing a redefinition of syntax rules based on the content of ordinary-language propositions); the emergence of the concept of propositional system (*Satzsystem*) as the basic unit of sense; and the concept of language as a calculus or a game, with the question of rules and meaning as determined by these rules pushed to the foreground.[13]

Another question is the position of BT in this middle period of the evolution of Wittgenstein's philosophy. For one, it undoubtedly was, in the view of Wittgenstein himself, the best aggregation of the insights he had developed since his return to Cambridge. It was under constant revision and correction, but Wittgenstein had it at hand at all time and used it when working on his other projects. As shown, for example, by Stephen Hilmy (1987: 25–39), TS 213 was Wittgenstein's central reference when drafting the first version of the *Philosophical Investigations* at the turn of 1936 and its later, post-war version, especially regarding Wittgenstein's late concept of philosophy as depicted in §§87–133 of the *Investigations*. Hilmy (1987: 37) argues that in view of the multiple overlaps between observations in TS 213 and the ideas in the *Investigations*, *The Big Typescript* would more legitimately merit the subtitle of 'Preliminary Study for the *Philosophical Investigation*' than *The Blue and Brown Books* do.

3. *The Big Typescript*: Form and Content

Unmatched by any other text by Wittgenstein, the panoply of themes and problems addressed in BT combined with its structure to produce a piece of writing that has stubbornly resisted any general description and left readers with several questions to which no straightforward answers can be found. For instance, it is difficult to state whether chapter titles gesture at questions that Wittgenstein aimed to solve through his remarks or whether they are just general formulations in a catalogue of observations on a given theme. To make this even more baffling, some chapters, such as 'Understanding', appear to aspire to the former, while others, for example, 'Expectation, Wish, etc.', are rather collections of notes referring to the eponymous issues. The titles of subchapters make a peculiar impression as well. Quotations from the text, as they are, they were supposed, Schulte proposes, to remind Wittgenstein that he had put them at those respective places even though they might as well appear elsewhere. According to Schulte, the views expressed in the titles sometimes diverge from, or even contradict, most of the remarks the subchapters contains. This happens, for example, in 'Concept of Meaning Originates in a Primitive Philosophical Conception of Language', where 'primitive' has a rather negative connotation whereas the observations themselves use 'primitive' in the sense of a simple, or overly simple, fashion of explaining how language works.[14] The chapters differ in the degree of elaboration and internal coherence. For instance, 'Phenomenology' develops thematically homogeneous thought-lines, whereas 'Idealism, etc.' partly continues the phenomenological chapter and partly analyses the expression 'having pain'. So far, all the endeavours mobilized to identify any consistent logic behind the sequencing of the BT chapters have proven futile. Chapters on psychological notions are interwoven with chapters on language-philosophical issues, with 'Understanding' and 'Meaning' followed by 'Proposition. Sense of a Proposition', only to veer to the psychological perspective in 'Immediate Understanding', pass to considerations entitled 'The Nature of Language', jump again to 'Thought. Thinking', head towards 'Grammar' and then turn to 'Intention and Depiction'. An honest attempt to decipher the structure of this book would take a detailed and comprehensive investigation of basically all its chapters, which is an enterprise that has not been undertaken yet.

At the same time, one can hardly be content with a general observation that the notorious thematic alternations in BT are a testimony to the fact that

Wittgenstein still hesitated over many issues at the time of its production and his thoughts meandered from one question to another without any obvious connections or references. Such an appraisal may be apt to some extent, and it appears to capture Wittgenstein's treatment of phenomenology quite well, but several parts of BT exhibit a more profound logic. For example, it is actually symptomatic that Wittgenstein begins not from the proposition but from understanding and meaning and only passes to the proposition and its sense in the third chapter. This is primarily related to his anti-psychologism, that is, his criticism of the view that understanding and meaning denote certain mental (psychical) states and processes; or, in broader terms, that the mind confers meanings on language expressions, that internal, mental processes determine whether the use of language has sense, and that they unfold outside of sings and, as such, outside of language. However, Wittgenstein claims in a somewhat enigmatic way: 'Just as there is no metaphysics, there is no metalogic; and the word "understanding", the expression "understanding a proposition", aren't metalogical. They are expressions of language, just like all others' (BT, 1). What Wittgenstein criticizes and consequently rejects here is not the idea that certain mental processes are involved when one, for example, understands an order or tries to understand what another person means when talking to one. Wittgenstein's insistence that 'understanding', 'having in mind' and 'meaning' are not metalogical entails his repudiation of the notion that the primary function of such concepts in our language is denoting certain mental states and processes, first of all when one talks about 'understanding a proposition'. This is why he argues that '[u]nderstanding doesn't begin until there's a proposition. (And therefore it doesn't interest us.)' (BT, 1). It is not of interest as a concept depicting internal psychic states in the same way as psychological understanding of meaning falls outside of Wittgenstein's considerations, which nevertheless does not implicate the disappearance of these 'psychological' concepts themselves from discourse. Instead, they only become language expressions as any other ones and cease to be approached as 'metalogical', that is, being 'beyond-logic'. What must be emphasized, however, is that, as Hilmy has pointed out, 'logic' does not refer here to the discipline practised, for example, by Russell or Gottlob Frege. For the middle Wittgenstein, the domain of logic is defined by the use 'of these expressions as any other ones'. In other words, it simply coincides with ordinary language.

As already stated, Wittgenstein in his middle period did not entirely relinquish the positions he had expounded in the *Tractatus Logico-Philosophicus*, in particular in their conceptual layer. When surveying the table of contents in *The Big Typescript*, one may be intrigued by chapters dedicated to psychological concepts: understanding, thinking, intention, expectation and wish. The truth is, however, that one should not construe Wittgenstein's ponderings on these as anticipating his later studies on the philosophy of psychology. His analyses do not delve into concepts that concern experiencing, and he does not aim to grasp the grammar of expressions depicting our 'interiority' – inner experiences, processes or states. He thus does not focus on matters that were to become the central thematic concerns of his writings on philosophy of psychology, to which he dedicated himself towards the end of his life. His new approach to ordinary language – the only one that can be an object of analysis – is still interlaced with his old, Tractarian way of thinking. Wittgenstein looks into the concepts of understanding, thinking, wishing, expecting, etc., not as psychological notions but as exemplifications of a general relationship between a proposition (language), compared to a picture as it was in the *Tractatus*, and that which it presents – thoughts and reality: an expectation and meeting an expectation, wishing something and fulfilling this wish, an intention and making it a reality, a command and executing it, thinking that p and p, understanding that p and p. In a sense, it is a case of new wine in old bottles, as Wittgenstein clothes his novel thoughts in some already used garments.

What thoughts are these? One answer is: that the correspondence of thinking and reality is not a correspondence of two independent entities which is based on the correspondence of their logical form; their correspondence is determined by grammar. The relationship between language and the world is an internal relation, in the sense that the world itself is not split into facts with which one can compare propositions to establish whether these are true or false. It is the grammar we use that divides this world into facts. This will be addressed in more detail in the following chapter, and meanwhile our focus will be on the notes from 1929 to 1932, in which Wittgenstein replaced the notion of logical syntax with the notion of grammar and, instead of examining general forms, sought to explain rules behind particular uses of language. The grammar of ordinary language encompasses the use of expressions of this language and does not concern the logical structures behind the everyday use of language, which form the requisite basis of all representation systems.

About one third of *The Big Typescript* is devoted to issues in the philosophy of mathematics, which in fact take up even more room in the notes. The chapters 'Foundations of Mathematics', 'On Cardinal Numbers', 'Mathematical

Proof', 'Proof by Induction. Periodicity' and 'The Infinite in Mathematics' are placed at the end of the work, but this does not mean that they are meant as a conclusion to the whole of the book. Essentially, considerations on mathematics in BT are an integral part of Wittgenstein's philosophy as such, and it is here that their links to Wittgenstein's general ideas concerning language, meaning and understanding are more pronounced than anywhere else. This facilitates exploring his philosophy of mathematics as connected to and against the backdrop of his philosophy as a whole, rather than as a discrete field or a subdiscipline, a perspective which was prompted by the publication of the 1937–44 notes in 1957 as a separate work entitled (by Wittgenstein's heirs) *Remarks on the Foundations of Mathematics*.[15]

As already mentioned, the thematic versatility and the range of subjects addressed in *The Big Typescript* make it barely possible to devise a general framework within which to meaningfully enclose them all. However, I believe that it is possible to identify a leitmotif that was pervasive in Wittgenstein's thought in the early 1930s and lies at the core of *The Big Typescript* as well. Specifically, Wittgenstein's reasoning at the time pivoted on the idea of language as a calculus, a game or a system of rules,[16] notions that Wittgenstein tended to use interchangeably. Such an approach to language was supposed to yield a perspicuous representation (*übersichltliche Darstellung*) of 'grammar', that is, of grammatical rules that delimit sense and indicate where and how language sets metaphysical traps for us. Wittgenstein would seek to show how language operated as a calculus or a game throughout BT and in multiple contexts produced, for example, by psychological concepts, mathematical propositions and the primary language of phenomenology. For instance, he referred in 'Grammar' to a 'notation that is more easily surveyed', by which he obviously did not mean either the logical notation of the *Tractatus* or phenomenological language as its possible complementation, but rather an enumeration of the rules for the use of our language. At the same time, these rules should not be understood as empirical propositions or their list as a description of language facts (i.e. a depiction of the actual use of language). In BT, Wittgenstein insists on a fundamental difference between a description of facts and a description of a calculus or a game. For example, when describing a real language, we talk about it the way we talk about chess pieces, that is, we list the rules that govern them rather than their physical properties. Thus, already in BT, a 'surveyable notation' – or a 'clearly surveyable representation' – denotes something more than just a description or an enumeration of observable patterns in the use of language expressions. It rather designates a description and a perspicuous catalogue of that which determines the sense of all speech, that is, rules which are acquired through manners of learning a language, explanations and justifications of meanings and forms of correcting erroneous uses of expressions.

When explaining the difference between his outlook in the *Tractatus* and his standpoint adopted in the early 1930s, Wittgenstein somewhat self-critically observed:

> In my old book [the *Tractatus*] the solution of the problem is still presented in a far too little homespun manner; there's still too much of the appearance that to solve our problems we should need some discoveries; everything is too little put in the form of grammatical obviousnesses of ordinary language (ordinary way of expression). Everything still too much requires discoveries.
>
> (MS 109, 213)

Apparently, Wittgenstein refers to these very insights, which were recorded in November 1930, when he states in 'Philosophy' in BT: 'All reflections can be carried out in a much more homespun way than I used to do. And therefore no new words have to be used in philosophy – the old ones suffice' (BT, 420). The description of the rules of grammar of our language – a surveyable representation of these rules – supplants the logic of language, which the *Tractatus* championed as revealing the hidden relation between language and the world. Thus, while the Tractarian aim of delimiting sense remains unchanged, this aim is supposed to be achieved in the BT period by ordinary – that is, grammatical – means, which leave everything 'the way it is'. We do not need new words. Which combinations of words make sense and which do not, as well as which are propositions and which are not, is no longer decided by logic or logical syntax. It is determined by grammar.

Wittgenstein continued to develop these ideas in his post-BT notes, first and foremost in *The Blue and Brown Books*, to finally find a proper expression for them in the *Philosophical Investigations*. When reading *The Big Typescript*, one can easily realize how substantial a portion of the remarks included in BT were transplanted, in a revised version, into the *Investigations*. This overlap implies that Wittgenstein's intense work after his return to Cambridge resulted in new insights into the issues related to the limits of sense in language use, which had preoccupied him since the *Tractatus*. He never stopped exploring them, though without any discernible linear progression. Rather, he tackled these issues from various angles, such as psychological concepts, phenomenological language, logic and mathematics.

4. Philosophy as working on oneself

Before winding up this argument, attention is due to a question that was neither conspicuously present in Wittgenstein's earlier work nor as emphatically addressed in his late considerations. Its special interest lies in that it concerns philosophy itself or, to put it more precisely, philosophical self-knowledge. Remarks included in the 'Philosophy' chapter of *The Big Typescript* were for the most part incorporated into the *Philosophical Investigations* (§§111–134). However, Wittgenstein did not re-employ one of these remarks, which directly captured what he devoted almost all of his life to. Specifically, the chapter opens with an insight that: 'As is frequently the case with work in architecture, work on philosophy is actually closer to working on oneself. On one's own understanding. On the way one sees things. (And on what one demands of them.)' (BT, 407).

Wittgenstein's earliest meta-philosophical comments are in all probability to be found in the *Notes on Logic* (1913), where he states that:

> In philosophy there are no deductions: it is purely descriptive.
> Philosophy gives no pictures of reality.
> Philosophy can neither confirm nor confute scientific investigation.
> Philosophy consists of logic and metaphysics: logic is the basis. …
> Philosophy is the doctrine of the logical form of scientific propositions (not only of primitive propositions).
> The word 'philosophy' ought always to designate something over or under but not beside, the natural sciences.
>
> (NB, 106–7)

These insights embody a positive concept of philosophy, but there is no reference in them to any philosophizing subject. First of all, philosophy is purely descriptive, a view that Wittgenstein will consistently endorse throughout his life. The fact that it does not involve deduction means that it does not start from any overriding principles, such as, for example, the Cartesian *cogito* principle, to infer other axioms of the system from them. It does not generate any images of reality, which means that it does not provide any knowledge of the world, does not discover anything and does not hold any cognitive engagement. This perception of philosophy will constantly accompany Wittgenstein. Still, philosophy has a domain of its own since it is a science of the logical form of scientific (empirical) propositions.[17] The assertion that philosophy consists of logic and metaphysics, with logic being its foundation, sounds cryptic and rather puzzling. It suggests that logical forms of expressions reveal the essential structure of reality – that the 'logic' (i.e. the logical structure) of reality is inferable from the logic of language. The point is that such an outlook would contradict the descriptive concept of philosophy as devoid of basic assertions (overriding principles) from which to derive other assertions. In the descriptive concept of philosophy, logic cannot be the basis of metaphysical postulates.

While Wittgenstein's earliest meta-philosophical comments are positive regarding the object and method of philosophy, his outlook changes in the *Tractatus Logico-Philosophicus,* even though it admittedly reiterates some of Wittgenstein's theses from the *Notes on Logic*.[18] What becomes entirely rejected is the concept of philosophy as a science of logical forms. There are no philosophical propositions describing logical forms, and philosophy cannot be a doctrine of anything; there are no 'productions' of philosophical thinking whatsoever. Puzzles of philosophy result from the fact 'that the logic of our language is misunderstood' (TLP, p. 3, also 4.003). When we grasp this logic and properly comprehend it, all philosophical problems will disappear; they will no longer be posed, because they are products of illusions that come into being when we use words in ways that breach their logical syntax (grammar). Hence, in the *Tractatus* period and later as well, Wittgenstein regards philosophy as a critique of language:

> Philosophy aims at the logical clarification of thoughts. Philosophy is not a body of doctrine but an activity. A philosophical work consists essentially of elucidations. Philosophy does not result in 'philosophical propositions', but rather in the clarification of propositions. Without philosophy thoughts are, as it were, cloudy and indistinct: its task is to make them clear and to give them sharp boundaries.
>
> (TLP, 4.112)

When this is accomplished, we will recognize that, while philosophizing in the traditional sense, we assume a wrong position vis-à-vis the world and language (thought), one of looking from the side. As a result, it seems to us that by looking from the side we can see who we are and what the world is like. However, when our thoughts are clarified, '[t]hen we will see the world aright' (TLP, 6.54).

Thus, philosophy has a positive facet to it and has its constructive uses. Specifically, it may help us see the world in a proper manner, provided that we discard its cognitive (metaphysical) ambitions and practise it within the bounds of linguistic critique, which will reveal and consequently curb the illegitimate claims of traditional philosophizing. At the same time, the Tractarian concept of philosophy does not envision any philosophical subject or self-awareness, either, at least not explicitly. While the exercise of philosophy alters our attitude to the world, it is, so to speak, an external activity. *The Big Typescript,* on the contrary, depicts philosophy as working on oneself. At the very beginning of its chapter on 'Philosophy', Wittgenstein states that challenges inherent in the practice of philosophy differ from those involved in doing science.[19] The difficulty of philosophy is associated with a change of attitude, to accomplish which one must conquer the resistance of the will: 'What has to be overcome is not difficulty of the intellect but of the will' (BT, 407). If philosophical efforts consist in working on oneself, the question is what that means, what this work is supposed to result in and finally why it should be similar to work in architecture. Do architects mainly work on themselves? Did Wittgenstein have his own experience as an architect in mind?[20] Not all of these questions can be answered. Wittgenstein's observations in this chapter imply that said change of attitude is linked to the fact that the words we use every day, without even noticing it, are natural to us and crop up automatically when we need them. We have a certain natural, pre-philosophical image – or rather a *proto-picture*[21] – of language, implanted deep inside us, often beyond our consciousness. Wittgenstein described this proto-picture in a note of 15 June 1931 (see MS 111, 16), which he then placed at the beginning of the chapter on 'Meaning' in *The Big Typescript*. As mentioned above, in this passage Wittgenstein used the word 'primitive' in the sense of this natural (simple) proto-picture of language and its relation to reality. Intimately familiar to us, this proto-picture is the same image that Wittgenstein labelled at the very onset of the *Philosophical Investigations* as the Augustinian picture (vision) of language, in which the paramount function of language was to name things. This very proto-picture held sway over Plato, Frege, Russell and even Wittgenstein himself in the *Tractatus*.

If now, that is, in *The Big Typescript*, Wittgenstein avers that work in philosophy entails working on oneself, he apparently means that the point is to make this proto-picture vanish so that it stops being a prism that refracts our perception of the operations of language. Philosophy as working on oneself is tantamount to working on a change of one's attitude, not to the world though, but to the language by means of which we describe this world. Admittedly, this is rather bizarre work, for its intended effect is self-destructive in seeking the ultimate dismantling of philosophy. Briefly, work in philosophy aims to put philosophy to an end. Regrettably, it is impossible, and our philosophical work on ultimately having no work to do never ends because, as long as there is language, so-called puzzles of philosophy will inexorably persist. As Wittgenstein puts it in BT:

> One keeps hearing the remark that philosophy really doesn't make any progress, that the same philosophical problems that occupied the Greeks keep occupying us. But those who say that don't understand the reason it must be so. That reason

is that our language has remained constant and keeps seducing us into asking the same questions. So long as there is a verb 'be' that seems to function like 'eat' and 'drink', so long as there are the adjectives 'identical', 'true', 'false', 'possible', so long as there is talk about a flow of time and an expanse of space, etc., etc., humans will continue to bump up against the same mysterious difficulties, and stare at something that no explanation seems able to remove.

And this by the way, satisfies a longing for the transcendental, for in believing that they see the 'limit of human understanding' they of course believe that they can see beyond it.

(BT, 424)

6

PS: Understanding, expecting, wishing, etc.

For a few months starting approximately at the end of October 1929, Ludwig Wittgenstein appears to have focused on two major problem fields in his manuscripts. One of them was phenomenology, which was discussed in Chapter 1, and the other was the philosophy of mathematics, which comprised general considerations on the nature of mathematical language and a range of particular issues, including the infinite and a critique of set theory addressed in the preceding chapter. A clear shift of focus came in the wake of Wittgenstein's abjuration of the phenomenological-language project, which Merrill Hintikka and Jaakko Hintikka (1986: 138*pass*) identify as a turning point in Wittgenstein's philosophy. From that moment on, his thought headed in another direction to delve into questions of grammar, primarily involving the understanding of expressions of ordinary language, the examination of examples of particular uses of these expressions and the comparison of language to a game. On 22 October 1929, Wittgenstein noted down: 'The idea that it would be possible to construct a phenomenological language which would properly say what we had (wanted) to express in philosophy is, I believe, nonsense. We have to make do with our ordinary language and just understand it correctly. This means that we must not let this language prompt us to talk nonsense' (MS 107, 176). Three days later, he wrote: 'Every proposition is a free play of marks and sounds without any connection to reality and [its] only relation [to reality] is the way it is verified' (MS 107, 177).

Having discarded phenomenological language, we are left with our ordinary language and the right understanding of its expressions, which is supposed to prevent us from uttering nonsense. In Chapter 2, Wittgenstein was shown to have understood verification as a way of establishing the sense of a proposition or as an attempt at answering the question 'How do you mean?' When saying that the method of the verification of a proposition is its only relation to reality, he means that the sense of a proposition, the way we understand it – and consequently its grammar – also determines this relation.

More or less from this moment on, Wittgenstein began to analyse the understanding and sense of various expressions of ordinary language. To start with, he focused on 'pain expressions' and expressions concerning space. He also devoted considerable attention to the grammar of colours. He interspersed these notes with general remarks on philosophy, in particular on concepts for describing relations between thought and reality. When compiling *The Big Typescript*, which (as explained in the preceding chapter) can be considered a representative selection of his notes from 1929 to 1933, he placed the problem of understanding and meaning at the very beginning of the work. In the *Tractatus*, understanding a proposition equalled knowing under which conditions it was true. In *The Big Typescript*, Wittgenstein's view was different: '"understanding a proposition" means acting in accordance with it' (BT, 15). He likened understanding a proposition to mastering a calculus (for example, multiplication) or to grasping a chess move: 'Isn't understanding a sentence analogous to understanding a chess move as a chess move?' (BT, 148).

Thus, understanding a proposition entails a certain *action*, a capacity to use it in language, rather than knowing its truth-conditions. Does it mean that we first understand something as a proposition and can only then use it? Is understanding a *cause* and use an *effect*? Inherited from Frege, Wittgenstein's anti-psychologism precluded such a solution. In the title of BT's first chapter, Wittgenstein wrote that '[u]nderstanding, meaning, drop out of our considerations' – they drop out as psychological processes unfolding in the mind. Language must speak for itself, which means, among other things. that if the sense of a proposition can only be explained by means of other propositions, language is the only thing we have at our disposal. We do not have to evoke non-propositional psychological acts and intuitive, albeit essential and fundamental, inner experiences that breathe life into dead signs. If meaning something, intention and sense were like the soul of a sign, it would perhaps be best to show it directly without any foreign mediation. This is what Edmund Husserl sought to do. To evoke his poignant phrasing, whether expressed or not, meaning leads a solitary mental life. In the second volume of his *Logical Investigations*, Husserl (2012: 181*pass*) argued that if we wanted to communicate, that is, simply express, the meaning of a language expression (*Ausdruck*), it took on the function of indication (*Anzeichen*), that is, it served as a sign of the speaker's *thought* or, in other words, a sign of mental experiences which conferred sense on signs.

Thus, meaning is something else than an expressed meaning; it is a thing in and of itself, primary and pure, uncontaminated by announcing, communicating, speaking or writing, in a word, by articulation, which is derivative and secondary.

Meaning has a monological dimension to it and is present when one talks to oneself. On such occasions, one does not address anybody else, and signs do not serve one as indications of one's unfolding mental acts. Such indications are entirely redundant and pointless, because the mental acts one experiences are immediately accessible to one; they are being experienced as the sign is being articulated. At this point, however, we can follow Wittgenstein and ask how one actually knows that *this* mental experience is *this* meaning: 'But if someone says: "How am I supposed to know what he means, all I see are his signs?", then I say: "How is he supposed to know what he means? – He too has only his signs"' (BT, 4). This immediate and propositional knowledge must nevertheless be somehow expressed in signs, just like talking to oneself is also premised on using signs. The very notions of 'immediate presence', 'immediate experience' and 'solitary mental life' are signs as well. To Wittgenstein, understanding signs does not involve understanding something that lies beyond signs. Hence, if one understands something, this thing is a proposition. In other words, according to Husserl, meaning is immediately given in an indivisible moment of time where there is no distance between experience and its content. In this single moment, the immediate experience of meaning is at the same time, as if in the blink of an eye, an immediate experience of there being no distance between 'thought' and its expression. When pondering the grammar of the words 'now' and 'here', Wittgenstein wrote in his notebooks: '"Now" is a word. What do I need this word for? "Now" – as opposed to what? – As opposed to "in an hour," "5 minutes ago," etc., etc. "Now" doesn't designate a system; rather, it belongs to one. It works no magic – any more than any other word' (BT, 524). Thus, 'now' refers to what is not-now, to what is before and after. As a result, in Husserl's parlance, 'the primordial givenness', the immediate presence of meaning or 'the actual now of the present moment' is constructed by grammatical rules that form a system of representation. Present experience at this very moment is only possible if this experience is bracketed off from the entire stream of consciousness, a feat that can be accomplished solely by means of signs and rules that govern them. As Wittgenstein insists, '[t]he description of what is psychological ought to be usable in turn as a symbol' (BT, 284).

Suppose, however, that one tries to 'show straight' meaning conceived of as the soul of a sign and to directly capture the mental act of understanding. According to Wittgenstein, 'If someone tells me something and I understand it, then this is as much something that happens to me as is hearing what he says. And here understanding is a phenomenon that occurs when I hear an English sentence, and that distinguishes this type of hearing from hearing a sentence in a foreign language' (BT, 7). Let us imagine that I have in front of me a coded sentence and the key necessary for deciphering the code. If I were asked whether I understood the sentence, I would answer: 'No, I must first decode it', and only when I had transposed the ciphered signs into Polish could I say: 'Now, I understand it.' According to Wittgenstein, if I wanted an insight into the essence of understanding, I would have to determine at what moment of transposing the code into Polish I came to understand the sentence. But this moment cannot be pinpointed. Instead, one can say that one understands the sentence because one is able to state what 'the sense of this sentence is'. One of Wittgenstein's fundamental views on understanding was that of understanding as bound up with explaining sense. The lack of understanding, that is, non-understanding, can be eliminated by explanation: 'Understanding correlates with explanation; and in so far as it doesn't, it is unarticulated and therefore doesn't interest us; or it is articulated and correlates with the proposition itself, whose sense we want to render' (BT, 11).

Peter M. S. Hacker (2013: 86) has observed that in *The Big Typescript*, Wittgenstein realized that thinking, understanding, meaning, etc., were not meta-logical concepts. Meta-logical concepts are concepts that refer to relations between propositions, thoughts, representations of states of affairs and reality. If conceived in meta-logical terms, understanding is a process unfolding beyond signs; it is a mental process through which signs obtain life, in the sense of becoming connected to reality. This understanding of *understanding* imposes itself so irresistibly that Husserl succumbed to it. For his part, Wittgenstein endeavoured to inspect this, say, natural idea of understanding, but at the same time he regarded it as wrong because it resembled the causal concept of meaning as something that enlivens dead signs.[1] In this context, Wittgenstein drew on command and its execution as his example. It appears obvious that one must first understand a command to execute it; understanding a command is a condition (cause) of its execution (effect). Does understanding a command, for instance, 'fetch a hammer', indeed involve envisioning going to a tool box and taking a hammer out of it? Wittgenstein replies: 'But there is no transition from knowing to doing. And there is no justification in principle for *that* being what corresponded to the command' (BT, 16). Another possible question is how long before executing a command one should understand this command. According to Wittgenstein, there is no intermediary stage between understanding a command and executing it. If there were such a stage, if understanding were a prior preparation for the execution of an order, it would have to be something that, so to speak, attached itself to the sign, something exterior to the sing that were not its execution.

Besides the chapter on understanding, *The Big Typescript* also contains chapters on intention, expectation and wish. Counterintuitively perhaps, they are entirely unrelated to the philosophy of psychology which Wittgenstein went on to develop in the late 1940s. These BT chapters do not aim to analyse the language of perceptions, and Wittgenstein does not explore in them the nature of expressions for inner experiences, which is what he does in the *Philosophical Investigations*. Wittgenstein's object in BT is rather different as he seeks to show the internal (logical) relation between meaning and its expression. The point is that there is no pre-existing thought, meaning, sense or intention which is then given an expression in language. Thought and language, thought and word form a whole and cannot be considered separately, just like a facial expression cannot be disjoined from the face itself. Let us think something and now let us think this in language – the distinction underlying this suggestion does not make sense. Wittgenstein later elaborated on and honed these insights in *The Blue and Brown Books* and in the *Philosophical Investigations*.

In the chapter 'Intention and Depiction', Wittgenstein compared intention to anger and hatred. For example, I am angry that he has come at this very moment. Of course I may not know *why* he makes me angry, but I cannot possibly not know *that* he makes me angry. 'He makes me angry' does not mean that I am angry and he is the cause of my anger, 'rather he, or alternatively, the image of him – etc. – occur within my hatred, are components of my hatred' (BT, 273). One cannot be in doubt about what makes one angry, what one fears or what one believes. The proposition 'I am convinced, but I don't know what about' makes no sense. 'I am scared but don't know by what' and 'I am angry but I don't know about what' sound similarly problematic. Interestingly, however, Wittgenstein's notes amassed in *The Big Typescript* still often rely on the language of the *Tractatus* even though they gradually depart from the Tractarian take on understanding, propositions and language. Wittgenstein states, for example:

> Intention, however, is exactly the same kind of thing as – for example – annoyance. And here it seems somehow that one can never recognize an intention, when viewed from the outside, as an *intention*; as if one has to intend it oneself in order to understand it as an intention. But that would mean not to view it as a phenomenon, as a fact! Of course this is the previous problem again, because the funny thing about it is that you have to be able to tell by looking at a thought (viewed as an independent fact) that it is the thought that such and such is the case. If you can't tell this by looking at it (just as you can't tell from a stomach-ache what caused it) then it's of no logical interest.
>
> (BT, 381)

A pertinent question is what this 'logical interest' in thought, intention and understanding actually targets and whether it is an interest in the logical syntax of language – in the very construction of a proposition itself which is supposed to indicate that this or that is the case. Apparently, 'logical interest' concerns something else. The point is that intentional propositions are not symbolic expressions of intention understood as an inner mental act that unfolds, as it were, beyond signs. A thought can only be scrutinized in a proposition whereas outside of a proposition, it requires an additional experience or sensation and lies, in this sense, outside of logic. This entails approaching thought neither as a phenomenon nor as a fact. Logic does not mean here the same thing as in the *Tractatus* since understanding and thinking are words as any other ones and their logical interest is essentially grammatical interest. In the chapter 'Intention an Depiction', Wittgenstein compares intention and its fulfilment to drawing a model of or copying an object. In the *Tractatus*, he presented his concept of depicting reality in and through language: 'What a picture must have in common with reality, in order to be able to depict it – correctly or incorrectly – in the way it does, is its pictorial form' (TLP, 2.17). A picture and what it presents have the same logical form in common. Dubbed the 'doctrine of isomorphism' by Hacker, this theory holds that the logical form of reality is depicted by the logical form of language. A proposition can be a picture of reality because it shares the common logical structure with reality or, more precisely speaking, with states of affairs. Wittgenstein explained that

> [a] gramophone record, the musical idea, the written notes, and the sound-waves, all stand to one another in the same internal relation of depicting that holds between language and the world. They are all constructed according to a common logical plan. (Like the two youths in the fairy-tale, their two horses, and their lilies. They are all in a certain sense one.) (TLP, 4.014)

Thus, the relationship between music, the score and grooves in the gramophone record is not based either on their external resemblance or on there being something external to them to which all the three of them refer. The similarity is internal and resides in their logical structure. As points on a map are a spatial projection of points on land, so propositions in language are a logical (internal) depiction of reality. However, propositions cannot depict this logical form itself – their own logical structure; instead, they can only show it: 'A picture cannot, however, depict its pictorial form: it displays it' (TLP, 2.172).

Nevertheless, when Wittgenstein abandoned the theory of logical atomism in the late 1920s and early 1930s, he discarded the doctrine of isomorphism as well. Still, he did not relinquish the comparison of language or a proposition to a picture. This analogy appears time and again in a variety of contexts in his notes from 1929 to 1933. The theme is discussed in two dedicated subchapters of *The Big Typescript* (21. 'Similarity of Proposition and Picture' and 22. 'Propositions Compared to Genre-Paintings. [Related to This: Understanding a Picture]'), where Wittgenstein also frequently employs picture-similes when analysing understanding, intention and expectation: 'One can compare understanding a description with drawing a picture based on that description. ... And indeed in many cases it is taken as the criterion of understanding' (BT, 15); and 'Only intention can measure up to the original. And that is shown by the fact that the expression of intention contains the description of the original as well as expression of the rule of projection' (BT, 276). Yet at the same time, this repeatedly rehearsed comparison to a picture – Wittgenstein's discourse evoking depicting, drawing, copying and painting – carries negative overtones since it serves to demonstrate the erroneousness of the Tractarian idea that thought and reality share the same logical form, which language – that is, a picture – depicts. Wittgenstein directly repudiates this misconception in his *Philosophical Grammar*:

> Here instead of harmony or agreement of thought and reality one might say: the pictorial character of thought. But is this pictorial character an agreement? In the *Tractatus* I had said something like: it is an agreement of form. But that is misleading.
>
> Anything can be a picture of anything, if we extend the concept of picture sufficiently. If not, we have to explain what we call a picture of something, and what we want to call agreement of the pictorial character, the agreement of the forms.
>
> For what I said really boils down to this: that every projection must have something in common with what is projected no matter what is the method of projection. But that only means that I am here extending the concept of 'having in common' and am making it equivalent to the general concept of projection.
>
> (PG, §113)

The doctrine of logical form, one of the central theories of the *Tractatus Logico-Philosophicus*, is now deemed fallacious. In this context, equating depiction with projection is highly relevant because, while the Tractarian approach is that the logical form of reality itself, which is independent of language, cannot be depicted in propositions, the method of projection indeed can. The method of projection is identical with the picture itself, and if it is not recognisable in the picture, which may happen, we are able to describe and symbolically present it. What Wittgenstein came to consider faulty in the Tractarian concept of the logical form of depiction was that it was independent of language and reality, that it was something that we could only see in them but could not convey in language. Thus, by retaining the comparison of a proposition (language) to a picture, Wittgenstein emphasized the limits of this comparison and its nonsense-breeding misuses. For example, in his considerations on intention, Wittgenstein observed:

> If I intentionally copy a particular shape, at a certain point the process of copying has this shape in common with reality. The shape is a fact of the copying process. A fact that is contiguous with the copied object and that coincides with it at these points of contact. Then one could say: Even if my pencil doesn't capture the original, my intention always does.
>
> (BT, 275–6)

Picture-comparisons only capture a certain property of language, but not its nature, unlike in the *Tractatus*. To say that a proposition is a picture highlights a certain characteristic in the grammar of the word 'proposition'. This characteristic is a very general one; specifically, a picture must have something in common with that which it is a picture of, in the same way that a proposition must have something in common with what it says, an intention with its realization, a command with its execution, and an expectation with the fulfilment of it. However, the shared thing is different in every case. All the instances that Wittgenstein addresses in *The Big Typescript* – proposition, understanding, thought, thinking, intention, expectation and wish – exemplify a general relation of thought to reality, of a picture to the pictured, but the question of agreement between them is the matter of the grammar of these words, of the way they are used in language. Such general comparisons are actually not pivotal because they do not explain much, but rather themselves need interpretation. Wittgenstein will tend to focus on concrete descriptions of the grammar of words which bear a reference to reality: expecting, wishing, commanding, understanding, thinking, etc. But now his major lens changes and is no longer defined by the isomorphism of the picture and the pictured as the basis of the thought-reality agreement: 'Agreement of thought and reality. Like everything metaphysical the (pre-established) harmony between thoughts and reality is to be discovered in the grammar of language' (BT, 189).

In his discussion of expectation in *The Big Typescript*, Wittgenstein claims, for example, that expectation and its fulfilment are connected in language. In the proposition 'I expect that he will come', the words 'he will come' seem to be used differently than in the assertion 'he will come'. Yet it is unclear what this difference actually is. When one expects a visitor, one usually repeatedly looks at one's watch, walks up and down the room, looks out of the window to see whether the visitor is coming, etc. However, one's behaviour bears little resemblance to expecting since one may walk to and from, have a glance at one's watch time and again or look out of the window without expecting this visitor to come. This behaviour is thus not characteristic of expectation that the visitor will come. One's expectation or wish for this visitor to come is an expectation (a wish) that *he* and not anybody else should *come* rather than, for example, call. However, this – the fact that one is waiting for *him*, for *this* particular visitor, to *come* – cannot be shown in and through one's behaviour; it can only be explained in language by clarifying the use of 'he' and 'come'. These are grammatical explanations that make up language and simultaneously provide the touchpoint between expectation and its fulfilment: 'Everything is carried out *in language*' (BT, 382). How about reality then? In his remarks on commands, Wittgenstein observes: 'It is as if in the command there were already a shadow of its execution. But a shadow of this *execution*. It is you who goes to this or that place in the command. – Otherwise it would just be a different command' (BT, 288–89). Expectation (or wish) casts a shadow on its fulfilment, because it is *he* whom one expects and waits to see. Wittgenstein also talks about commands or wishes 'anticipating' their execution or fulfilment, whereby he avails himself of the English word 'foreshadowing'.[2] But to say that wishing that *p* should be the case through the happening of the event p is nothing else than a sign-rule (*Zeichenregel*) that holds: the wish that *p* should be the case = the wish which is fulfilled by the event p. It seems consistent with Wittgenstein's view that reality is not a property that is missing in expecting something, wishing something, commanding or intending; it is not something that will only become their property when the expectation and the wish have been fulfilled, the command has been executed and the intention has been realized. Nor is reality like daylight, which gives things their colours while they remain colourless at night. Briefly, reality is not addition to expectation, wish, command, thought or intention. That would be as nonsensical as the statement that an imagined colour is dull in comparison with the real one. As Wittgenstein puts it, our words cast their shadow on reality,[3] and objects, facts and events, like a figure and its shadow, touch words and in this sense become elements in the system or representation as examples, models and samples, serving to explain grammatical rules that govern the use of expressions: 'The agreement of thought and reality consists in this: if I say falsely that something is red, then, for all that, it isn't red. And when I want to explain the word "red" to someone, in the sentence "That is not red," I do it by pointing to something red' (PG, §113).

To conclude, multiple concepts, such as understanding, are divested of their meta-logical quality in *The Big Typescript* and become words like any other ones. When, in Chapter 84, Wittgenstein considers belief, he immediately refers to kindred words, such as expectation, hope, fear, wish, doubt and search. Having rejected the idea of phenomenological language, we are only left with our ordinary language, so we must study words the way they are used, along with their grammar, that is, the rules for their use. In BT, Wittgenstein does not entirely abandon the discourse of the *Tractatus Logico-Philosophicus*. Understanding, thinking, expecting, wishing and intending are not of interest to him as psychological concepts, and he is still quite far from the position espoused in the *Philosophical Investigations*. The concepts listed above are simply examples of a general relation between language and the world, between a picture and that which it presents. But as understanding ceases to be a meta-logical word, so does a picture (or image) cease to be such a word. Although in the early 1930s Wittgenstein uses notions typical of the *Tractatus*, he is evidently aware of their limitations and insufficiency in conveying the ideas he wants to convey. Focusing on concrete language phenomena will undermine his notion that language operates in one way, for example as being a picture of reality. Sometimes it is, and sometimes it is not.

7

Magic, rituals and philosophy

Wittgenstein on Frazer's *The Golden Bough*

1. Reading *The Golden Bough*

In some of his notes from the 1930s, Ludwig Wittgenstein reflected on the books he was reading, specifically, on Ernst Renan's *Histoire du peuple d'Israël* (*History of the People of Israel*) and James George Frazer's *The Golden Bough*. While remarks on Renan's work (dated on 3 November 1930) take up less than one page, observations concerning *The Golden Bough* are far longer. Wittgenstein told Maurice Drury that 'he had long wanted to read Frazer's *The Golden Bough* and asked to get hold of a copy out of the Union Library and read it out loud to him. I got the first volume of the full edition and we continued to read from it for some weeks' (Rhees 1984: 119).[1] Written between 19 June and 6 July 1931, a time Wittgenstein spent in Vienna, the notes referring to Frazer's study do not directly reference reading sessions with Drury. The remarks were included in TS 211, that is, an early version of *The Big Typescript* but, tellingly perhaps, they were not incorporated into its final version (TS 213), where Wittgenstein only retained a few excerpts (mainly in Chapter 93) to ultimately leave a single trace of reading *The Golden Bough* in §122 of the *Philosophical Investigations*. He also mentioned Frazer in the May Term lectures of 1933 and in notes in MS 143, known as 'loose sheets of varying size', which form the second part of 'Bemerkungen über Frazers *Golden Bough*' ('Remarks on Frazer's *Golden Bough*'), published by Rhees in 1967.[2]

When Wittgenstein embarked on reading *The Golden Bough*, Frazer's study enjoyed considerable popularity and was acclaimed as a significant piece of scholarship even though its outlook was already outdated in anthropology. *The Golden Bough* was, namely, the last great work of evolutional anthropology. Its first two-volume edition appeared in 1890, and the last one, consisting of twelve volumes, was published in 1915. Frazer lined up magic, religion and science in a chronological sequence of three successive levels in the evolution of the human spirit. He examined an array of cultures to find resemblances and analogies implying that magic was a composite of primitive ideas and customs that formed the earliest stage in the evolutionary development of humanity. According to Frazer, 'magic is a spurious system of natural law as well as a fallacious guide of conduct; it is a false science as well as an abortive art' (1922: 15). Hence, when reading *The Golden Bough*, Wittgenstein held in his hands a book that represented a style of thinking that was becoming obsolete and at the same time boasted a refined literary, even poetic, quality. Still, neither the anthropological content nor the stylistic merits of the study seem to have really mattered to Wittgenstein. What was of interest to him was rather a worldview, a certain mode of explaining human thought and action and a theory of meaning underlying this explanation, which Wittgenstein deemed basically wrong.

One of the aims Fraser pursued in *The Golden Bough* was to explain a bizarre ritual of the succession of the King of the Wood, a priest at the sanctuary of Diana Nemorensis in the forest surrounding Lake Nemi in the vicinity of Aricia. The candidate for the king could only succeed to this office by killing his predecessor. There was one crucial condition to this, though. Before killing the king, the candidate had to pluck a branch of a designated tree in the holy grove. The point was that this could be done exclusively by a slave who had escaped from his master. When a runaway slave plucked a branch of the tree guarded by the priest, he could fight the priest and, having defeated him, become the next Rex Nemorensis. The ancients identified this branch with the Golden Bough which, following Sybil's prophecy, Aeneas plucked before his perilous descent to Hades. Frazer sought to answer two major questions: 'First, why had Diana's priest at Nemi, the King of the Wood, to slay his predecessor? Second, why before doing so had he to pluck the branch of a certain tree?' (1922: 11). In Frazer's view, these questions could not be answered by examining ancient sources alone:

> The strange rule of this priesthood has no parallel in classical antiquity, and cannot be explained from it. To find an explanation we must go farther afield. ... For recent researches into the early history of man have revealed the essential similarity with which, under many superficial differences, the human mind has elaborated its first crude philosophy of life. Accordingly, if we can show that a barbarous custom, like that of the priesthood of Nemi, has existed elsewhere; if we can detect the motives which led to its institution; if we can prove that these motives have operated widely, perhaps universally, in human society, producing in varied circumstances a variety of institutions different but generically alike;

if we can show, lastly, that these very motives, with some of their derivative institutions, were actually at work in classical antiquity; then we may fairly infer that at a remoter age the same motives gave birth to the priesthood of Nemi.

(1922: 3)

Frazer concluded that the magic beliefs and practices of, to use his diction, 'savage' people could be elucidated by recourse to the model of instrumental rationality based on the notion of means and ends. Within this framework, the reason why 'savages' undertake certain actions at a particular time and place is always their desire to achieve a defined aim. In the case of the Nemi ritual, the king had to be killed in his prime, because otherwise his soul would not have retained the vitality necessary to keep the world from falling apart. According to Frazer, the rite was a vestige of the time when people had believed that the combat-confirmed replacement of an aging priest with a younger and more vigorous one would ensure plentiful harvest for their community. In Frazer's view, all other customs and rituals were also driven by instrumental motives, as exemplified by the bringing on of rain: 'when the end of March draws on, each householder betakes himself to the King of the Rain and offers him a cow that he may make the blessed waters of heaven to drip on the brown and withered pastures' (1922: 141). From the viewpoint of instrumental rationality, asking for rain is of course a blunder, and the establishment of the King of the Rain office is foolish. Wittgenstein does not agree with this interpretation, observing that:

> The people pray for rain *when the rainy period comes*. But surely that means that they do not really believe that he [= the Rain-King] can make it rain, otherwise they would do it in the dry periods of the year in which the land is 'a parched and arid desert'. For if one assumes that the people formerly instituted this office of Rain-King out of stupidity, it is nevertheless certainly clear that they had previously experienced that the rains begin in March, and then they would have had the Rain-King function for the other part of the year. Or again: toward morning, when the sun is about to rise, rites of daybreak are celebrated by the people, but not during the night, when they simply burn lamps.
>
> (RGB, 137)

Frazer argues that the longevity of the rain ritual was due to the utter difficulty of discovering a fault in magic as the spell for bringing on rain would anyway be fulfilled sooner or later. The same was also true for other rituals, such as killing by burning an image:

> For example, when an Ojebway Indian desires to work evil on any one, he makes a little wooden image of his enemy and runs a needle into its head or heart, or he

shoots an arrow into it, believing that wherever the needle pierces or the arrow strikes the image, his foe will the same instant be seized with a sharp pain in the corresponding part of his body; but if he intends to kill the person outright, he burns or buries the puppet, uttering certain magic words as he does so.

(Frazer 1922: 17)

According to Wittgenstein, by anchoring his explanations in the notion of means and ends, Frazer presented people's magical and religious beliefs in a way that made them *errors*. Consequently, he could present magic as a false science and a collection of faulty guidelines for conduct. For his part, Wittgenstein radically disagreed with such an interpretation, claiming that the analogy between the magical vision of the world and the scientific one was thoroughly misconceived, and that magic was no false physics, false medicine or false technic: 'Rather, the characteristic feature of ritualistic action is not at all a view, an opinion, whether true or false' (RGB, 129). In Wittgenstein's view, magic, like religion, cannot be true or false because it does not contain any beliefs, that is, propositions which could be verified or falsified and consequently ascertained as true or false. Rather, magic is an expression of human desires, fears and hopes and is, as such, symbolic and expressive. The burning of an image, making offerings to the King of the Rain and the like activities are not just mistakes but disclose a wish that something should happen. Wittgenstein draws a clear line between magic and actions based on wrong or simplistic ideas about things and processes. Frazer fails to perceive this difference and confounds superstitions, that is, false empirical hypotheses, with magic, seeking to explicate the latter as an assemblage of wrong beliefs about the causes of phenomena which can be correctly explained and consequently dispel *wrong* magical theories.[3]

According to Wittgenstein, 'savage' people's knowledge of nature does not fundamentally differ from ours, but their magic is different. When one is angry, one sometimes hits the ground or a tree with a cane, but one does not really believe that the ground or the tree are to blame for one's anger or that hitting them will make a difference. What one does is simply vetting out one's anger: 'And all rites are of this kind. Such actions may be called instinct-actions' (RGB, 137). Thus, they cannot be called true or false, and they can be perfectly understood without historical explanations, such as, for example, that one's predecessor believed that hitting the ground would help or that it resembled whipping, though this may indeed be true. It was, however, on such historical explanations that Frazer relied in juxtaposing and comparing resources from geographically remote regions of the world and temporally distant epochs in search of analogies and similarities across the cultures of ancient Greece and Rome, European peasantry, uncivilized contemporaneous tribes and peoples of the East, Australia, Africa and South America. He was convinced that if such analogies and similarities were found, they would shed light on the genesis of a given ritual and thus help understand it.

In Wittgenstein's view, Frazer's explanations were wrong not because they were historical, but because they were no explanations in the first place. They were founded on the interrogative word 'why', as were his two central questions about the King-Priest. In this context, one of Wittgenstein's later observations delivers an illuminating angle: 'People who are constantly asking "why" are like tourists, who stand in front of a building, reading Baedeker, & through reading about history of the building's construction etc., etc., are prevented from *seeing* it' (CV, 46, italics original). Frazer's historical explanations only worked as a distraction from what really mattered, and they in fact entirely precluded perceiving and grasping the real meaning of the rituals he described. Emphatically, what Wittgenstein objected to was not historical explanation as such but a very particular detail of it, specifically, the causative mode of Frazer's expositions. In Wittgenstein's view, Frazer was more preoccupied with looking for causes and geneses of rituals rather than with deciphering their meanings as such.

What their real meanings were is indicated by Wittgenstein's discussion of the description and interpretation of the festival of Beltane in the second part of 'Remarks on Frazer's *Golden Bough*'. In Frazer's rendering:

> All over Europe the peasants have been accustomed from time immemorial to kindle bonfires on certain days of the year, and to dance round or leap over them. Customs of this kind can be traced back on historical evidence to the Middle Ages, and their analogy to similar customs observed in antiquity goes with strong internal evidence to prove that their origin must be sought in a period long prior to the spread of Christianity. ... Not uncommonly effigies are burned in these fires, or a pretence is made of burning a living person in them; and there are grounds for believing that anciently human beings were actually burned on these occasions. ...
>
> After kindling the bonfire with the *tein-eigin* the company prepared their victuals. And as soon as they had finished their meal, they amused themselves a while in singing and dancing round the fire. Towards the close of the entertainment, the person who officiated as master of the feast produced a large cake baked with eggs and scalloped round the edge, called *am bonach beal-tine* – i.e., the Beltane cake. It was divided into a number of pieces, and distributed in great form to the company. There was one particular piece which

whoever got was called *cailleach bel-tine* – i.e., the Beltane *carline*, a term of great reproach. Upon his being known, part of the company laid hold of him and made a show of putting him into the fire; but the majority interposing, he was rescued.

(1922: 798, 810)

Frazer explains the festival of fire genetically or evolutionarily, arguing that this observance stems from prior customs that date back to antiquity, when people were killed as an offering to deities of crops and fertility to ensure bountiful harvest. Embellishing an effigy to be burned and the designation of the Beltane hag to be thrown into the fire are remnants of that ancient ceremony. By compiling and juxtaposing various rites of fire festivals across cultures and times, Frazer concludes that the major aim of these feasts lay in chasing away witches, who were deemed to cause all the failures and calamities that befell people, livestock and crops. The custom of burning effigies of witches or sorcerers is just a substitute of burning evil men and women alive, because sympathetic magic holds that the culprits themselves are burned when their images go up in flames. According to Wittgenstein, this may indeed be the case – the festival of Beltane may in fact be a mitigated version of human sacrifice – but citing this historical reason does not in and of itself provide a satisfactory explanation.

According to Wittgenstein, retracing the historical origin of fire festivals is not necessary for understanding them as they can be comprehended on the basis of their own 'inner nature', that is, the idea of human sacrifice. Wittgenstein argues:

> I believe it is clearly the inner nature of the modern practice itself which seems sinister to us, and the familiar facts of human sacrifice only indicate the lines along which we should view the practice. When I speak of the inner nature of the practice, I mean all circumstances under which it is carried out and which are not included in a report of such a festival, since they consist not so much in specific actions which characterize the festival as in what one might call the spirit of the festival; such things as would be included in one's description, for example, of the kind of people who take part in it, their behavior at other times, that is, their character; the kind of games which they otherwise play. And one would then see that the sinister quality lies in the character of these people themselves.
>
> (RGB, 145)

Frazer paid too little attention to the 'inner nature' of the Beltane festival and focused too much on the historical explanations of its origin, which prevented him from realizing that the upsetting and bleak quality of these practices ensued from the fact that they affected us directly, as it were, without historical knowledge having any part in it, by evoking the terrifying idea of human sacrifice. While Wittgenstein acknowledges the relevance of anthropological data and historical resources, he objects to squeezing them into an evolutionary and genetic framework. This will be discussed in more detail below, and at this point it is enough to note that what Wittgenstein calls for is such a presentation of empirical data that would help one fathom the meaning of the Beltane festival against the background of other practices in which its participants engaged. This would enable one to grasp the spirit of the custom, which is not immediately available in reports and descriptions of the rites themselves. One could then realize that the sinister quality of the world actually resides in human nature, in one's sensations at the thought that a human being once burned another human being. Such a description would enable one to capture one's own attitude as implied by one's experience of the idea of burning humans in sacrifice to deities. However, what Wittgenstein fails to consider in 'Remarks' is that one may actually not understand those people, that their mode of life is entirely different, and that one cannot find any shared instinct in it.

This is where Wittgenstein's other objection to Frazer's interpretation of the festival of Beltane surfaces. The point is that the profound and sinister nature of fire festivals derives from our own experiences and sensations, which make the customs reported by Frazer (e.g. lot-drawing with the use of cake) especially unsettling. Wittgenstein avers that witnessing or getting to hear about customs like this is similar to seeing a person harshly rebuke another person for a minor reason. In such situations, the pitch and facial expression of the speaker make us realize that this individual can be frightful under certain circumstances. The question about the source of the profundity and menace of fire festivals is, as it were, a question about the source of the profundity and menace of human sacrifice. Wittgenstein's reply suggests that 'the deep and the sinister do not become apparent merely by our coming to know the history of the external action, rather it is we who ascribe them from an inner experience' (RGB, 147). Festivals such as Beltane are not simply an incidental human invention, and their persistence depends on a far more solid foundation – on some more general human propensity. This is a psychological factor, and as such it can work without any historical hypotheses: 'Indeed, if Frazer's explanations did not in the final analysis appeal to a tendency in ourselves, they would not really be explanations' (RGB, 127). Frank Cioffi (1998: 214–15) claims that such a psychological explication is as much an explanatory hypothesis as is Frazer's historical assumption about the origin of the ritual. If events such as the killing of the King of the Wood were to happen simply because they were terrible, citing that as a cause would be as uncertain as citing other causes. Similarly, grasping the inner nature of the eighteenth-century Beltane festival and knowing what it meant to its participants cannot offer a better solution to the riddle of its effect on us than discovering its origin can. This objection can be countered by observing, as Jacques Bouveresse does (2008: 11), that there is at least one thing that dispels all the doubts and hesitations. Namely, if we want to find a germane expression for the feelings inscribed in the practices depicted by Frazer, the practices themselves offer us what we are looking for. Whether an old custom really symbolizes what it seems to symbolize can obviously always be doubted, but the relation between what this custom symbolizes and the depictions that make it mean what it does to us is neither hypothetical nor uncertain. If somebody wanted to make an impression on us by telling us about the old fire festival of Beltane, they would not have to relate to us how it historically came into being; it would be enough for them to present its content without adding anything. Frazer mistakenly concludes that the burning of an effigy is a reminiscence of the ritual of burning people as sacrifice to the corn-deity to ensure plentiful harvest. While this may be the case, this does not have to be the only cause. We do things not only because they are useful and expedient. The burning of an effigy may be powered by feelings that have little or altogether nothing to do either with the practices of old or with utility. More than that, the account of the history of the ritual may divert our attention from its content and divest it of all mysteriousness. The lot drawn as a piece of cake and the straw puppet burned on the bonfire may be perturbing without any explanation, or perhaps even more harrowing, as historical explanations channel our attention towards something merely hypothetical and thus cushion, if not forestall, the impact of the very matter of the tale. Wittgenstein enquires:

> But why shouldn't it really be only (or certainly in part) the *thought* which gives me the impression? For aren't ideas terrible? Can't I be horrified by the thought that the cake with the knobs has at one time served to select by lot the sacrificial victim? Doesn't the thought have something terrible about it? – Yes, but what I see in those stories is nevertheless acquired through the evidence, including such evidence as does not appear to be directly connected with them, – through the thought of man and his past, through all the strange things I see, and have seen and heard about, in myself and others.
>
> (RGB, 151)

In his commentary on this passage, Bouveresse (2008: 10) stresses that Wittgenstein replaces the idea of the ritual pointing to other similar past customs of human sacrifice with the idea of the human being and the bizarre and unsettling nature of human behaviour. Wittgenstein's answer to Frazer's question why the King-Priest of Nemi had to kill his predecessor was: 'Because it is dreadful. That is, precisely that which makes this incident strike us as dreadful, magnificent, horrible, tragic, etc., as anything but trivial and insignificant, is also *that* which has called this incident to life. Here one can only *describe* and say: this is what human life is like' (RGB, 121, italics original). This insight is corroborated by Frazer's depiction itself, as Frazer begins his narrative from a reference to Turner's painting of the golden bough and uses a diction that implies his intention for his readers to sense that something stupendous and terrifying is at hand. The succession to the office of the King of the Wood, the festival of Beltane and scapegoating rituals, all reveal the sinister side of human nature. Historical sources may be doubted, but one cannot doubt what one directly feels, what one harbours inside and what a given ritual in a way helps one unleash: 'The crowd of thoughts which cannot come out, because they all want to rush forward and thus get stuck in the exit' (RGB, 123). If the lot-drawing custom comes across as deep and ominous to us, this does not require any historical descriptions or explanations. It is such in and of itself as it resonates with and spurs a part of human nature.

While Wittgenstein does not entirely rebuff historical explanations, he insists that they are incapable of capturing the expressive and symbolic meaning and relevance of ritual practices to both their actors and to us. He not only claims that what arrests us in the festival of Beltane is its meaning and not its history but also suggests in what way genetic explanations may help us identify this meaning. Specifically, Wittgenstein believes that historical explorations yield a knowledge of similarities from which 'the relatedness of the *facts*' can be gleaned: 'As one might illustrate an internal relation of a circle to an ellipse by gradually converting an ellipse into a circle; *but not in order to assert that a certain ellipse actually, historically, had originated from a circle* (evolutionary hypothesis), but only in order to sharpen our eye for a formal connection' (RBG, 133, italics original). Nevertheless, we must never lose sight of what is 'a formal connection' here, what makes it possible to perceive similitudes which necessarily presuppose differences. This interplay of variations and resemblances is what Wittgenstein brings into spotlight:

> Besides these similarities, what seems to me to be most striking is the dissimilarity of all these rites. It is a multiplicity of faces with common features which continually emerges here and there. And one would like to draw lines connecting these common ingredients. But then one part of our account would still be missing, namely, that which brings this picture into connection with our own feelings and thoughts. This part gives the account its depth.

> In all these practices one, of course, sees something that is similar to the association of ideas and related to it. One could speak of an association of practices.
>
> (RGB, 143)

The passage comes from the second part of RGB, that is, from the period when Wittgenstein had already developed his own take on the notion of 'family resemblance' (*die Familienähnlichkeit*), on which his reasoning above builds. In this context, Wittgenstein's May Term lectures of 1933, in which he again referred to Frazer's *The Golden Bough* and in particular to his interpretation of the Beltane festival, offer an interesting and salient viewpoint. In comparison with Wittgenstein's remarks from June 1931, which make up the first part of RGB, a new insight appeared in Wittgenstein's critique of Frazer. According to Moore's notes from the lecture of 9 May 1933, Wittgenstein observed that Frazer's account of the burning of an effigy at the festival of Beltane (i.e. as a residue of the old custom of human sacrifice to appease the deity of corn and ensure abundant harvest) failed to explained why the story of this ritual affected us irrespective of its historical origin. Wittgenstein put Frazer's account on a par with Darwin's evolutionary account of emotions: 'Why do we shew our teeth when angry? Because our ancestors wanted to bite. Why does our hair stand up when frightened? Because our ancestors, like other animals, frightened their enemy by looking bigger … The charm of the argument is that it reduces something that's important to utility. (Important in sense that it impresses us.)' (Wittgenstein 2016: 331). If we wonder what the Frazer-Darwin method has in common with methods of philosophizing, a clue is offered by Wittgenstein's remark: 'If I could talk about Ethics, connection would be clearer. I was recommending "descriptive method" = method which tells you various things in right order = order which impresses you, without pretending to thread them on historical thread' (2016: 331). The reference to ethics concerns the example of identifying the meaning of 'good' with that which is shared by all the things we call good. 'Game' and 'beauty' are other examples of this kind. Admittedly, Wittgenstein does not directly talk about 'family resemblance' in his lectures, but this is without a doubt the type of relation that he has in mind; rather than being interested in searching for links which produce one common element ('essence in medieval philosophy'), he proposes exploring a network of interlacing and intersecting similarities that can be likened to family members resembling each other in various respects: the colour of the eyes, the shape of the nose, smile, etc. The question 'what is a game?' is best answered simply by marshalling examples of games: football, tennis, chess and the like – these are games. In the following lecture, Wittgenstein relied on an analogous approach to discuss beauty: 'It is not true that "beautiful" means what's common to all the things we call so: we use it in a hundred different games' (2016: 335).

This type of anti-essentialist interpretation was not yet present in the notes Wittgenstein recorded in June 1931, of which the first part of RGB is composed, although they have been shown to contain phrasings that anticipate the notion of 'family resemblance', which made its way to Wittgenstein's discourse a mere two months after writing down his first remarks on *The Golden Bough*, precisely speaking on 19 August 1931 (MS 111, 119). In terms of 'family-resemblance' relations, Frazer's idea that the account of Beltane appeals to us because it is a remainder of a rite in which people were actually burned fails to render our actual sentiments: 'It does impress us, because it has relation to burning a human being, but not necessarily the relation of having developed therefrom. What impresses us is seeing this event along with other similar events' (Wittgenstein 2016: 343). In the last of his May Term lectures, Wittgenstein asserted: 'What satisfies my puzzlement about Beltane, is not kind of causal explanation which Frazer gives – which is a hypothesis; but simply describing lots of things more or less like Beltane' (2016: 352).

Nonetheless, all this does not entail that the notion of 'family resemblance' ousts all the insights of Wittgenstein's critique in the first part of RGB, in which he interprets magical practices as expressive and instinctive behaviour. In the lecture of 5 May, Wittgenstein observed: 'Frazer talks of magic performed with an effigy & says primitive people believe that by stabbing effigy they have hurt the model. I say: Only in some cases do they thus entertain a false scientific belief. It may be that it expresses your wish to hurt' (2016: 326). Wittgenstein thus admitted three options: firstly, he did not deny as positively as in the first part of RGB that magical practices could sometimes be interpreted as a 'false scientific belief'; secondly, he perceived them as possibly instinctive actions; and, thirdly, he posited that these actions could be expressive of one's wish. What primarily mattered to Wittgenstein was not to seek out one sole cause (origin) or a single explanation, as Fraser did for magic and Darwin for emotions. The new insight mentioned before as arising in the May Term lectures resided in a closer entwining of Wittgenstein's critique of Frazer with the issue of meaning conceived in relation to 'language games' and 'family resemblance'. However, it is disputable whether this indeed represented a decisive shift from Wittgenstein's observations from June 1931, as Marco Brusotti (2014: 288) would have it. We shall return to this below.

Meanwhile, it should be noticed that this new insight associated with Wittgenstein's preoccupation with language meanings stands in a fraught relation to the notion of expressive and instinctive actions. In the above quotation from the second part of RGB, Wittgenstein states that, in the description of similarities among various customs, we should identify an element that complements the picture of intersecting and overlapping resemblances and tethers it to our own feelings and thoughts. In this sense, a formal relation (the hypothesis of development) can be said to presuppose a substantive relationship, which is a connection between 'a phenomenon' and 'an instinct that I myself possess'. Wittgenstein contrasts 'explanation', which he conceives of as a causal explanation, with the purely descriptive method: 'Here one can only *describe*' (RGB, italics original). The difference between 'explaining' rituals and 'describing' them is a difference between attending to, respectively, their 'cause' and their 'inner nature'. Notably, the explanation/description dichotomy was already present in the *Tractatus*, where Wittgenstein mentioned distinguishing things from others by means of description (see TLP, 2.02331), claimed that '[a] complex can be given only by its description' (TLP, 3.24), argued that 'only the description of expressions may be presupposed' in logical syntax (TLP, 3.33) and insisted that 'to give the essence of a proposition means to give the essence of all description, and thus the essence of the world' (TLP, 5.4711). At the same time, the *Tractaus* also deplored that '[t]he whole modern conception of the world is founded on the illusion that the so-called laws of nature are the explanations of natural phenomena' (TLP, 6.371), whereas the laws of nature, such as Newton's mechanics, are also essentially a description of the world rendered as a homogeneous whole: 'Mechanics is an attempt to construct according to a single plan all the *true* propositions that we need for the description of the world' (TLP, 6.343, italics original). Wittgenstein expressly contrasted description and explanation in the *Philosophical Investigations* as well, demanding that: 'All *explanation* must disappear, and description alone must take its place' (PI §109, italics original). Description is meant here in the way that was first proposed in 'Remarks on Frazer's *Golden Bough*', that is, as a 'perspicuous representation' (*die übertsichtliche Darstellung*)[4]: 'The concept of perspicuous representation is of fundamental importance for us. It denotes the form of our representation, the way we see things (A kind of "world-view" as it is apparently typical of our time. Spengler.)' (RGB, 133). It was no coincidence that Spengler was invoked in this context since Wittgenstein was reading his *The Decline of the West* at the time. Spengler, who repudiated causal explanations in history, drew a distinction between *organic* and *mechanical* perceptions and presentations of the world, distinguishing 'the content of images from that of laws, the picture and symbol from the formula and the system, the instantly actual from the constantly possible' (1926: 6). In Spengler's view, causal explanations proper to the natural sciences, which deal with dead forms, must not be transferred onto history, which depicts the humanly produced world. He defined the aim of his morphology of world history as the interpretation of cultural forms as symbols and expressions.[5] Wittgenstein must have felt an ideological kinship with Spengler's anti-scientistic approach. He pitted description, conceived as 'perspicuous representation', against historical explanation, touting the former as another viable form of presenting (*Darstellungsform*) empirical data: 'The historical explanation, the explanation as an hypothesis of development, is only *one* way of assembling the data – of their synopsis. It is just as possible to see the data in their relations to one another and to embrace them in a general picture without putting it in the form of an hypothesis about temporal development' (RGB, 131). He went on to specify this difference in more detail:

> 'And so the chorus points to a secret law' one feels like saying to Frazer's collection of facts. I *can* represent this law, this idea, by means of an evolutionary hypothesis, or also, analogously to the schema of a plant, by means of the schema of a religious ceremony, but also by means of the arrangement of its factual content alone, in a 'perspicuous' representation.
>
> (RGB, 133, italics original)

In the passage, Wittgenstein cites Goethe's *Die Metamorphose der Pflanzen* (*The Metamorphosis of Plants*). A 'secret law' indicated by the 'chorus' of plants, that is, their multiplicity and diversity, is the Goethean idea of the primal plant (*die Urpflanze*), meaning a certain model or schema of the plant which does not appear in reality but which enables us to identify and study real plant-forms. Yet Wittgenstein departs from Goethe's model in this respect,[6] as he does not evoke the notion of the 'primal plant' or, more generally speaking, the 'primal phenomenon' or the 'primal form'. His words clearly imply that a 'secret law' actually cannot be grasped either in the form of an evolutionary hypothesis or in the form of a schema revealed in all empirical symptoms; rather, it can only be captured 'by means of the arrangement of its factual content alone, in a perspicuous representation'. Of course, a perspicuous representation may be composed of canonical models, measures or norms, which are not objects of study themselves, such as the standard metre in Paris or the 'colour octahedron'.[7] Wittgenstein assembled a long list of such measures, norms and models, especially related to the learning of language: colour charts, schematic drawings, animal exhibits, collections of objects, etc. Regarding the anthropological facts cited by Frazer, one can follow him and arrange data in alignment with the evolutionary hypothesis, but one can also do so by relying on the constructs of a model or a schema of religious ceremony, the way Goethe sought to order the vegetal world on the basis of the idea of the primal plant or the type. (Regrettably, Wittgenstein never spelled out what such a schema would look like.) One can also present this 'secret law' in a perspicuous representation of facts that makes connections between individual facts or events directly perceivable.

Nonetheless, the 'perspicuous representation' of anthropological facts should not be put in opposition to the identification of connections between phenomena and the instinct that one possesses oneself. In Wittgenstein's view, 'explanations' based on a 'perspicuous representation' and 'explanations' founded on one's inclinations, 'experiences in one's own interior', are not mutually exclusive. Just the other way round, our instincts and sensations are this 'secret law', a common trait that recurs in multiple forms. When the anthropological material is presented in a suitably perspicuous manner, this trait will become perceptible and the 'secret' law indicated by the 'chorus' of customs and rituals will be brought to light. This is a prerequisite for understanding the meaning of ritual practices of primitive people if these practices are construed as symbolic behaviour that expresses the primal impulses and responses that are distinct to human nature in magical or religious forms. In Wittgenstein's view, the necessary point of reference for grasping the meaning of magical rituals of primitive societies is provided by the common human sense of wonder triggered by things in which we are steeped – 'the phenomena of death, birth, and sexual life, in short, everything we observe around us year in and year out, interconnected in so many different ways' (RGB, 128–9). However, if we disregard all this and consider our wonder-informed response to the world we inhabit irrelevant to comprehending foreign customs, we will interpret instances of magical behaviour as mere mistakes.

To sum up, the descriptions of succession to the priesthood of Nemi and lot-drawing at the festival of Beltane are non-hypothetically connected to what appears to us as terrifying and tragic, rather than as normal and innocuous. If we sought a suitable expression for 'the majesty of death' or 'the deep and the sinister of human sacrifice', the account of the Beltane festival and the death of the King of the Wood would be apt choices. Wittgenstein, as it were, discards the historical connections established by Frazer by reflecting on these rituals as such and perhaps using the power of the imagination to disentangle their sense and meaning from the historical and cultural modes of their articulation so that these rituals come to appear quite natural. They appear this way because they convey the fears and anxieties that intrinsically haunt us, whatever the form of their expression. They captivate us because they tie in with propensities we sense in ourselves. Wittgenstein concludes:

> One sees how misleading Frazer's explanations are – I believe – by noting that one could very easily invent primitive practices oneself, and it would be pure luck if they were not actually found somewhere. That is, the principle according to which these practices are arranged is a much more general one than in Frazer's explanation and it is present in our own minds, so that we ourselves could think up all the possibilities.
>
> (RGB, 127)

Wittgenstein's point is that we already know where these rituals come from, and this realization does not take any special ethnographic or historical knowledge. They might as well have been fabricated by an inventor of engaging tales; more than that, we could ourselves make up similar ones, and they would anyway be compelling to us, because their principle inheres in us ('this is what human life is like'). They unveil the dark side of human nature, which we are afraid to reveal and falter to discuss. The knowledge of the origin of these rituals and of the fact that there were multiple similar rites and customs can only blunt their therapeutic edge and render them more tolerable by making us think 'been there, seen that' – that there is nothing strange or special about them, that this has already been done. Such a knowledge breeds complacency while Wittgenstein's object was rather different as he urged us to reflect on our responses and attitudes to the very possibility of these sinister tendencies being intrinsic to us.

2. Wittgenstein and Obscurantism

Some commentators and researchers have not found Wittgenstein's critique of Frazer and his own interpretation of ritual behaviour convincing and on the mark. According to Cioffi, Wittgenstein's argument that ritual practices were not explainable in empirical ways and that they could be understood without such explanations was amiss and resulted from Wittgenstein's unwarranted circumscription of empirical research, instead of which he proposed another type of explanation. His explanations were based on discerning connections, discovering 'formal relations' or arriving at a 'perspicuous representation', which provoked accusations of obscurantism. Cioffi (1998: 183–4) identifies three types of obscurantism: limits obscurantism, method obscurantism and sensibility obscurantism. Limits obscurantism simply negates the possibility of explaining phenomena by recourse to empirical knowledge. Method obscurantism attributes explicative power to reflection or introspection alone. Sensibility obscurantism evokes non-epistemic rationales, such as 'consolation', 'satisfaction' or 'reassurance'.

While Cioffi believes that, in 'Remarks on Frazer's *Golden Bough*', Wittgenstein is guilty on all the three charges of obscurantism, he mainly focuses on the two former ones. Limits obscurantism surfaces in Wittgenstein's statement that Frazer's attempt at explaining the ritual of succession to the Nemi priesthood is wrong and that 'one must only correctly piece together what one *knows*, without adding anything, and the satisfaction being sought through the explanation follows of itself' (RGB, 121, italics original). It can be pointed out in Wittgenstein's defence that the *history* of this ritual is an altogether different matter than its *meaning*. However, in Cioffi's view, the meaning of a custom is not fully separable from its genesis. For example, is the meaning of the Catholic mass independent of the origin of this ceremony? Most rituals, or at least some of their aspects, can only be explained by referring to their historical circumstances. However, this is not the most essential thing in this case as Wittgenstein insists that Frazer's empirical explorations are inadequate for a deeper reason. In a note from June 1931 which was later included in the edition of RGB, Wittgenstein wrote: 'The religious actions, or the religious life, of the priest-king are no different in kind from any genuinely religious action of today, for example, a confession of sins. This, too, admits of being "explained" and not explained' (MS 110, 182). The point is that religious practices are inherently expressive and performative rather than instrumental. We will 'explain' the Nemi ritual when we recognize the feelings that it expresses and that accompany similar practices. Yet if Cioffi believes that Wittgenstein thought the Nemi ritual to be explainable not on the basis of historical considerations but solely through 'a tendency in ourselves', he errs twice. The opposition between the explainable and the non-explainable is not identical with the instrumental-vs.-expressive dichotomy. Not all customs are equally natural, and not all of them are founded on conventions, such as hitting the ground or a tree with one's cane to vent one's anger. Crossing oneself needs an explanation, and one can be provided both when it is a purely expressive or symbolic act and when it is an apotropaic one. The expressive does not have to be immediately clear and understandable to us without any explanation, and instrumental actions may sometimes be such as in, to cite Wittgenstein's own example, attempting to persuade disease to leave the patient.

However, there is something that indeed defies explanation; specifically, these are the acts of expression that are not grounded in conventions and are bound up with 'an instinct which I myself possess'. Crossing oneself as an expression of piety certainly lends itself to a historical explanation, but an impulse to do so does not. According to Cioffi, the reason why Wittgenstein believed that the ritual of the succession of the King-Priest at Nemi and similar practices could not be explained did not result from their expressive nature but from his view of them as primal and, as it were, pre-phenomenal (*Ur-phenomenal*). Nevertheless, Cioffi does not identify the nature of these primal practices – whether they were expressive, instrumental or else. Instead, he falls back on a vivid comparison, proposing that we imagine trying to explain the place a scarecrow or a snowman take in our lives to a person who does not know these figures. Explaining why people sometimes put up scarecrows is not difficult; they do so simply to drive away birds and thus protect crops. The snowman is an entirely different case. It does not protect against anything and has no other instrumental function. The reasons why we sometimes build snowmen vary; sometimes we do it for fun, and on other occasions out of sadness, simply because there is snow or even for no discernible reason at all. This activity is sometimes expressive of something, and sometimes it is not. We do so just because 'this is what human life is like', just because we feel like doing so. According to Wittgenstein, Frazer misguidedly approached the Nemi ritual the way we approach the scarecrow while it was in fact an expression of our own primal tendencies and should therefore be viewed as an instance of snowman-building. There is an epistemic affinity between the two: 'But magic brings a wish to representation; it expresses a wish' (RGB, 125).

Cioffi apparently undermines this epistemic affinity and doubts that the motives behind killing the King-Priest can be understood without recourse to their history or to the system of beliefs in which this custom was embedded. Even if one agreed with Wittgenstein that the rite had been driven by the desire to express 'the majesty of death', one would anyway need to resort to empirical considerations in order to establish whether that had in fact been *the* impulse powering the emergence of the ritual.[8] This is a tricky question indeed. We know in what relation we stand to the scarecrow and the snowman, but we do not know the connection between the community of Nemi and the ritual combat. Consequently, we cannot know whether finding out new data about it will improve our understanding of the events or not. In Cioffi's view (1998: 191), Wittgenstein deems celebration an autonomous and primal human tendency. His interest is limited to the most general characteristics of the Nemi ritual, including the sense of the terrifying, the sinister and the tragic. As a result, he does not enquire why the priest was supposed to fight for his life or why exclusively a runaway slave could pluck the Golden Bough. He does not ask why actually the urge to express the 'majesty of death' was brought to fulfilment in a fight resembling a showdown of gladiators.

At the same time, we can observe that we, as it were, recognize the expressive impulses manifest in ritual behaviour even though their specific form was historically shaped by the cultural symbolic system and can only be explored through retracing and piecing it together. The problem is that it is notoriously difficult to tell apart the natural impulse itself and its historical trappings. More than that, it is unclear whether such a distinction can legitimately be made in the first place. In other words, it is not in the least obvious whether there is something ahistorical and natural in us – something that is independent of history and culture, can be known in an immediate fashion and is achievable 'through introspection', as Wittgenstein states. Wittgenstein readily offers an answer:

> It was not a trivial reason, for really there can have been no reason, that prompted certain races of mankind to venerate the oak tree, but only the fact that they and the oak were united in a community of life, and thus that they arose together not by choice, but rather like the flea and the dog. (If fleas developed a rite, it would be based on the dog.)
>
> (RGB, 139)

Thus Wittgenstein insists that ceremonies are inscribed in a 'community of life' and are addressed to the deceased, death, birth, the sun and the moon, the rain season, harvest time, seasons of the year, animals one hunts, foes one fights, etc. Without study and research, it would be a steep challenge to make a clear-cut distinction between rituals born from an expressive urge and those prompted by practical needs. This holds for the community of Nemi as well, and in Frazer's view, only the historical method may help us ascertain which tendencies held sway over its members. The historical method may admittedly not yield a complete and comprehensive explanation of ritual practices, but perhaps we should be content with what is actually possible to explain. Rigorous adherence to understanding as defined by Wittgenstein often breeds misunderstandings. His critical assessment of Frazer's method in *The Golden Bough* did not result exclusively from his belief that the Nemi ritual could not be empirically explained or that it could be explained without empirical research. It proceeded above all from the fact that what mattered more to Wittgenstein was *our* attitude to such practices and explaining *our* feelings triggered by them. He was not really preoccupied with Frazer's view that the Beltane festival of fire was a vestige of a ritual in which people had really been burned, and he denied that our terror and the sense of menace were evoked by the suffering of the sacrificed person, because diseases involving great pain did not impress us in this way. He focused on the conditions in which the game of horse and rider could feel sinister, on Frazer's tone in relating ritual succession to Nemi priesthood, on the way the Beltane festival moved us regardless of its historical explanations, just like the fact 'that on certain days children burn a straw-man could make us uneasy, even if no explanation for it were given' (RGB, 151), and on cake-based lot-drawing being as sinister and terrifying as betrayal with a kiss. Listening to accounts of such practices is like discovering that under certain circumstances a human being is capable of burning another human being. All these practices harbour a menacing and mysterious quality that horrifies but at the same time irresistibly attracts us, because it resonates with the deeply concealed recesses of human nature. According to Wittgenstein, our response to manifestations of ritual life is the same as to aesthetic experiences. Like products of art, ritual practices communicate something to us, and we should strive to decipher the message. In Cioffi's view (1998: 196), such an approach represents method obscurantism and should be replaced with hermeneutic enquiry.

*

Cioffi's interpretation and objections certainly deserve a closer scrutiny. He is obviously right to argue that several questions concerning the ritual of succession to the Nemi priesthood – such as why the contender had to pluck a branch of a designated tree before the fight and why horses were banned from the holy grove – can only be answered through historical research. However, two issues must be set apart, which both Frazer and Wittgenstein failed to do.[9] One of them is how it happened in the first place that such and not any other acts had to be performed in the Nemi ceremony at a certain point. The other issue is what these acts meant. The former can be established on the basis of historical enquiry, but the latter is essentially hermeneutical and can only be determined in relation to the way the ceremony unfolded and to the behaviour, beliefs and reasons espoused by its participants. If they were unaware of the origin of the ritual in which they took part, the knowledge of its genesis would not help explain its meaning. Several ceremonial practices do not need any explanation; they simply are the way they are. But they may also be imbued with certain expressive and/or symbolic meanings, and their temporally and spatially remote historical origin may have no bearing on what they mean to their participants. According to Peter M. S. Hacker, who defends Wittgenstein against Cioffi's criticism, the aetiology of ritual practices is to their meaning or inner nature what etymology of a word is to the meaning of this word. Like in grammar, in rituals there is no remote action.

The division into historical and hermeneutic matters does not invalidate the charge of 'limits obscurantism' that Cioffi levels at Wittgenstein. Cioffi cites the Catholic confession of sins as an example of a religious ritual which can be explained. Specifically, its explanation is to be found in the dogmas of Catholic faith and in the historical tradition. Hacker finds Cioffi's claims problematic for three reasons. First, Wittgenstein does not rule out referencing the beliefs of the ritual participants and himself insists that 'an opinion – a belief – can itself be ritualistic or part of a rite' (RGB, 129). Second, confession practices in the Catholic church cannot actually be explained; they can at best be described. In this sense, beliefs implicated in confession-related dogmas (e.g. the belief in absolution by the priest) belong to the very practice of confession. Evoking them augments our knowledge of this religious act and, as such, is part of its depiction. Third, the explanatory power of beliefs does not hinge on their truth or falseness but on the fact that one holds such beliefs and that this faith is expressed in the ceremony. Their truth, if it can indeed be ascertained, is irrelevant to understanding them. No historical event becomes incorporated into a ceremonial practice exclusively as a historical fact. The eating of unleavened bread on Passover is not explained by the fact that the children of Israel ate such bread when fleeing Egypt, but by the fact that today pious Jews believe that this is what happened. What is relevant here – that is, what helps us understand this custom – is our desire to commemorate something that matters to us. Thus, if Frazer is right to claim that it is impossible to understand the killing of the Nemi king-priest in his prime without knowing that, historically speaking, the king's soul had to be fresh and young or otherwise the world would have fallen apart, this belief is neither a mistake nor a historical fact but part of the ritual.

Hacker (2001: 86) also overturns the accusation of 'method obscurantism', which consists in explaining old rituals by reference to human instincts. Cioffi suggests that Wittgenstein was more preoccupied with what the old rituals meant *to us* than with aetiological and hermeneutical explorations. His object was to arrive at a specific form of understanding of *conditio humana*. If Wittgenstein contends that 'one must only correctly piece together what one *knows*', Cioffi construes this as meaning that what one knows refers to one's knowledge of oneself and of the human condition – human instincts and reactions in existentially salient situations. This construal is denounced by Hacker as mistaken, though he agrees that Wittgenstein regarded knowledge of all these issues as requisite for the understanding he pursued. What one 'must only correctly piece together' are the empirical data compiled by Frazer. They must simply be arranged in a way that makes sense but not with a view to proposing any new hypotheses of development. According to Hacker, Wittgenstein's allegedly obscurantist claim that all attempts at explaining rituals are futile should be juxtaposed with his remarks concerning perspicuous representation, a conception evoked above.[10] Besides, Wittgenstein did not actually dismiss empirical explanations. As his May Term lectures indicate, he allowed three kinds of explications of magical an ritual actions: as instinctive actions, as symbolic and expressive actions and as 'false scientific beliefs'. Frazer's descriptions of succession to the Nemi priesthood and the festival of Beltane, in which rituals were reduced to a single historical cause, were simply incomplete in Wittgenstein's view.

Hacker is on the mark when he says that Wittgenstein's is by no means a case of the obscurantist rejection of anthropological data as irrelevant to the hermeneutic understanding of meaning. On the contrary, such materials have their significant uses, but not as a basis for the evolutionist hypothesis that magic is a species of proto-science. The collection of facts cited by Frazer importantly places a particular ceremony against the background of an entire family of similar practices and, in this sense, it may boast explanatory power. Briefly, Frazer's explanations can be convincing, but this does not result from their historicity. Wittgenstein simply calls for arranging the anthropological data in another fashion than Frazer did, specifically, for discovering patterns of similarities and differences of ceremonial forms of expression.[11] His method of searching for structural analogies and disanalogies – to put it simply, the method of 'perspicuous representation' and family resemblance – brings to mind Spengler's take on culture. Spengler's conception held that all cultures developed upon the biological scheme of birth, flourishing and decline, and thus that they had each their beginning, period of burgeoning and fall, which he called civilization. The resources supplied by Frazer should be treated the way Spengler handled his data, by offering a perspicuous representation of multiple cultures on the basis of Goethe's idea of the primal plant or the type. Frazer failed to do so because he embraced the positivist paradigm, which explored phenomena in their evolution. Wittgenstein viewed this as a different way of seeing things and a different worldview than that of *The Decline of the West*. In other words, Frazer espoused a scientific worldview, in which knowledge was predicated, as it was in science, on constructing models or theories that explained the empirical world.

To know a phenomenon was tantamount to identifying the general law under which this phenomenon fell. Wittgenstein sought to pit another worldview, another mode of world perception, against science as the only legitimate method of knowledge.[12]

In the notes preceding the remarks concerning *The Golden Bough*, Wittgenstein reflects briefly on Ernst Renan's *History of the People of Israel*.[13] At one place, he briefly cites the book: 'In Renan's *Peupel d'Israël* I read: "Birth, sickness, death, madness, catalepsy, sleep dreams, all made an infinite impression and, even nowadays, it is given to only a small number to see clearly that these phenomena have causes within our constitution"' (MS 109, 200; CV, 7). Events catalogued by Renan awed people not because they were extraordinary, but because there was no causal explanation for them. Wittgenstein objects to the notion that primitive peoples wondered at everything in their environment. The idea that primitive peoples '*had* to fear all the forces of nature & that we of course do not have to fear' (MS 109, 202; CV, 8, italics original) is, he believes, an equally primitive prejudice. The fear referenced by Wittgenstein is not a fear of the unknown or the inexplicable. The fact that we know that wind is caused by a difference in air pressure does not automatically strip it of mystery, of a certain spiritual or symbolic quality which makes a perplexing, nearly mystical impression on us. Wonder in this sense is connected to the awakening of the human spirit rather than to primitivism. For Wittgenstein, the time that it befell him to inhabit was again a time of the slumber of this spirit, a time which erased fear and marvel. The scientific worldview also made inroads into Renan's and Frazer's books, which addressed human affairs in a fashion that belittled awe and wonder as mistakes or silliness, though Wittgenstein hoped that this would change in the future: 'But we cannot exclude the possibility that highly civilized peoples will become liable to this very same fear again & their civilization and the knowledge of science will not protect them from this. All the same it is true that the *spirit* in which science is carried on nowadays is not compatible with fear of this kind' (MS 109, 202, italics original).

3. The Relevance of 'Remarks on Frazer's *Golden Bough*' to the Development of Wittgenstein's Late Philosophy

As mentioned at the beginning of this chapter, Wittgenstein's notes on *The Golden Bough* were not included in *The Big Typescript*, which stands today as a representative selection of his thoughts and observations from the 1930s and which Wittgenstein himself seems to have regarded as such. A handful of passages were retained mainly in Chapter 93 of BT, and the sole trace of the reading of Frazer left in the *Philosophical Investigations* is to be found in §122, which addresses 'perspicuous representation', one of the central notions of Wittgenstein's late philosophy. This begs the question whether it is indeed the only remnant of his reflection on Frazer's study and whether Wittgenstein's ponderings on the book affected the development of his philosophy in any way.

Brusotti (2014: 2) busies himself with these questions in his comprehensive and superbly researched study *Wittgenstein, Frazer und die 'Ethnologische Betrachtungsweise'* (2014). Brusotti is primarily fixed on establishing whether Wittgenstein's 1931 criticism of *The Golden Bough* can be considered an early exercise in the 'ethnological approach' to philosophical problems, to which he referred in a later period, closer to the *Philosophical Investigations*.[14] Brusotti argues that it was not from Frazer that Wittgenstein learned this approach; nor can it be viewed as a response to the Scottish anthropologist. Wittgenstein's position in June 1931 was still nowhere near either 'the ethnological approach' or his stance in the *Investigations*. His criticism of Fraser should rather be examined in conjunction with the rest of manuscript MS 110, in which it was originally included. Only from this perspective is it possible to properly assess the relevance of these remarks to the development of Wittgenstein's late philosophy. One should not presuppose that these remarks formed an avenue towards the standpoint that he called 'the ethnological approach' in philosophy. Brusotti claims that the genesis of this approach was linked to the gradual transition from the universalist perspective of the *Tractatus Logico-Philosophicus* to the clear acknowledgement of cultural differences. In 'Remarks on Frazer's *Golden Bough*', Wittgenstein considers cultural differences merely a surface beneath which a substantial identity of human nature is to be nested. He emphasizes commonalities and things we share with remote and foreign cultures. This is indeed at a far remove from his later position, where semantic differences are stressed and conceptual relativism is embraced. Brusotti also observes that the 1931 critique of Frazer was affected by the ideas Wittgenstein had developed when exploring ethical questions and problems of religious language. Pivotal in this context were his reflections on the performative character of ethical propositions, which budded in 'A Lecture on Ethics' (1929) and were then carried on in relation to ritual practices in the remarks on *The Golden Bough* in MS 110. 'He would only much later extend his anti-intellectualist reasoning onto language games in general', states Brusotti, '[b]ut already in February 1932, ethics was for him a model of an approach that presumed a normative dimension of speech' (2014: 6). This implies that the remarks on *The Golden Bough* accounted for a stage in Wittgenstein's journey towards the concept of language games, which we know from the *Investigations*, and that they should be read as contributing to the framework which emphasized the connectedness of language with actions and 'forms of life'. However, shortly later, Brusotti observes that Wittgenstein's criticism of Frazer derived from a dynamic notion of signs as an alternative to the causal theory of meaning. According to Wittgenstein, signs were part of a calculus or a sign system rather than of a mechanism in which meaning depended on the causal influence of individual signs on us. The meaning of signs hinged on the role they played in this calculus or this system. This held not only for language but also for images, gestures and patterns, which should be analysed within their proper sign systems. Brusotti (2014: 8) claims that Wittgenstein first directed his criticism of the causal theory of meaning against Bertrand Russell and Charles K. Ogden as the champions of this theory and later accused Frazer of explaining phenomena through the causal method.

For the sake of clarity, the problem of the relevance of 'Remarks on Frazer's *Golden Bough*' could be phrased as the question whether Wittgenstein's reading and critique affected the development of his later concept of language, as presented in the *Philosophical Investigations*, or whether, the other way round, his criticism of Frazer was propelled by the ideas of language Wittgenstein espoused at the time, specifically, his critique of the causal theory of meaning, as Brusotti suggests. Brusotti's argument is cautious and well balanced. He stresses that by reading *The Golden Bough*, Wittgenstein acquired a new awareness of cultural differences, though he still treated them in the Spenglerian vein as symbols and indications of shared instincts and feelings of the 'ceremonial animal' that the human being is. At the same time, many of Wittgenstein's views from the time of his first confrontation with Frazer in 1931 were to change as his understanding of language mutated.

Before discussing this interpretation, a methodological remark is in order. Brusotti claims that Wittgenstein's critique of Frazer from June 1931 should be read in the context of manuscript MS 110, in which it was originally included.[15] This is somewhat of a difficulty since, when going through MS 110, one easily notices that the remarks on Frazer have nothing in common with the preceding and following notes, in which Wittgenstein mused on the grammar of miscellaneous language expressions: colour terms, numerals, names, etc. All these notes do not add up to any clearly appreciable context. More than that, they are chaotic and thematically disparate. This begs the question about the limits of the context. These may of course be expanded, yet the problem remains unsolved, because it is still up to the interpreter to determine what this context is composed of.[16] This is all the more the case with Wittgenstein's notes from the 1930s as they form a sprawling and intricate maze of thoughts, intuitions, allusions, commentaries and sometimes personal remarks which is notoriously difficult to navigate. Wittgenstein's notes on *The Golden Bough* come across as entirely disjoined from the grammatical context of considerations in MS 110. As already mentioned, with minor exceptions, the Frazer-related insights were not knitted into *The Big Typescript*.

If these remarks were to be located in a context, this context would more suitably be provided not so much by 'the ethnological approach' in philosophy as rather by 'A Lecture on Ethics' from 1929 or a later lecture on faith and, at the same time, by Spengler's *The Decline of the West*. 'The ethnological approach' is characteristic of Wittgenstein's late work and the philosophical shake-up it accomplished. When Wittgenstein was putting down his first responses to *The Golden Bough* in June 1931, he was still very far from the standpoint developed in the *Philosophical Investigations*. His philosophical thought was only looking for new solutions in an attempt to overcome difficulties spawned by the *Tractatus*. Emphatically, 'the ethnological approach' is attached to the notions of 'language game', grammar, rules, following the rule and 'forms of life', none of which come forth in the 'Remarks' and whose role and meaning in Wittgenstein's discourse were developed later.

What is it that lies at the core of 'the ethnological approach' and why should it not be associated with 'Remarks on Frazer's *Golden Bough*'? In a note from the end of 1931, Wittgenstein stated: 'Savage peoples have games (or rather we call them so) for which they have no rules, no list of them. Let's now imagine the work of a researcher who travels across the lands of these peoples and makes lists of rules for their games. This is an exact analogy to what a philosopher does' (MS 112, 196). The philosopher is pictured as one that surveys grammatical facts and is thus a kind of field researcher or an ethnologist-linguist that drafts catalogues of rules for the language or languages of foreign tribes. However, one would be wrong to conceive of these grammatical rules as of empirical propositions and of their list as of a description of language facts, that is, an account of the actual use of language. In 1931, Wittgenstein had not yet arrived at clarity on rules though he was certainly aware of the issue itself. It was only later that he concluded that the rules of grammar were not empirical propositions for describing observable regularities in the use of langue expressions. 'The ethnological approach' meant thus something more than the compilation and description of language facts; rather, it denoted a description and perspicuous representation of that which determines the sense of all speech. Rules of grammar are acquired in the manners of learning language, in explanations of meaning, in its justifications and in the forms of criticizing and correcting wrong uses of words. Briefly, the ethnological approach in philosophy was bound up with issues of grammar and meaning, and these issues were for their part fundamentally predicated on the comparison of language to a game, which was not limited either to the problem of rules or to the problem of rule-governed action. In a note quoted above, Wittgenstein mentions 'savage peoples that have games', which means that they can play these games but neither possess a list of their rules nor can name them. It is not uncommon to learn how to play a new game without mastering or formulating its rules. In Wittgenstein's view, 'following the rule' is a practice and playing a game is part of our human natural history. Of course, playing a game inevitably connotes the application of rules, but whether it is correct or not is rather a matter of practice, which Wittgenstein called 'conventions' in *The Blue Notebook* and 'forms of life' in the *Investigations*.

As a field linguist, the philosopher traverses charted and uncharted lands, describing the rules of various grammars that determine the meanings of words used by the natives of these territories. In making an account of the grammar of their languages, he must depict their everyday practices – their forms of life – because, in Wittgenstein's view, words are always used in the context of actions, and they are always and for ever inseparably bound with these actions, with what is customarily done. Wittgenstein's approach is both ethnological and historical, but, as Hacker (2010: 20) observes, his is a 'historicism *without history*' (italics original). In his later works, Wittgenstein rarely refers to the real history of numbers, proof, counting, etc., or to the history of notions such as 'soul' and 'mind'. He does not consider the grammar of colour terms in Japanese or in any of the Papuan languages. Instead of a historical account of the arithmetic systems of ancient Egypt, Babylon or China, instead of references to empirical language facts, Wittgenstein tends to depict invented languages and made-up cultures in order to imagine other possible systems of representation. A prefiguration of this 'history *without history*' can perhaps be found in a thought offered in 'Remarks on Frazer's *Golden Bough*': 'All these *different* practices show that it is not a question of the derivation of one from the other, but of a common spirit. And one could invent (devise) all these ceremonies oneself. And precisely that spirit from which one invented them would be their common spirit' (RGB, 151).

From this perspective, 'Remarks on Fazer's *Golden Bough*' is not an exercise or a practice study in 'the ethnological approach', which emphatically presupposed the understanding of language that Wittgenstein had not developed yet when registering his observations on Frazer's study in June 1931. These notes display some proximity to his views on ethics and religion, their role in human life and the language they use. At the same time, they include concepts and contexts which were later developed in the *Philosophical Investigations*, notably, the notion of 'perspicuous representation'.

As already mentioned, magical thinking and magical rituals were regarded by Wittgenstein as expressive and symbolic, rather than instrumental. While this expressive and symbolic sense was rendered in various ways, depending on time and place, identical human feelings and instincts were always to be found beneath differences and cultural specificity. The way we talk about ethics offers a model for such an approach. Brusotti (2014: 27*pass*) claims that this normative and expressive way of talking appears shortly after 'A Lecture on Ethics'. However, the 'Lecture' itself contains its seeds as Wittgenstein defines ethics as considerations on what really matters: 'the enquiry into the right way of living, or into what makes life worth living, or into the meaning of life' (LE, 5). But when it appears to us that we could talk or think about all this, it turns out not to be the thing. Ethics, like the mystical, is pure experience and is therefore inexpressible. When one wants to express an ethical value, which is an absolute value and not of this world, as it were, for whatever is of this world is relative and can always be otherwise, one in fact wants to cross the limit of the world and thus the limit of significant language use. Wittgenstein believes that efforts to say something about ethics and religion essentially involve grappling with language, 'running against the walls of our cage', as he put it. These travails are perfectly and absolutely futile:

> Ethics so far as it springs from the desire to say something about the ultimate meaning of life, the absolute good, the absolute valuable, can be no science. What it says does not add to our knowledge in any sense. But it is a document of a tendency in the human mind which I personally cannot help respecting deeply and I would not for my life ridicule it.
>
> (LE, 12)

Wittgenstein equates ethical content with religious content, or more precisely speaking, the language of ethics with the language of religion. Expressions they use are similes or allegories which cannot be relinquished to directly express the facts they convey, because there are no such facts. There is no other content to be found behind or beneath these similes and allegories. They simply express our inner experiences which are of absolute value to us. Ethical content cannot be put in a propositional form, but it can, as Wittgenstein claims, be described the way literature sometimes goes about presenting human fates. At such moments, literature helps us evoke the sense of absolute values and express what is constantly on our minds and guides our lives.

Frazer's descriptions of ritual practices in *The Golden Bough* could work in a similar way if only one looked into their inner nature as a 'document of a tendency in the human mind'. If one wanted, for example, to express 'the majesty of death', the depiction of the succession of the Nemi king-priest would perfectly fit the bill. Likewise, if one wanted to present the absolute value of the feeling of guilt, Dostoevsky's writings would be a perfect illustration. Magical beliefs, like ethical and religious beliefs, are located beyond facts and consequently beyond language. As such, they cannot be true or false, because they are actually no beliefs in the first place, but symbols, images or performatives. They are measured not by truth or falseness but by the *power* of their impact on us in directing our lives, which is as great as the risks we would be prepared to incur to uphold them.

'A Lecture on Ethics' (1929) provided a background for the interpretation of ritual practices as expressive and instinctive actions. However, when Wittgenstein picked up some threads of the critique of *The Golden Bough* in the 1933 May Term lecture and evoked ethics in order to show the link between this critique and the method of philosophy, his reference already had a different resonance. Rather than elaborating on the approach encapsulated in 'A Lecture on Ethics', it focused on the grammar of the word 'good' and foregrounded explorations of the meaning of language expressions. This, however, does not exactly mean, unlike Brusotti (2014: 288) would have it, that the lectures of May 1933 marked a decisive step in Wittgenstein's philosophy by giving unquestionable precedence to his new views on meaning over the question of the viability of causal explanations of magical and ritual practices. Brusotti examines Wittgenstein's remarks on Frazer in the chronological order: from the notes from 1931 (MS 110), to the May Term lectures of 1933, to 'loose sheets' (MS 143) that make up the second part of RGB. Such an account produces an impression of a linear succession of ideas and nurtures the notion that Wittgenstein's thinking developed in a sequence of discrete steps. In fact, however, one would be hard-pressed to detect such a progression in Wittgenstein's remarks on Frazer, where his concepts expand radially and multiple ideas and insights overlap and interlace. 'Family resemblance' and the anti-essentialist take on meaning in the lectures of 1933 do not supplant the expressive and symbolic model; rather, as has been shown, the two approaches coexist side by side like in the notes from

1931, albeit not to such an extent, of course. What happens is a shift in emphasis and not a change of the viewpoint. Hence, the relevance of 'Remarks on Frazer's *Golden Bough*' should be perceived in Wittgenstein's resolute belief about the uniqueness and autonomy of the understanding of the human world, that is, in his anti-scientistic worldview, which merges with his concepts of language and meaning into an organic whole. While, from this perspective, 'Remarks on Frazer's *Golden Bough*' is not an exercise in 'the ethnological approach', it does contribute to the shaping-up of this whole.

8

Wittgenstein as a philosopher of culture

Ludwig Wittgenstein did not study culture. His research chiefly focused on language, its logic and its grammar, which he conceptualized as a set of rules governing the use of words. A considerable proportion of Wittgenstein's writings was devoted to the language of mathematics or simply the philosophy of mathematics. This does not mean, however, that Wittgenstein did not broach culture-related themes. On the contrary, he did so time and again in his diaries, which he kept throughout his life. Georg Henrik von Wright culled these scattered, variously dated notes and published them as *Vermischte Bemerkungen* in 1977. While Wittgenstein's remarks on music, art, literature and culture in general are without a doubt interesting and importantly illumine his personality, this chapter swerves in a different direction in order to explore the cultural meaning of Wittgenstein's philosophy as such, particularly in its post-Tractarian iteration, in which language and thought are conceived of as expressions of the 'form of life' (German: *Lebensform*), that is, a socially instituted pattern of practices exercised by a community. If the 'form of life' is simply referred to as culture, what Wittgenstein insists on is that language and thought are interwoven with our customary practices and should not be understood in disjunction from their cultural foundation. This begs the question of how deeply Wittgenstein's thinking is embedded in this cultural foundation and how far his philosophy can be legitimately interpreted as a philosophy of culture.

1. In Spiritual Alienation: Spengler

As already mentioned, after his return to Cambridge in 1929, Wittgenstein's object was to write a book – his second – to follow the *Tractatus*, as attested by some of his notes from late 1930, for example, drafts of prefaces to a future publication. There are a handful of such introductions, and all of them articulate ideologically coloured convictions. One of such passages was used by Rush Rhees as a 'Foreword' to his edition of TS 209, which was published as *Philosophische Bemerkungen* in 1964.[1] This 'Foreword' is completely at odds, *prima facie* at least, with the content of the *Philosophical Remarks*, which for the most part deals with the philosophy of mathematics. To make things even more puzzling, Rhees only picked two short excerpts from the longer text of the draft preface, and they were sourced from MS 109, that is, from outside the corpus of *Philosophische Bemerkungen*, encompassing manuscripts numbered from MS 105 to MS 108. The remaining, though not all, passages were published by von Wright in *Culture and Value*. They contain no reference to a concrete book, which also makes Rhees's arbitrary manoeuvre quite problematic.

The passages selected by Rhees encapsulate Wittgenstein's attitude to the spirit of his time – the spirit of Western civilization. The 'Preface' to the *Philosophical Remarks* proclaims, for instance:

> This book is written for such men as are in sympathy with its spirit. This spirit is different from the one which informs the vast stream of European and American civilization in which all of us stand. That spirit express itself in an onwards movement, in building ever larger and more complicated structures; the other in striving after clarity and perspicuity in no matter what structure. The first tries to grasp the world by way of its periphery – in its variety; the second at its centre – in its essence.
>
> (PR, 7)

Another remark, which is situated in the proximity of this excerpt in the notes from which it comes, reads: 'The spirit of this civilization [European and American civilization] the expression of which is the industry, architecture, music, of present day fascism & socialism is a spirit that is alien & uncongenial to the author' (MS 109, 205; CV, 8). In Wittgenstein's view, progress lay at the core of Western civilization:

> Our civilization is characterized by the word progress. Progress is its form, it is not one of its properties that it makes progress. Typically it constructs. Its activity is to construct a more and more complicated structure. And even clarity is only a means to this end & and not an end in itself. For me on the contrary clarity, transparency, is an end in itself. I am not interested in erecting a building but in having the foundations of possible buildings transparently before me. So I am aiming at something different than are the scientists & my thoughts move differently than do theirs.

It is all one to me whether the typical western scientist understands or appreciates my work since in any case he does not understand the spirit in which I write.

So I am really writing for friends who are scattered throughout the corners of the globe.

(MS 109, 207; CV, 9)[2]

The unmistakable Spenglerian tone of this passage should not come as a surprise since Wittgenstein was reading *The Decline of the West*[3] at approximately the same time and, like Oswald Spengler, whom he counted among his most powerful influences,[4] he felt that his epoch was a time of 'non-culture' – 'a time without culture' (*die Zeit der Unkultur*). This was not supposed to mean a time of the decay of human values, but of some expressions of these values. Wittgenstein extolled art as the highest expression of human values, deserving the name of Great Culture and, in the vein of Spengler, regarded the cult of science and technology as a demise and petrification of the living and vigorous body of culture, producing a merely mechanical, dead structure that Spengler called 'civilization'. Civilizations 'are a conclusion, the thing-become succeeding the thing-becoming, death following life, rigidity following expansion, intellectual age and the stone-built, petrifying world-city following mother-earth and the spiritual childhood of Doric and Gothic. They are an end, irrevocable, yet by inward necessity reached again and again' (Spengler 1926: 31). The culture–civilization dichotomy was the opposition between the Greek soul and the Roman intellect, non-philosophical one, estranged from art, pursuing concrete targets and geared to practical aims. The man of civilization was painted by Spengler as a determined, entirely a-metaphysical 'man of fact', incapable of creating great painting, music or architecture and merely possessed of purely extensive capacities.

There is no telling how far Wittgenstein actually endorsed Spengler's pessimistic prophetic vision, though it begs no doubt that he did not share all his views. In any case, *The Decline of the West* must have struck a sensitive chord in Wittgenstein and resonated with his ruminations on his time, which he followed Spengler in labelling as civilization. This reading also helped him articulate his attitude to the spirit of *that* time, strange, odious, distrust-inspiring and reservation-breeding as it was. Above all, Wittgenstein perceived a negative effect of science, which – via technology – transformed human community into industrial society and inevitably engendered the collapse of culture. Maurice Drury recounts in his recollections of Wittgenstein that one day the philosopher stormed into his room in dismay and, when asked about the reasons for his agitation, replied: 'I was walking about in Cambridge and passed a bookshop, and in the window were portraits of Russell, Freud and Einstein. A little further on, in a music shop, I saw portraits of Beethoven, Schubert and Chopin. Comparing these portraits I felt intensely the terrible degeneration that had come over the human spirit in the course of only a hundred years' (Rhees 1984: 112). Of course, Wittgenstein did not mean that Russell, Freud and Einstein were not outstanding and worthy people; what perturbed him was that in the time of civilization – *in der Zeit der Unkultur* ('in a time without culture' [CV, 9]) – great personages turned away from art and applied themselves to other areas in which 'somehow the value of the individual finds expression' (CV, 8).

It was also this alien and abhorrent spirit of the time that should be blamed for Wittgenstein's abiding worry that he would be misunderstood. The spirit he himself described and cherished was, in his view, different, so his words might not appeal to his contemporaries and sound foreign and as if not of this time. Haunting Wittgenstein from the early 1930s on, these apprehensions reverberate in the preface to the *Philosophical Investigations* from 1945, where he confesses that he is making the insights contained in the book 'public with misgivings. It is not impossible that it should fall to the lot of this work, in its poverty (*Dürftigkeit*) and in the darkness of this time, to bring light into one brain or another – but, of course, it is not likely' (PI, 4). Although today we cannot know with any certainty whether 'the darkness of this time' was supposed to refer to the Second World War or to the entire age of civilization, some of Wittgenstein's other declarations from that period[5] corroborate the latter conjecture.

What spirit exactly Wittgenstein wrote about and how that spirit differed from the spirit of civilization is not easy to specify, and it cannot be directly inferred from his worldview-coloured remarks. These are sparse, quite laconic and scattered casually across his writings; as such, they sound like an offhand register of trepidations and fears rather than an outcome of systematic reasoning. On their own, they barely add up to anything more than trivia. However, in Wittgenstein's second philosophy, people's language and thought are always part of 'language games', which are inseparably bound up with what he called a 'form of life' (*Lebensform*). Almost at the onset of the *Investigations*, Wittgenstein explains that 'to imagine a language means to imagine a form of life' (PI, §19), and in *The Brown Book* he explicitly equates language with culture: 'Imagine a use of language (a culture) in which there was a common name for green and red' (BB, 134) and further: 'We could also easily imagine a language (and that means again a culture) in which there existed no common expression for light blue and dark blue' (BB, 134). Consequently, 'the darkness of this time' must in one way or another express itself in language and thought as well. This is indeed the case, meaning that the turmoil in our forms of life is reflected in the restlessness of the mind, that is, in the puzzles of philosophy. These, Wittgenstein insists, ensue from the confusion of language, from disturbances within 'language games' and thus from disruptions in our social practices. Von Wright (1982: 215) asked whether and to what extent these three aspects of Wittgenstein's philosophy – that is, (1) his idea of language and thought as expressions of 'forms of life'; (2) his attribution of philosophical confusions to the ruptured operations of 'language games' and thus of 'forms of life'; and (3) his denouncement of scientific-industrial civilization – were conceptually interconnected. The Spenglerian dimension is interlaced with other aspects in ways that exceed the historical and psychological contexts. If there were no conceptual interrelatedness here, Wittgenstein's attitude to his time would be irrelevant to his philosophy, though meaningful to understanding his personality. According to von Wright, a problem arises regarding the second point, that is, Wittgenstein's position on the philosophy that emerges from language confusion bred by breaching the correct use of language. Since Wittgenstein's idea was that philosophy and life were intertwined, confusion in language was a reflection of confusion in people's forms of life.

2. Stanley Cavell: The *Philosophical Investigations* as a vision of culture

Von Wright's question whether Wittgenstein's attitude to his epoch is relevant to understanding his philosophy has been answered in the positive by Stanley Cavell,[6] who posits that the *Philosophical Investigations* can be construed as a picture of civilization or a series of sketches, to draw on Wittgenstein's own wording, that detail what Spengler called our 'spiritual history'. It is not so evident, however, how passages, scenes and particulars of the *Investigations* should be described to show that the book expresses an attitude to the spirit of the time and presents a picture of culture. If anything, the *Investigations* is a study on the operations of our language and does not say a word about culture, civilization or community. Of course, Wittgenstein does not address all these issues directly, and Cavell seems to suggest that the Spenglerian ideas are more or less deeply buried in the vignettes and sketches dealing with language, meaning, use, etc. As underlined throughout this book, Wittgenstein considered language part of the culture of a given community; to reiterate: 'to imagine a language means to imagine a form of life'. Cavell evokes the opening of the *Investigations*, which features a quotation from St Augustine relating how a child inherits language. Cavell believes that it portrays culture as a process of inheritance that unfolds in and through generational conflicts, as Freud claimed. The figure of a child is incorporated into this image of civilization in a far more meaningful way than in other philosophical treatises, perhaps except Rousseau's *Emile*. Like youth in Nietzsche and Kierkegaard, childhood calls for acceptance and attention from culture and never forgets the cost of acquiring those or having them refused and missing. The words of Augustine recalling how he learned language as a child resound throughout the *Investigations*. We shall revisit this moment.

The axial insight of Cavell's interpretation is:

> That what Wittgenstein means by speaking outside language-games, which is to say, repudiating our shared criteria, is a kind of interpretation of, or a homologous form of, what Spengler means in picturing the decline of culture as a process of externalization .... In the *Investigations* Wittgenstein *diurnalizes* Spengler's vision of the destiny toward exhausted forms, toward nomadism, toward the loss of culture, or say of home, or say community: he depicts our everyday encounters with philosophy, say with our ideals, as brushes with skepticism, wherein the ancient task of philosophy, to awaken us, or say bring us to our senses, takes the form of returning us to the everyday, the ordinary, every day, diurnally.
>
> (1988: 261–2; italics original)

Cavell appears to argue that what Spengler thought of as a universal historical process of externalization that had brought about the decline of Western culture is *diurnalized* by Wittgenstein, who identifies this externalization with stepping beyond 'language games' and contriving bold, intricate and sophisticated thought-constructions which, for all their refinement, are disjoined from any form of life and in this sense resemble castles in the air. The incorrect use of words, the pursuit of universality and an infatuation with the scientific method (scientism), which Wittgenstein explicitly censured in *The Blue Book*, would thus be tantamount to the twilight and loss of culture. Spengler (1926: 174) interpreted externalization as an atrophy of organic forms, which he regarded as *parasymbols* of all cultures. They are expressed in the sense of form proper to every individual, as well as to community, culture and age, whereby they define and establish the style of all manifestations of life. They are, as it were, fundamental schemas or concepts that determine people's perception and experience of the world. When the time of civilization arrives, these forms no longer suit the world and become dead even though they continue to be used: '*Pure* Civilization, as a historical process, consists in a progressive *taking-down* of forms that have become inorganic or dead' (Spengler 1926: 32, italics original).

In Cavell's view, discourse that falls outside the limits of language games and is typically found in traditional philosophy is similar, if not analogous, to Spengler's vision of the decline of culture. Wittgenstein's description of philosophers transgressing the boundaries of 'language games' and thus of the correct use of words conjures up the same picture that Spengler painted. The evocation of the decline of culture springs from the very core of Wittgenstein's discourse. Cavell tries to capture and show this, revealing various forms of similarities and analogies. One such resemblance lies in the notion of the loss of home or, more precisely, of everydayness as the abode of words: 'When philosophers use a word – "knowledge", "being", "object", "I", "proposition/sentence", "name" – and try to grasp the *essence* of the thing, one must always ask oneself: is the word ever actually used in this way in the language in which it is at home [*seine Heimat hat*]?' (PI, §116, italics original). According to Cavell, words are always out, 'in exile' and 'never at home' in philosophy. The point is that the correct use of expressions occurs within a given 'language game', which is based on a set of rules and criteria for sense shared by a given community. When philosophers cross the boundaries of our ordinary language use in a certain 'language game' and, consequently, venture beyond social conventions and practices, they position themselves outside of this community, so to speak. This breeds philosophical confusion which involves the loss of whereabouts in language and thus in culture, as well as the loss of connection to our common practices: 'A philosophical problem has the form: "I don't know my way about"' (PI, §123). By discarding the shared criteria and rules for correct language use, philosophy also discards a part of their natural cultural legacy and seeks to go beyond our form of life and to institute itself (alongside science) as the only legitimate perspective of reason.

According to William J. DeAngelis (2007: 73), Cavell's idea is that an analogy to Spengler's 'dead forms' is to be found in Wittgenstein, as philosophers' transgression of the limits of 'language games' is driven by their notion that it is only beyond the compass of ordinary 'language games' that something philosophically momentous can be said. Philosophy treats 'language games' as exhausted and dead forms which are useless and thus have to be relinquished for philosophy to fulfil its mission. However, hardly anything in either of Cavell's texts substantiates this reading. Cavell does not elaborate on the idea of 'dead forms'. If one were to search for an analogy, one would have to keep in mind that Spengler described civilization that continued to use these dead forms. Meanwhile, in going beyond the limits of 'language games', philosophy confers on words a specific and abstract sense disconnected from the form of life, as a result of which these words become dead to us. Wittgenstein proposed asking whether a word is ever used in a philosophical way in the language which is its home (*Heimat*). His own answer was a straightforward and resounding 'no'. It is not our ordinary 'language games' but the forms produced by philosophy that would correspond to inorganic forms, exhausted and dead.

Philosophy has two facets to it, though. It is a *pharmakon*, which can be both a medicine and a poison. Philosophy causes confusion, the loss of whereabouts and the severance of bonds, but it is also a remedy to all these aberrations. As already mentioned, in philosophy, words are, as it were, 'out' and 'in exile', and they need to be steered back home, to *Heimat*: 'What *we* do is to bring words back from their metaphysical to their everyday use' (PI, §116, italics original). What Cavell sees in the *Investigations* is not only an image of the decline of culture in Spengler's vein – a vision of the loss of orientation in language and culture – but also an attempt at overcoming the unsound tendencies that cause dead forms, nomadism and, consequently, decline. Comparable to philosophy's ancient mission of awakening human consciousness, this task takes the form of the return to everydayness. To rehearse Wittgenstein's dim hope and stark misgivings from the preface to PI: 'It is not impossible that it should fall to the lot of this work, in its poverty (*Dürftigkeit*) and in the darkness of this time, to bring light into one brain nor another – but, of course, it is not likely' (PI, 4). The admission of poverty is not a simple self-effacing expression of humility; it is bad news and a warning that the therapy prescribed in order to illumine the darkness of this time will be applied in the book. The question is what it is actually that the *Investigations* is poor in.

3. Wittgenstein and Hölderlin

The German word *Dürftigkeit* used by Wittgenstein brings to mind Friedrich Hölderlin's elegy 'Bread and wine':

> Meanwhile I often think it is
> Better to stay asleep, than to exist without companions,
> Just waiting it out, not knowing what to do or say
> In the meantime. What use are poets in times of need? (trans. James Mitchell)

When Hölderlin wrote about times of need (*dürftige Zeit*), he meant modernity as an age in which gods were gone – they 'live,/But up over our heads, up in a different world'. The time of lack, poverty and need deprives human life of a solid foundation and strips it of an objective meaning that exceeds individual goals and individual gain/loss calculations. In metaphysical terms, it is a time in which the unity of the spirit and nature has been forfeited, a time of split into *res cogitans* and *res extensa*; it is a time of subjective values, of a de-divinized world, divested of ethics and spirituality, a mechanical and material world in which only concrete, pragmatic goals matter. It is marked by the disintegration of genuine community, by chronic individualism and ubiquitous loneliness. Hölderlin contrasts this miserable time with Greek antiquity, when gods dwelled among humans, a period that, to him, embodies a world of genuine unity of the spirit and nature, the individual and the collective. In that world of old, values were directly embedded in being, and the truth had an ontological dimension. That world is gone. Christ, the last of gods, announces the end of the day, but he illumines darkness with a torch and promises a return. In times of need, in an age emptied of divine sense, in the night of metaphysical poverty, when human life has lost its higher purpose along with its non-subjective foundation, poets are all we have left. They are there to remind us of the Greek days of genuine unity and spiritual community, to restore the element of divinity to things and to infuse hope into the course of human affairs.

Hölderlin's times of need and poverty correspond to the age of civilization inhabited by the 'man of fact', an a-metaphysical type incapable of truly great deeds or of creating works of art. Arguably, 'times of need' from 'Bread and Wine' and Wittgenstein's 'darkness of this time' – that is, civilization – are distressingly redolent of each other, even though nowhere in the entire *Nachlass* does the philosopher mention the poet's name. This notwithstanding, the affinity is unmistakable:

> It is very *remarkable*, that we should be inclined to think of civilization – houses, streets, cars, etc – as separating man from his origin, from the lofty, eternal, etc. Our civilized environment, even its trees & plants, seems to us then cheap, wrapped in cellophane, & isolated from everything great & from God as it were. It is a remarkable picture that forces itself on us here.
>
> (CV, 57, italics original)

Wittgenstein locates the origin and onset of the time of the night in the expansion of science and the scientific method, which has sprawled to subsume the human world and culture. Prompted by the instinct of imitation, we erect huge edifices and spin grand metaphysical theories in this world, whereby we, unnoticeably as it were, come to stand aside, move beyond the everyday and our common, simple words and break our bonds with what is close and familiar to us in our 'pursuit of universality'. Chasing God's view from above, we hope to see the objective essence of the world and the meaning of our life. These aspirations are informed by the desire for the absurd. As Wittgenstein repeated, one cannot reach beyond language by means of language, or at least philosophy cannot do that. We can only imitate this reaching-beyond and pretend to have found great treasure, which is exposed as a mere trinket in daylight. The 'poverty' of the *Investigations* should be understood as philosophy's disavowal of the claim to being a privileged standpoint from which we examine language and, thus, culture. This poverty or lack is an asset because it heralds the return to everydayness. This begs the question of what everydayness is in fact. Hölderlin also eulogized the day, the ordinary human moments as the opposite of the night, which symbolized life away from gods and the rending of cultural legacy: 'Full of stars, unconcerned probably about us – /Astonishing night shines, a stranger among humans ....'

However, Hölderlin's vision located the long-awaited day and coveted, divinity-suffused everydayness far away – in sunlit and joyful Greece, which we can merely call to mind when listening to poets' words. Meanwhile, the return to the everyday in Wittgenstein is primarily bound up with philosophy and language; it is a return to the ordinary use of words in common linguistic practice, a return to ordinary human games, a return to our familiar forms of life and community, which is wrecked by the urge to go beyond what we usually do and by the aspiration to assume the divine position of looking from nowhere. In his elegiac vision, Hölderlin evokes grand figures and myths of history, Greek gods, Christ and the power of poetic imagination. Such is the task of poetry. The type of philosophy espoused by Wittgenstein recoiled from such notions and commitments. Wittgenstein admonished: 'Everything ritualistic (everything that, as it were, smacks of the high priest) is strictly to be avoided because it straightaway turns rotten.' Nonetheless, he immediately rushed to add: 'Of course a kiss is a ritual too & it isn't rotten; but no more ritual is permissible than is as genuine as a kiss' (MS 109, 209; CV, 10). It is not the point of this chapter to establish whether Hölderlin's poetry is rotten or whether it is like a kiss for us. What nevertheless should be noted is that the poetic symbols and metaphors of 'Bread and wine' are laden with philosophically invested concerns: the disintegration of the integrity of man and the world and the loss of the unity of the subject as such, which was most momentously instantiated in the Kantian duality of knowledge and action, necessity and freedom.[7] Something more is thus at stake than just the experience of disintegration, loss, confusion and alienation, shared by the poet and the philosopher.

What is of interest to us in this chapter is the unity of the human being and the world as envisaged by Wittgenstein himself: 'A culture is like a big organization which assigns each of its members a place where he can work in the spirit of the whole; and it is perfectly fair for his power to be measured by the contribution he succeeds in making to the whole enterprise' (MS 109, 205; CV, 6e). Yet the whole to which Wittgenstein refers is no longer there, and we have ourselves been instrumental in its dissolution. Our desire to go beyond our customary practices has proven our doom. According to Wittgenstein this urge and this aspiration crucially originate in 'our preoccupation with the method of science' (BB, 18). This method consists in reducing the explanations of natural phenomena to the possibly fewest basic laws of nature. Their eyes fixed on the scientific method, philosophers continually ask questions and answer them the way science does, while '[t]his tendency is the real source of metaphysics, and leads the philosopher into complete darkness' (BB, 18). The prefatory 'darkness of this time' of the *Investigations* is the same darkness into which the philosopher is plunged by emulating the natural scientist. Wittgenstein's profound belief was that the development of science and technology, along with the adulation of progress fuelled by them, had a pernicious effect on our culture and consequently on our self-understanding. His cultural pessimism was connected to his late philosophy by his opposition to scientism, which proclaimed that multiple spheres of human activity, such as philosophy, literature, art and music, could be studied and explored as if they were sciences.[8]

In Wittgenstein's view, the difference between philosophy and science was that the latter furnished us with a *knowledge* of the world, providing explanations of processes and events that take place in it, while the former was first and foremost about *understanding* ourselves. Science discovered new empirical facts and constructed theories and laws to explain those, and philosophy explored our concepts. Philosophy thus was not a theory but an *activity* striving for conceptual clarity: 'Philosophical investigations: conceptual investigations. The essential thing about metaphysics: it obliterates the distinction between factual und conceptual investigations' (Z, §458). The essential question was why it did so – why philosophy treated words in a specific, generalizing manner which made one think that if one learned to use, for example, the word 'time', one automatically came to possess a general picture of time, differing from the meanings of this word in various 'language games'; in other words, why we thought that if words such as 'a tree', 'a book' and 'a car' had their ontological designates, words 'time', 'truth', 'number' and 'meaning' had them as well, but not among empirical things. This analogy goaded us to ask 'What is time?', 'What is truth?', 'What is number?' and 'What is meaning?' The path to metaphysics was opened, and it knew no closure because these questions could not be definitively answered.

Ray Monk (1999: 67) argues that the difference between science and philosophy in Wittgenstein is the difference between theoretical and non-theoretical understanding. Scientific – theoretical – understanding is produced by empirically verifiable or falsifiable theories and hypotheses. Non-theoretical understanding is not reducible to one facet. While it resembles the understanding of poetry, music and other people, there is much more to it than that. For instance, a person that understands words in their language can not only properly use them but also paraphrase, accurately explain and/or apply them in a fitting context, etc. In the same way, a person who understands children can talk and play with them, answer their questions and comprehend their gestures, facial expressions, movements, etc. Such a person does not need to be versed in educational theories and can comfortably rely on their life experience and the skill of interaction with children acquired via this experience. In this context, understanding is something else – a different ability – than, for example, the understanding of contemporary music or modern painting. Those who understand the latter do not themselves have to be able to paint or deal with painters; instead, they must competently use proper metaphors to describe modern painting, to compare it with other kinds of painting, to cite its successful and unsuccessful specimens, etc. This suggests that there are various understandings: 'understanding integral calculus', 'understanding Schönberg's music', 'understanding abstract geometrical painting', 'understanding women', 'understanding English', 'understanding chess rules', 'understanding how the combustion engine works', 'understanding a poem', 'understanding the Pauli principle', 'understanding animal behaviour', 'understanding the ten commandments', etc. Whether or not all these understandings have something in common, it is not really necessary to identify this in order to understand each of these respective things. Surely, a person who understands children does not automatically understand English, $E = mc^2$ and Rilke's poetry as well?

Wittgenstein was most acutely distressed by strivings to understand human feelings, desires, experiences and sensations in a theoretical way, an aspiration that endorsed the scientistic claim that scientific knowledge was superior to all other methods of knowing and understanding. Towards the end of the second part of the *Investigations*, which in the latest edition by Hacker and Schulte is no longer the second part but 'Philosophy of Psychology – A Fragment' ('Philosophie der Psychologie – ein Fragment'), Wittgenstein asks: 'Is there such a thing as "expert judgement" about the genuineness of expressions of feeling?' (PI II, §355). Of course, people vary in the aptness of their judgements, and this faculty can be trained to an extent, but not in any courses or classes. Instead, it can be acquired and perfected in repeated observations which are not graspable in any generalization, because there is no particular technique involved, and whatever guidelines or even rules there may be, they do not add up to a system: 'The genuineness of an expression cannot be proved; one has to feel it' (PI II, §357). Apt judgements – for example how sincere a long-unseen old acquaintance is when saying 'we must catch up over a beer someday' – can only be made on separate occasions. To Wittgenstein, any attempts at formulating overall instructions would look like 'ruins of the system', because the whole of the enigma is in the 'imponderables' – in the nuances of the look, the tone, the gesture. One can recognize the look of candour and tell it from pretended sincerity, but one can also be entirely unable to do so for inexperience, inborn good-naturedness or incorrigible naivete. It is far from obvious how one acquires 'the feel' in some matters, but it is quite obvious that one cannot learn it the way one learns the rules of a calculus or even the rules of language. Understanding people can never be a science. Rather, it resembles the understanding of music, which Wittgenstein referenced time and again.[9] In his view, understanding music involves a certain mode of expression which comprises movements and the manner in which one that understands plays or hums a piece of music; it may also comprise similes, metaphors and images one employs. One that understands music will listen with a different facial expression than one that does not:

> Appreciating music is a manifestation of human life. How could it be described to someone? Well, above all I suppose we should have to describe *music*. Then we could describe the relation human beings have to it. But is that all that is necessary, or is it also part of the process to teach him to appreciate it for himself? Well, developing his appreciation will teach him what appreciation is in a *different* sense, than a teaching that does not do this. And again, teaching him to appreciate poetry or painting can be part of an explanation of what music is.
> (CV, 80–1)

4. '....nur *dichten*'

Hölderlin appointed to poets the mission of retaining and transmitting thoughts of things divine. In times of need – a time of lack and poverty, when words do not arise like flowers – it has befallen them to prophesize the future, to revive the memory of the day and to reforge memory into hope. To Wittgenstein, the significance of philosophy lay in bringing words back to their *Heimat*, that is, in reminding about their natural use in everyday 'language games' ('The work of the philosopher consists in assembling reminders for a particular purpose' [BT, 415]) – in dispelling the metaphysical darkness in which philosophy and science – or, rather, philosophy as science – make claims to being the sole depositary of the truth. At the same time, however, besides heading straight home along a familiar road, philosophy can also stray into complete darkness; it can represent the possession of our minds by our means of expression, besides relying on these means to instil clarity and transparency into our perception of the world. Philosophy cannot regain home and lucidity as a science in disguise. If not as this, then as what? In one of the notes made in 1933/1934 and included by von Wright in *Culture and Value*, Wittgenstein stated: 'I believe I summed up where I stand in relation to philosophy when I said: really one should write philosophy only as one *writes a poem* [*eigentligh nur dichten*]' (CV, 28, italics original).

The German word *dichten* has no exact equivalent in English. In the first English edition of *Culture and Value*, Peter Winch translated this sentence as 'Philosophy ought really to be written as a *poetic composition*.' Neither of the versions fully conveys the meaning of the original, and they can easily foster a mistaken idea that Wittgenstein intended to write poems or turn philosophy into poetry. Meanwhile, the German verb *dichten* indeed means 'to write poetry' but also, more generally, 'to fable', as in the title of Goethe's *Dichtung und Wahrheit* (translated into English somewhat misleadingly as *Poetry and Truth* but also, more accurately, as *Truth and Fantasy from My Life*), where *Dichtung* stands for something fictitious and is contrasted with truth. Wittgenstein's point was that philosophy should be practised (written) the way one practised (wrote) poetry.[10] Elsewhere, in a less well-known note, he remarked: 'If I don't want to teach correct thinking, but new ideas, my aim is to "revalue values" and I think of Nietzsche, also because the *philosopher should be a poet*' (MS 120, 145, italics mine). Conspicuously, Wittgenstein crossed out both passages referencing poetry and the poet. We shall treat this deletion as a second impulse or as an imposition of control on the primary, immediate sense. This intuition is corroborated by Wittgenstein's musings from October 1946: 'Why is it, when I write philosophy, it is as if I was writing a poem? It is as if there was something tiny, something with a wonderful meaning. Like a leaf or a flower.'[11]

If we thus were to try and define the sense of the first (authentic, uncontrolled) impulse and specify what Wittgenstein meant by practising philosophy like poetry and by the philosopher preferably being a poet, we would perhaps first think of Wittgenstein's aphoristic style, especially in the *Tractatus*, which has caught the attention not only of professional philosophers but also of several writers and artists.[12] Wittgenstein's aphorisms nevertheless differ from those of Karl Kraus, Friedrich Nietzsche and Georg Lichtenberg, authors he knew and appreciated. None of Wittgenstein's adages is actually a self-contained whole; rather, they flow along in shoals of related remarks and, as a rule, say what they say, only rarely availing themselves of metaphors or similes. At the same time, a handful of them have come to live a life of their own, including outside of philosophy: '*The limits of my language* mean the limits of my world' (TLP, 5.6), 'What we cannot speak about we must consign to silence' (TLP, 7), 'There are, indeed, things that cannot be put into words. They *make themselves manifest.* They are what is mystical' (TLP, 6.522). Composed of such sentences, the *Tractatus* does not in the least resemble a traditional philosophical treatise. It does not develop discourse based on argumentative reasoning, but is persuasive in a barely accountable fashion even when one fails to grasp what Wittgenstein's aphorisms are all about. They sound cryptic, are peculiarly numbered and often curt, but on closer inspection allowing for their historical context, without which they tend to be unintelligible, they accurately convey the essence of things.

In the *Philosophical Investigations*, the aphoristic style transfigures into a conversational or dialogic form, if not into thinking aloud, frequently interspersed with phrases such as 'let us imagine …', 'let us think of …', 'let us assume …', etc. The author poses questions to us and to himself, now putting himself in the reader's shoes, now guiding him/her on the right track of thinking: 'So you are saying that the word "pain" really means crying? – On the contrary: the verbal expression of pain replaces crying, it does not describe it' (PI, §244). At the same time, aphoristic expressions are not entirely eliminated – 'The philosopher treats a question; like an illness' (PI, §255) – though they do not appear all too often. If anything, they morph into longer passages in colloquial language, purged of technical terms and concepts. While this was also largely true about the *Tractatus*, that book still exhibited the conceptual influences of Bertrand Russell and Gottlob Frege.

Still, what is the most striking aspect of the *Investigations* and Wittgenstein's other late writings is a unique species of the imagination – spinning made-up stories in order to show and comprehend the operations of our language and to make a survey of its grammar. Wittgenstein announces that he is not interested in the possible causes behind the origin of our concepts: 'we are not doing natural science; nor yet natural history – since we can also invent fictitious natural history for our purposes' (PI II, §365). This approach embodies a 'history without history', as discussed in the previous chapter. The *Philosophical Investigations* opens with a quotation from St Augustine's *Confessions*, recollecting how he learned language as a child: 'When grown-ups named some object and at the same time turned towards it, I perceived this, and I grasped that the thing was signified by the sound they uttered, since they meant to point it out' (PI, §1). This account presents a specific picture of human language in which words name objects and sentences are combinations of such words. We should endorse it because it appears natural, accepted as if unwittingly and pre-existing any theories and positions; it is a picture that is deeply rooted in us. Wittgenstein, as it were, persuades us to accept it; that is, he proposes assuming a certain philosophical view of language. What happens later is pivotal to the entire *Investigations*. Specifically, Wittgenstein does not pit his own conception of language and meaning against this, so to speak, referential semantics. What matters is what he does not say about it: he does not say it is wrong, inconsistent, based on false tenets, at odds with Augustine's other claims, etc. Briefly, he does not say anything that usually qualifies as an argument in a philosophical critique. One does not know in advance what is wrong in this picture. Instead, Wittgenstein suggests:

> Let us imagine a language for which the description given by Augustine is right: the language is meant to serve for communication between a builder A and an assistant B. ... For this purpose they make use of language consisting of the words 'block', 'pillar', 'slab', 'beam'. A calls them out; B brings the stone which he has learnt to bring at such-and-such a call. – Conceive of this as a complete primitive language.
>
> (PI, §2)

By concocting this simple example, Wittgenstein needed just a few lines to undermine the foundation of entire referential semantics and, to boot, to blur the natural and most obvious picture of language in which words signified objects. The point is that sometimes they just do not, but are commands for acting in a particular manner. In this way, Wittgenstein rattled the whole of philosophy.

How profound this shock was is evinced by countless references that bespeak the exceptional suggestiveness and memorability of §2.

Wittgenstein's writings abound with 'fantasizing' of this kind, with the story of a wood seller in 'Some Remarks on the Foundations of Mathematics' and a visit to a shop to purchase five red apples in the *Investigations* vividly exemplifying his fables. Wittgenstein also resorted to innumerable examples, comparisons and sometimes drawings to offer a 'perspicuous representation' of the meanings of expressions in our language and thus of our form of life, that is culture:

> We also say of a person that he is transparent to us. It is, however, important as regards our considerations that one human being can be a complete enigma to another. One learns this when one comes into a strange country with entirely strange traditions; and, what is more, even though one has mastered the country's language. One does not *understand* the people. (And not because of not knowing what they are saying to themselves.) We can't find our feet with them.
>
> (PI II, §325, italics original)

Rather than involving the penetration of the abyss of the self, 'the finding of our feet' is premised on the knowledge of the rules and practices observed by these people. Understanding people, their language and beliefs in disjunction from and prior to their form of life is but an illusion. The return to everydayness should also be comprehended as a return to our common practices, norms and models of conduct perpetuated by social conventions: 'What is true or false is what human beings say; and it is in their language that human beings agree. This is agreement not in opinion, but rather in form of life' (PI, §241). It is at the same time a return to simplicity and to the uninterrupted operations of rules. What complicates these operations and jettisons us out of the course of life are certain questions inopportunely asked 'from the side', from outside of 'language games' – questions that originate in our culture itself.

Notes

Preface

1. Cf. Hacker (2013: 152–3).
2. Wittgenstein's writings (manuscripts and typescripts) from this period are available today through *Wittgenstein's Nachlass: The Bergen Electronic Edition* (Oxford: Oxford University Press, 2000) and online as *Wittgenstein Source Bergen Nachlass Edition* (http://wittgensteinsource.org). A large portion of this material was also published in the *Wiener Ausgabe*, edited by Michael Nedo (Wien: Springer, 1993).
3. Cf. Wittgenstein 2016. Notes taken by other students attending Wittgenstein's lectures are available as well. See Wittgenstein 1979 and Wittgenstein 1980.
4. Cf., for example, Engelmann (2013); Kienzler (1997); Stern (1991).

Introduction

1. Cf. Schulte (1998: 380); Stern (2015: 183).
2. Cf. Hilmy (1987: 98).
3. Cf. Pichler (2018: 56).
4. For examples of such interpretations, see Stern (2018).
5. A similar view is championed by Stern, who states: 'Wittgenstein was drawn, during this transitional period in the early 1930s, toward a conception of philosophy on which its aim is to clarify, in a systematic way, the rules of our language in a philosophical grammar. However, by the time he composed the first draft of the *Philosophical Investigations* in 1936–37 he had given up this conception of philosophical grammar in favor of piecemeal criticism of specific philosophical problems' (2015: 211).
6. See BB, 70–2.
7. Cf. Gibson and O'Mahony (2020: 104).
8. What a daunting task it is to identify such a moment and how much such an identification depends on the interpretation of Wittgenstein's philosophy as a whole can be suggested by the multitude of answers Wittgenstein scholarship offers to the question when his late philosophy makes its first appearance. Stern has found as many as nine of them. Cf. Stern (2005: 172–88).
9. Cf. Wittgenstein (2016: 67).

10 Cf. Wittgenstein (1993: 113–14).
11 The letter dated on 20 November 1936.
12 'Eine der wichtigsten Aufgaben ist es ja, alle falschen Gadankengänge so charakteristisch auszudrücken, daß der Leser sagt "ja, genau so habe ich es gemeint". Die Physiognomie jedes Irrtum nachzuzeichnen. Wir können ja auch nur dann den Andern eines Fehlers überführen, wenn er anerkennt, daß dies wirklichg der Ausdruck seines Gefühls ist. [… wenn er diesen Ausdruck (wirklich) als den richtigen Ausdruck seines Gefühl anerkennt]. Nämlich, nur, wenn er ihn als solchen anerkennt, *ist* er der richtige Ausdruck. (Psychoanalyse)' (MS 110, 230).
13 The passage from the Skinner-Archive entitled 'Communication of Personal Experience', which was supposed to be an extension of *The Brown Book* does not change anything in this respect (Gibson and O'Mahony 2020: 149–84).
14 On this issue, see Pichler (2004: 129–31).
15 See Schulte (2013: 85).

Chapter 1

1 Cf. Kienzler (1997: 79–88); Nedo (1994: x); Rothhaupt (2010: 51–64).
2 See Munson (1962: 37–50); Van Peursen (1959: 181–97).
3 See Spiegelberg (1968: 244–56).
4 According to Ray Monk's count, there were fifteen publications on Wittgenstein's phenomenology before 2009 (2014: 335–6). While Monk's list is in fact incomplete, the papers he has omitted are rather few.
5 Such studies are included, for example, in Oskari Kussela's book from 2018.
6 This has been posited by Nicholas Gier (1981: 95).
7 Byong-Chul Park also subscribes to this view and contends that Carnap's influence is indirectly substantiated by the Mach-like quality of Wittgenstein's phenomenology, as *Aufbau* was written from the standpoint that exhibited affinity with some of Mach's ideas. See Park (1998: 18). For his part, James M. Thompson suggests that Wittgenstein came in touch with phenomenology via Heidegger. See Thompson (2008: 68–70). Cf. also Vrahimis (2014: 342–4).
8 See Carnap (2003: 233, §152).
9 See Spiegelberg (1968: 250).
10 For a more detailed discussion, see Monk (1991: 252).
11 On this issue, see Janik and Toulmin (1972: 212–18). Jaakko Hintikka (1996: 58) points out an interesting but rather infrequently noticed circumstance that Husserl admitted in one of his Amsterdam lectures in 1925 that his phenomenology continued on and radicalized Mach's phenomenology. Husserl wrote: 'In the struggle of philosophy and psychology for a strictly scientific method, a new

science appeared at the turn of the century, and along with it a new method of philosophical and psychological inquiry. This new science is called *phenomenology*, because it emerged together with its new method from a certain radicalization of the phenomenological method previously used by individual natural scientists and psychologists. For people such as *Mach* and *Hering*, the sense of this method lies in responding to the lack of underpinnings for theorizing, which threatened "solid" sciences; it was a response against theorizing within non-intuitive conceptual structures and mathematical speculations, which did not yield an intuitively graspable clarity of sense and theoretical result' (1968: 302).

12 On Hertz's and Boltzmann's influence on Wittgenstein, see Preston (2017: 110–25).
13 See BT, 492.
14 See Ramsey (1923: 465–78).
15 See Engelmann 2013: 13. Monk also expresses a similar view (2014: 126–8). For his part, Thompson (2008: 79) posits that, for Wittgenstein, phenomenology was 'an *a posteriori* method of logical investigation of phenomena capable of rendering complete descriptions of both the world and experience'. According to Thompson, Wittgenstein was looking, at that time, for a way to rehabilitate his earlier 'picture theory', which was not capable of comprehensively describing the world and its representation, as demonstrated by the colour exclusion problem. Propositions about colours, like all other statements of degree, fell outside this theory. Wittgenstein believed that the problem could be solved through a phenomenological analysis of direct experience.
16 Cf. MS, 106, 124.
17 However, phenomenological language must not be called, by analogy, a concept writing (*Begriffsschrift*), which is what Wolfgang Kienzler and Engelmann do (cf. Engelmann 2013: 17–19; Kienzler 1997: 115). The point is that Wittgenstein's phenomenological language was supposed to avoid the contradictions and ambiguities of ordinary language not through constructing an ideal notation in the sense of Frege's *Begriffsschrift* or Russel's 'theory of types', but through showing that language itself at the level of structure, like in the *Tractatus*, excluded nonsense. Importantly, one of the beliefs Wittgenstein never relinquished was that logical properties of language were inexpressible, and thus that constructs such as *Begriffsschrift* or 'theory of types' were redundant.
18 Cf. Engelmann (2013: 18).
19 One problem with Engelmann's interpretation is that it uses the Tractarian *talking/showing* distinction and the notion of external and internal properties. In the *Tractatus*, Wittgenstein defines internal properties as those of which it is unthinkable that a given object does not possess them (TLP, 4.123). However, such properties cannot be expressed in language; they can only be shown in correctly constructed propositions. For example, it is impossible to convey in language

that 'light blue is a lighter colour than dark blue'. This is simply *seen* from the proposition itself, that is, from the logical syntax (grammar) of this proposition as such. Yet in his notes from 1929 and the early 1930s, Wittgenstein abandons his theory about what cannot be talked about but solely shown. He rarely refers to the notion of internal and external properties (or relations) or to the belief about the inexpressibility of the logical (internal) properties of language, even though the notion of 'description' admittedly remains ambiguous.

20 Cf. Thompson (2008: 73–7).
21 See Engelmann (2013: 35).
22 Cf. MS, 107, 29.
23 In his conversations with Schlick and Waismann, Wittgenstein critically referred to the works of the mathematicians Johannes Hjelmslev and Felix Klein, who sought to derive Euclidean geometry from the natural geometry of visual space. In the latter, there are patches rather than points, the arc of a huge circle is indistinguishable from a straight line, and multisided polygons are seen as circles. Wittgenstein observes that 'circle', 'point' and 'tangent' have different grammars in Euclidean space and visual space, respectively. For example, a patch can always be imagined as having a contour, unlike a point. Cf. WVC, 55–9.
24 This view is shared by Park (1998: 3–4), who believes that the problem of phenomenology, which concerns direct experience, pervades Wittgenstein's entire philosophy. Still, if phenomenology is as generally defined as Hintikka and Park do it, multiple philosophers could be given the moniker of a phenomenologist.
25 A similar view is espoused by Gier (cf. Gier 1981: 113).
26 Monk claims that Wittgenstein's phenomenology, like Husserl's, entailed looking for the simple and the primary, for what entirely foregoes the hypothetical. Moreover, Wittgenstein resorts to a device that resembles the Husserlian *epoché*, which results in differentiating between a natural attitude to the world and a phenomenological attitude. Monk discerns this similarity in Wittgenstein's distinction between a film picture on the screen and pictures on the film strip. Consequently, phenomenology would be concerned with the film on the screen, and the natural attitude with the frames of the film (see Monk 2014: 329–30). Some similarity can indeed be perceived in this respect, for example, in attempts at describing phenomena themselves and their immediate experience in a language stripped of scientific concepts and categories or in focusing this description on seeing and visual space. Nevertheless, there are differences as well. The comparison of visual space to a book to which it does not matter whether it belongs to anybody may suggest that Wittgenstein's original project of phenomenology cast space as an object, that is, in an entirely objectivist way. He removed all the connections between visual space and the subject, insisting that calling visual space subjective, which is characteristic of our ordinary language, resulted from the physical

(scientific) mindset. What Wittgenstein called visual space or the visual field differed from what Maurice Merleau-Ponty, Husserl's French continuator, understood by this. For Merleau-Ponty, the visual field is always somebody's visual field and is formed by subjective acts of seeing and sensing. When delineating this field, one should start from the world rather than from oneself. Objects are always seen against a background and in configuration with other objects, never in disjunction from them. They are seen from one side or another, from this or that angle, as built of something, having a certain surface, etc. What they are to us depends on how they are experienced by us. When Wittgenstein says that the space described by our ordinary (secondary) language consists of visual, gustatory and tactile impressions and is a space where one can turn and where 'up', 'down', 'right' and 'left' are distinguishable, he suggests that the phenomenological description takes place at another level – between the objective description (science) and the subjective one (ordinary language) – and is, as it were, established by phenomena as such rather than by our impressions.

Chapter 2

1   Cf. Hacker (1996: 134); Monk (1991: 295).
2   A similar view is embraced by Hans-Johann Glock (1996: 382) and Michael Hymers (2005: 210).
3   Wittgenstein expressed such views in his lectures in the early 1930s. See Wittgenstein (1980: 66).
4   Shanker (1987: 42).
5   An interpretation of Wittgenstein's verificationism as proving his shift from realism to anti-realism has been offered, for example, by Crispin Wright (cf. Wright 1980: Chapters X–XI). For a discussion and critique of this reading, see Shanker (1987: 42–59).
6   Cf. Wrigley (1989: 275).
7   Cf. Wrigley (1989: 277–80).
8   On 24 December 1929, that is, shortly after writing 'Some Remarks on Logical Form', Wittgenstein noted in his diary:

> The new take on 'elementary propositions' holds that a proposition may be either more or less *close* to truth. (For red is closer to orange than to blue, and 2m closer to 201cm than 3m.) …
>
> [P]ropositions turn out to be even more like yardsticks than I previously believed. – The fact that *one* measurement is right automatically excludes all others. I say automatically: just as all the gradation marks are on *one* rod, the propositions corresponding to the graduation marks similarly belong together,

and we can't measure with one of them without simultaneously measuring with all the others. – It isn't a proposition which I put against reality as a yardstick, it's a *system* of propositions [*System von Sätzen*]. (MS 108, 35; PR, 82, italics original)

9   Cf. Medina (2002: 42).
10 Slightly earlier, Wittgenstein wrote: 'How a proposition is verified is what it says. This proposition says how it is verified. Compare the generality of genuine propositions with generality in arithmetic. It is verified in a different way and is thus a different generality. Verification is not *one* token of the truth, it is the *sense* of the proposition' (MS, 107, 143; PR, 200, italics original); and 'Every proposition is a free play of marks and sounds without any connection to reality, and [its] only connection to reality is the way it is verified' (MS, 107, 177).
11 Karl Seitz was the mayor of Vienna from 1925 to 1934.
12 Cf. Hacker (1996: 58). To specify, the notion of 'symptom' appears once at the beginning of *The Blue Book*, but Wittgenstein does not refer to it later.
13 Cf. Engelmann (2013: 25–8).
14 Andreas Blank (2011: 630) believes that Wittgenstein did not abandon verificationism because he found it incompatible with the rejection of logical atomism, but because he sought to develop his own version of verificationism independent of logical atomism. Blank emphasizes the role of discerning various aspects of the logical multiplicity of propositions and facts, in this way trying to show a connection between verification and 'seeing-as'.
15 Cf. McGuinness (2002: 180).

Chapter 3

1   David Hilbert used a similar notion of *Formelspiel* (game with formulas), which was also known to Wittgenstein (cf. WVC, 119).
2   Frege's critique of formalism coincides here with his critique of psychologism.
3   Frege writes: 'Why can no application be made of a configuration of chess pieces? Because, obviously, it does not express a thought. If it did, and if a move in chess in accordance with the rules corresponded to a transition from one thought to another, then applications of chess would be conceivable … Now, it is applicability alone which elevates arithmetic above a game to the rank of a science' (2013: 100, §91).
4   That is why Wolfgang Kienzler seems to miss the point when he objects that as Frege links the scientific rank of arithmetic to its applicability, he 'makes his philosophical analyses of arithmetic and numbers dependent on something external to it, on its applicability in geodesy, physics or astronomy' (1997: 203).

5   Michael Dummett (1991: 257–9) maintains that Frege understands the applicability of mathematics as exemplifying the applicability of more general logical truths. He also discusses the internal and external applicability of arithmetic and some differences between Frege's concepts as expounded in the *Grundlagen* and in the *Grundgesetze*.
6   Cf. Frege (2013: 101–2, §93).
7   See Dummett (1991: 255).
8   According to Kienzler (1997: 205), Frege's main objection to formalism was not the problem of distinguishing between the game itself and the theory of the game, but rather the impossibility of putting together a really complete list of rules, which would be necessary to prevent any imaginable contradiction among them.
9   Mathieu Marion refers to Wittgenstein's early position as 'logicism without classes' (1998: 26). For a criticism of the logistic interpretation, see Rodych (1995), and Wrigley (1998).
10 This view is shared, for example, by Dummett. He claims that we cannot simply oppose the notion of use to Frege's notion of sense (1981: 34).
11 For this reason, Mühlhölzer calls Wittgenstein's entire philosophy (and not only his philosophy of mathematics) a kind of 'formalism' (2008: 116).
12 Mühlhölzer is of a similar opinion. He observes that Frege did take rules of use into account as constitutive of the sign. What Frege indeed failed to notice was the full potential of the alternative embraced by Wittgenstein, whose assessment should be taken exactly as highlighting this potential. According to Mühlhölzer, Wittgenstein's entire philosophy of mathematics developed this potential (2010: 32). Kienzler (1997: 201) claims that Frege did notice the third option but dismissed it so firmly that Wittgenstein could offer it as a new idea.
13 To explain how signs acquire content through use, Sören Stenlund (2018: 75–86) refers to the distinction the *Tractatus* makes between *sign* and *symbol*. Following 3.32, the sign is what is perceptible by the senses in the symbol. As opposed to signs, symbols have meanings, yet not in the form of objects but through their use and function in symbolism. However, Stenlund passes over theses 3.321–3.325, in which Wittgenstein explicitly states what he needs this distinction for. Namely, he needs it in order to show that it occurs in everyday language that signs (words) signify in various ways, that is, they belong to different symbols ('Green is green'), or that two words which signify in different ways are used in a sentence in the same way, as is the case with the word 'is'. In mathematics, signs are not used in different ways, and symbolism that employs the same sign, such as '3 + 1', in different ways is not used (26). At the beginning of the quotation from the conversation with Schlick above, Wittgenstein – like most logicians and mathematicians – uses the terms *sign* and *symbol* as synonymous. Given this, I believe that Stenlund may be missing the point when he asserts that Frege failed

to recognize the difference between sign and symbol and, consequently, that his critique of Thomae's formalism is off the mark.

14   He did this in *The Blue Book* as well.
15   Frege himself addressed this issue when commenting on his context principle in the *Grundlagen*: 'If the second principle [context principle] is not observed, one is almost forced to take as the meanings of words mental pictures or acts of the individual mind' (1953: xxii).
16   Not only in his later philosophy in fact, for as early as in the *Tractatus*, Wittgenstein identified a fault in Russell's 'theory of types' in that it necessitated taking into account the reference of a given type of signs. In TLP, 3.331, Wittgenstein states: 'Russel must be wrong, because he had to mention the meaning (*Bedeutung*) of signs when establishing the rules for them.'
17   'I'm almost inclined to say: In a game there is (to be sure) no "true" or "false", but then again in arithmetic there is no "winning" and "losing"' (BT, 374).
18   This is how the problem of grasping a thought is interpreted by, for example, Dummett (1993: 101).
19   The fact that in Frege thought is independent of language is highlighted by Tyler Burge (1992: 633–50).
20   See also TLP, 6.21.
21   The example may be a reminder of the discussion of Leibniz's proof of $2 + 2 = 4$ criticized by Frege in *Grundlagen der Arithmetik* §6.
22   On this notion, see Glock (1996).

Chapter 4

1   It is rather puzzling that publications on Wittgenstein's criticism of set theory are few and far between.
2   Cf. Kuratowski and Mostowski (1978: 16).
3   The worldview-related aspect of Wittgenstein's critique of set theory is highlighted by Georg Henrik von Wright (von Wright 1982: 201–17).
4   For Wittgenstein, 'a series of forms' was a 'series that is ordered by an *internal* relation' (TLP, 4.1252, italics original). This definition was modelled on the notion of the series and the definition of natural number based on this notion and introduced by Frege. Cf. Frege (1993: §29).
5   Emphatically, as Hans-Johann Glock explains, numbers are not outcomes of a mathematical operation, but they result from a logical operation on propositions and correspond to the stage of producing molecular propositions out of elementary propositions. Given this, Wittgenstein wrote in TLP, 6.2, that

'[m]athematics is a logical method,' which did not mean that he considered logic primary to mathematics. Cf. Glock (1996: 266).
6   On this issue, see Rotter (2006: 71). Krzysztof Rotter identifies a clear intuitionist thread in Wittgenstein's first philosophy, which is particularly pronounced in his insistence on the effective decidabiliy and the effective constructability of all concepts, including the basic concepts of logic and mathematics.
7   Cf. Marion (1998: 34).
8   See Rodych (2000: 285).
9   See Ramsey (1950: 237–44).
10 Ramsey (1950: 241*pass.*).
11 For more discussion on this issue, see Methven (2015: 201–2).
12 This phrase is found in George E. Moore's notes. Cf. Wittgenstein (2016: 219).
13 See Methven (2015: 224).
14 See Glock (1996: 147).
15 This note was later incorporated into *The Big Typescript* (see BT, 749).
16 See Putnam (2007: 236, 246).
17 As far as I know, contemporary set theory does not use this division either.
18 Cf. WVC, 228.
19 On this issue, cf. Moore (1991: 206–8).
20 Hilary Putnam regards such a negative approach to infinity in mathematics as entirely ill conceived. In his view, even the intuitionist approach includes a positive assertion that there is always a possibility to continue a given series. It is an axiom of arithmetic that every number has a successor. See Putnam (2007: 240).
21 See Cantor (1932: 378–439).
22 José Ferreirós (2007: 18–19) points out that the philosophical atmosphere in Germany in the nineteenth century encouraged endorsing actual infinity. For example, Hegel referred to potential infinity as 'the bad infinite' and contrasted it with *qualitative infinity* proper to the Absolute. For his part, Cantor quoted Leibniz in one of his works: 'I am so much in favour of an actual infinite that instead of admitting that nature abhors it, as is commonly said, I hold that it affects nature everywhere in order to indicate the perfections of its Author. So I believe that every part of matter is, I do not say divisible, but actually divided, and consequently the smallest particle should be considered as a world full of an infinity of creatures' (Cantor 1932: 179, qtd. in Ferreirós 2007: 18–19).
23 Victor Rodych (2000: 283–87) argues that Wittgenstein's adoption of the finitist position vis-à-vis the concept of set implied his rejection of quantification over infinite domains. Our reasoning, however, indicates that the opposite may have been the case.
24 By cardinal numbers, Wittgenstein meant the natural numbers.
25 Wittgenstein elaborated on this idea first and foremost in Chapter 139 of *The Big Typescript*, entitled 'Kinds of Irrational Numbers (π', P. F)'.

26 See MS, 112, 33. This remark was later incorporated into *The Big Typescript*, 755.
27 See Da Silva (1993: 93).
28 Wittgenstein was not the first thinker to call for an arithmetical construction of the irrational numbers. A similar reasoning was promulgated by Weyl in *Das Kontinuum* (1928), a study in which he rejected the irrational numbers that were not arithmetically defined cuts of rational numbers. Jairo J. da Silva also draws attention to mathematician August W. Rehberg, Kant's contemporary, who championed an intentional theory of the irrational numbers. See Da Silva 1993: 95.
29 This aspect of Wittgenstein's critique of Dedekind is foregrounded by Stuart Shanker (1987: 187*pass.*). Putnam (2007: 245) claims that the fact that Wittgenstein questioned mathematical continuity, which he believes lies at the core of contemporary mathematics, shows that his approach was wrong.
30 See Bernays (1959: 19).
31 On this issue, see Marion (1998: 211).
32 Dedekind (1909: 9).
33 However, Mathieu Marion seems to agree with Wittgenstein, concluding that despite Dedekind's declarative intentions the definition of the real numbers as cuts was indeed geometrically underpinned, which is indicated by Dedekind's statement that '[o]f the greatest importance, however, is the fact that in the straight line L there are infinitely many points which correspond to no rational number. … If now, as is our desire, we try to follow up arithmetically all phenomena in the straight line, the domain of rational numbers is insufficient and it becomes absolutely necessary that the instrument R constructed by the creation of the rational numbers be essentially improved by the creation of new numbers such that the domain of numbers shall gain the same completeness, or as we may say at once, the same continuity, as the straight line' (Dedekind 1909: 8–9). According to Marion (1998: 211), Dedekind's intention was to complement the domain of the rational numbers with irrational numbers and, in this way, to arithmetically achieve the continuity that is proper to the straight line. Thus what Dedekind did was extending the principle of geometrical continuity onto arithmetic. According to Wittgenstein, Dedekind's proof that there were infinitely many cuts of the rational numbers was legitimized by the vision of continuity, while it should have been the other way round, that is, the vision should have been legitimized by proof.
34 Cf. MS, 108, 179.
35 Cf. Floyd and Mühlhölzer (2020: 140–1).
36 Cf. RFM, II, 21.
37 Mühlhölzer (Floyd and Mühlhölzer 2020: 136) claims that Wittgenstein perceived a serious disproportion between the simplicity of Cantor's method and the fundamental and seminal mathematical result achieved through this method. This lies at the core of Wittgenstein's philosophical consideration in the second part of

RFM and represents the most fruitful perspective of his investigations. Mühlhölzer (Floyd and Mühlhölzer 2020: 171) also stresses that although the 'hocus-pocus', that is, the extensionalist model, was developed in the form of axiomatic systems, it came at a price. Most currently used mathematical methods and techniques do not accept set-theoretical axioms.

38   Cf. Floyd and Mühlhölzer (2020: 33).
39   'Cantor shews that if we have a system of expansion it makes sense to speak of an expansion that is different from them all. – But that is not enough to determine the grammar of the word "expansion"' (RFM, II, 30).
40   Cf. Schroeder (2014: 22*pass*.).
41   Rodych dubs it an '*extra*systemic application criterion'. See Rodych (2000: 302).
42   See RFM, II, 16.
43   In *Lectures and Conversations on Aesthetics, Psychology, and Religious Belief*, Wittgenstein suggested that many of the explanations offered by psychoanalysis were endorsed because there was a magnetism and appeal to them: 'The picture of people having subconscious thought has a charm. The idea of an underworld, a secret cellar. Something hidden, uncanny' (LCA, 25). Freud's interpretations particularly captivate us and appear irresistibly attractive not because they are founded on solid empirical knowledge, but because they essentially express a certain *mindset*. In Wittgenstein's view, Cantor's theory is steeped in a similar charm and loveliness:

> E.g. I pulled Ursell's proof to bits. But after I had done, he said that the proof had a charm. Here I could only say: 'It has no charm for me, I loathe it.' Cf. The expression 'The Cardinal number of all Cardinal numbers.'

> 38. Cf. Cantor wrote how marvellous it was that the mathematician could in his imagination [mind–T] transcend all limits.

> 39. I would do my utmost to show it is this charm that makes one do it. Being Mathematics or Physics it looks incontrovertible and this gives it a still greater charm. If we explain the surroundings of the expression we see that the thing could have been expressed in an entirely different way. (LCA, 28)

44   See RFM II, 16. These ideas reverberate in §412 of the *Philosophical Investigations*, where Wittgenstein dwells on 'giddiness, which occurs when we are doing logical tricks. (The same giddiness attacks us when dealing with certain theorems in set theory.)'
45   Regarding this, Rotter (2006: 99) identifies an evolution from intuitionist radicalism to descriptiveness and pragmatism in Wittgenstein's ideas in the 1940s. This tendency, which can be called grammatical, seems to have already surfaced in the early 1930s, as suggested by Wittgenstein's criticism of Dedekind's definition of infinite set.
46   Cf. Floyd and Mühlhölzer (2020: 141).

47 Cf. Frascolla (1994: 97).
48 Cf. Dauben (1990: 134–7).
49 I discuss this in Chapter 8.

Chapter 5

1   See MS, 109, 205–6 and 211–12.
2   Cf. Krüger (1993: 309). In Wolfgang Kienzler's view (1997: 83–8), it is not TS, 208 as such but Wittgenstein's work on it that is a decisive factor in establishing the beginning of Wittgenstein's late philosophy. While reworking TS, 208, in Kienzler's account, Wittgenstein proceeded in a very systematic fashion to produce a kind of philosophical inventory aimed at separating the ideas and insights he considered meaningful at the time from those he believed wrong. Kienzler refers to revising TS 208 as the 'resumption' (*die Wiederaufnahme*), which channelled a shift towards Wittgenstein's late philosophy.
3   This view is represented by, for example, Alois Pichler (2004: 80).
4   In TS, 211, Wittgenstein arranged his manuscripts in the sequence of MS, 111; MS, 110; MS, 109; MS, 112; MS, 113 and the beginning of MS, 114.
5   For detailed information on the dating of the manuscripts used to compose TS, 213, see Krüger (1993: 303–13).
6   Cf. Nedo (2000: VII).
7   See Kienzler 2006: 14. A similar view is held by Rhees (1974: 488) and Michael Nedo (1994: XII), with the latter insisting that, contrary to common belief, Wittgenstein's typescripts from this period are not revisions of and improvements on the manuscripts; rather, the typescripts simply replace them with a view to facilitating further work on them.
8   The title was first used in print by Georg Henrik von Wright. In his editorial note to *Philosophical Grammar*, Rhees refers to it as 'The large typescript of 1933'. See Rhees (1974: 488).
9   Cf. BB, v–vi.
10 On this issue, see Stern (1991: 203).
11 This statement is to be found in TLP, 2.1512–2.15121.
12 Cf. e.g. Glock (1996: 67*pass*.).
13 For a discussion of this issue in relation to the 'middle Wittgenstein', see Engelmann (2013: 93–111).
14 Cf. Schulte, 'Introduction' to TS, 213, www.wittgensteinsouce.
15 On this issue, cf. Weisberg (2006: 248–9).
16 Cf. Engelmann (2013: 215*pass*.).

17 This take on philosophy was doubtlessly affected by Russell's lecture 'On Scientific Method in Philosophy', in which Russell stressed the intimate interrelation (if not identity) of philosophy and logic, insisting that the former was a theory of logical forms. Cf. Russell (1917: 97–125).
18 See 4.111: 'The word "philosophy" must mean something whose place is above or below the natural sciences, not beside them.'
19 See BT, 406.
20 The remark on working on oneself in philosophy and architecture is dated on 14 October 1931 (cf. MS, 112, 46). It cannot be ruled out that it drew on Wittgenstein's own experiences as an architect. Wittgenstein and his friend, architect Paul Engelmann, are known to have helped design and build a house for Wittgenstein's sister Margarette between 1926 and 1928.
21 See Hacker (1986: 129).

Chapter 6

1 Russell advocated this conception in *The Analysis of Mind*. In February 1930, Wittgenstein wrote some critical remarks about Russell's theory, particularly about his account of desire as an external relation between a desire and what satisfies it (cf. MS, 107, 289–295; PR, 63–64). Wittgenstein insisted that this relation was *internal* like the relation between a proposition and what makes it true, an expectation and its fulfilment and an order and its execution. It is noteworthy that these remarks were not incorporated into BT, and that Wittgenstein did not refer to internal and external relations in his account of desire there. For more comments on Wittgenstein's remarks from 1930, see Hacker (1993: 108–12).
2 See BT, 365.
3 On this issue, see Hacker (1986: chapter VII).

Chapter 7

1 In all probability, when noting these remarks Wittgenstein had an abridged (one-volume) edition of *The Golden Bough* from 1922 at his disposal. Like Wittgenstein, Frazer was a fellow at Trinity College, where he lectured on 'The Fear of the Dead in Primitive Religion' in the academic year 1932/1933. At that time, Wittgenstein held his lectures in a hall adjacent to Frazer's and most likely attended the latter's lecture when his own one was rescheduled from Monday, 8 May, to Tuesday, 9 May. Josef Rothhaupt, who provides this piece of information, also cites some

similarities in the content of Frazer's and Wittgenstein's lectures. See Rothhaupt 2016: 74–80.

2   See Ludwig Wittgenstein, 'Bemerkungen über Frazers *Golden Bough*,' *Synthese*, 17 (3) (1967): 233–53. The first part of this edition is composed of notes from 1931 (MS 110, 177–300). The second part comprises later passages the dating of which is unclear and which were included in MS, 143. Rush Rhees argues that they were produced much later than the notes in part one, in 1936 at the earliest, though probably as late as after 1948. However, Rothhaupt (2016: 11–85) claims that the May Term lectures of 1933, recorded by George Moore, prove that these notes were produced in 1933, rather than in 1936. Wittgenstein talked about fire festivals in Europe, including the festival of Beltane. Thus, there is good reason to believe that the notes in MS, 143 were compiled in 1933 in preparation for his lectures (and possibly further work). Cf. also Brusotti (2014: 398–405).

3   Cf. Hacker (2001: 79).

4   For a more detailed discussion of perspicuity and perspicuous representation, see Baker and Hacker (2005: 303–34). On references to and conceptual contexts of the notion of 'perspicuous representation' in 'Remarks on Frazer's *Golden Bough*', see Brusotti (2014: 192–205).

5   He further specified the two divergent approaches to history: Consequently, in a research such as that lying before us there can be no question of taking spiritual-political events, as they become visible day by day on the surface, at their face value, and arranging them on the scheme of 'causes' or 'effects' and following them up in the obvious and intellectually easy directions. Such a 'pragmatic' handling of history would be nothing but a piece of 'natural science' … What concerns us is not what the historical facts which appear at this or that time *are*, per se, but what they signify, what they point to, *by appearing*. (Spengler 1926: 6–7, italics original)

6   On this issue, see Rothhaupt (2016: 25).

7   'The colour-octahedron is grammar because it tells us that we can talk about a reddish blue, but not about a reddish green, etc. The representation via the octahedron is a surveyable representation of the grammatical rules' (BT, 441).

8   Brian McGuinness makes a rather unfounded claim that Wittgenstein subscribed to a barely tenable idea that we could always understand primitive rituals through evoking the inclinations we ourselves felt. Moreover, he contends that '[w]e feel that we could invent primitive usages' (McGuinness 1982: 37). However, as Cioffi notes with undisguised sarcasm: 'Is McGuinness aware of any inclination in himself to determine whether someone is a witch by feeding poison to a chicken? … There is no more reason to think that McGuinness could have invented the Azande poison oracle than that the Azande could have invented the Mass' (Cioffi 1998: 191–2).

9   See Hacker (2001: 83).

10 Rodney Needham, who comments on 'Remarks on Frazer's *Golden Bough*' as an anthropologist, observes that the 'what one knows' criterion is thoroughly uncertain. Ethnographic and anthropological reports must not be a priori considered objective knowledge as they first and foremost demand assessment and careful interpretation. Contrary to Wittgenstein's insistence, ethnographers must in fact add quite a lot in order to arrive at a reliable cognitive evaluation of the empirical material provided by ethnographers. It is by far not enough to piece it together correctly (see Needham 2018: 236). It is probable that Wittgenstein would have agreed with this view, but what he had in mind was something else: a *way (form)* of arranging the ethnographic material rather than its *content*. 'What one knows' must evidently be based on strong foundations, and Wittgenstein does not negate that the data provided by Frazer – his descriptions of rituals – have such reliable underpinnings, but they are ordered in a hypothetical way that Wittgenstein believed was faulty.

11 See Hacker (2012: 88–91).

12 The anti-scientistic tenor of 'Remarks on Frazer's *Golden Bough*' is highlighted by Coliva (2017: 39–59).

13 Renan also wrote a book about the Nemi ritual, entitled *La Prêtre de Némi*, which was known to Frazer. See Brusotti (2014: 42, 36n).

14 See MS, 162b, 67.

15 Brusotti analyses these remarks as evolving, from the first part edited by Rhees (i.e. notes from 1931) through Moore's notes from the May Term lectures of 1933 to the second part comprising later notes from MS, 143.

16 Apparently, an attempt at outlining the philosophical context of 'Remarks on Frazer's *Golden Bough*' has been undertaken by Heinz Wilhelm Krüger (2014: 101–28). Regrettably, Krüger only focuses on an immanent analysis of the determinacy of sense and meaning in Wittgenstein's manuscripts from the 1930s and in the *Philosophical Investigations* and fails to define the connection between these issues and comments on Frazer's study.

Chapter 8

1 The English edition appeared in 1975.

2 Interestingly, the passages in which Wittgenstein reveals his attitude to his time also contain a remark about the *Tractatus*, suggesting that his worldview was intimately connected to his philosophy, and his thought was always interwoven with life, with the choice between the past and the present: 'In my old book [the *Tractatus*] the solution of the problem is still presented in a far too little homespun manner; there's still too much of the appearance that to solve our problems we should need some discoveries; everything is too little put in the form

of grammatical obviousnesses of ordinary language (ordinary way of expression). Everything still too much requires discoveries' (MS, 109, 213).

3   On Spengler's influence on Wittgenstein, see DeAngelis (2007); Haller (1988); Lurie (1989); Kienzler (2013).

4   Besides Spengler, Wittgenstein also named Boltzmann, Hertz, Schopenhauer, Frege, Russell, Kraus, Weininger and Sraffe as people who had had an important impact on him. See CV, 16.

5   See DeAngelis (2007: 41–2).

6   See Cavell (1988: 258). An expanded version of this paper is to be found in Cavell (1989).

7   The theme of subjective unity and similar ways of regaining it in Wittgenstein and Hölderlin is discussed by Richard Eldridge (Eldridge 2004: 211–28), who points out that they both insist on the impossibility of theoretical explanation of subjectivity and on the importance of transitions, modulation, thought, attitude, mood and feeling, as crucial to a person's life. Eldridge argues: 'The central idea of Hölderlin's poetology is that the successful poem will embody *transitions* or *modulations* among experiences and moods of independence and attunement, thereby showing that these experiences and moods can be coherently integrated with one another within a life. Against this background Wittgenstein can be seen to offer in his own itinerary similar transitions or modulations between independence and attunement and so likewise to offer us, through identification with his voices, the possibility for us to acknowledge fundamental conditions of human life' (2004: 213).

8   See Monk (1999: 66).

9   For example, in CV, 79–90 and in Z, §§159–167.

10 The translatory difficulties involved in translating Wittgenstein, including the quoted remark, are discussed by Perloff (2011: 278–80). See also Schalkwyk 2004: 56–9. For his part Wolfgang Kienzler claims that *dichten* refers to Wittgenstein's work on his own writing, which he repeatedly corrected, revised and reworked. This meaning dovetails with Spengler's insight that '[n]ature is to be handled scientifically, history poetically' ('Natur soll man wissenschaftlich traktieren, über Geschichte soll man dichten', Spengler 1920: 139.) See Kienzler (2006: 17).

11 Qtd. in Nedo (2020: 168).

12 See Perloff (1996: 6–10).

References

Albinus, J., J. Rothhaupt and L. Seery, eds. (2016), *Wittgenstein's Remarks on Frazer: The Text and the Matter*, Berlin and Boston: De Gruyter.

Baker, G. P and P.M.S. Hacker (2005), *Wittgenstein: Understanding and Meaning. Volume I of An Analytical Commentary on the* Philosophical Investigation: *Part I: Essays*, Oxford: Blackwell Publishing.

Beale, J. and I.J. Kidd, eds. (2017), *Wittgenstein and Scientism*, London and New York: Routledge.

Bengtsson, G., S. Säätelä and A. Pichler, eds. (2018), *New Essays on Frege: Between Science and Literature*, Cham: Springer.

Bernays, P. (1959), 'Comments on L. Wittgenstein's "Remarks on Foundation of Mathematics"', *Ratio*, 2 (1): 1–22.

Black, M. (1964), *A Companion to Wittgenstein's Tractatus*, Ithaca, NY: Cornell University Press.

Blank, A. (2011), 'Wittgenstein on Verification and Seeing-As, 1929–1932', *Inquiry*, 54 (6): 614–32.

Block, I., ed. (1981), *Perspectives on the Philosophy of Wittgenstein*, Oxford: Basil Blackwell.

Bouveresse, J. (2008), 'Wittgenstein's Critique of Frazer', in J. Preston (ed.), *Wittgenstein and Reason*, pp. 1–21. Oxford: Blackwell Publishing.

Brusotti, M. (2014), *Wittgenstein, Frazer und die 'Ethnologische Betrachtungsweise'*, Berlin and Boston: De Gruyter.

Burge, T. (1992), 'Frege on Knowing the Third Realm', *Mind*, 101 (404): 633–50.

Cantor, G. (1932), *Gesammelte Abhandlungen mathematischen und philosophischen Inhalts*, hrsg. E. Zermelo, Berlin: Verlag von Julius Springer.

Carnap, R. (1963), 'Intellectual Autobiography', in P.A. Schilpp (ed.), *The Philosophy of Rudolf Carnap*, pp. 1–84. Illinois: The Library of Living Philosophers, volume XI, Open Court, La Salle.

Carnap, R. (2003), 'The Logical Structure of the World and Pseudoproblems in Philosophy', translated by R.A. George, Open Court, chicago and La Salle, Illinois.

Cavell, S. (1988), 'Declining Decline: Wittgenstein as a Philosopher of Culture', *Inquiry*, 31 (3): 253–64.

Cavell, S. (1989), *This New yet Unapproachable America: Lectures after Emerson after*, Chicago: The University of Chigaco Press.

Cioffi, F. (1998), *Wittgenstein on Freud and Frazer*, Cambridge: University Press, Cambridge.

Coliva, A. (2017), 'Rituals, Philosophy, Science and Progress: Wittgenstein on Frazer', in J. Beale and I.J. Kidd (eds.), *Wittgenstein and Scientism*, pp. 39–59. London and New York: Routledge.

Crary, A., ed. (2007), *Wittgenstein and the Moral Life. Essays in Honor of Cora Diamond*, Massachusetts: The MIT Press.

Da Col, G. and S. Palmií, eds. (2018), *The Mythology in our Language*, Chicago: Hau Books.

Da Silva, J.J. (1993), 'Wittgenstein on Irrational Numbers', in K. Puhl (ed.), *Wittgensteins Philosophie der Mathematik. Akten des 15. Internationalen Wittgenstein-Symposiums*, pp. 93–100. Wien: Verlag Hölder-Pichler-Tempsky.

Dauben, J.W. (1990), *Georg Cantor: His Mathematics and Philosophy of the Infinite*, Princeton: Princeton University Press.

Dawson, R. (2016), 'Wittgenstein on Set Theory and the Enormously Big', *Philosophical Investigation*, 39 (4): 313–34.

DeAngelis, W.J. (2007), *Ludwig Wittgenstein – A Cultural Point of View: Philosophy in the Darkness of this Times*, Burlington: Ashgate.

Dedekind, R. (1872), *Stetigkeit und irrationale Zahlen*, Braunschweig: Friedrich Vieweg und Sohn.

Dedekind, R. (1909), *Theory of Numbers: I. Continuity and Irrational Numbers; II. The Nature and Meaning of Numbers*, trans. W.W. Beman, Chicago: Open Court Publishing Company.

Dummett, M. (1978), *Truth and Other Enigmas*, London: Duckworth.

Dummett, M. (1981), 'Frege and Wittgenstein', in I. Block (ed.), *Perspectives on the Philosophy of Wittgenstein*, pp. 31–43. Oxford: Basil Blackwell.

Dummett, M. (1991), *Frege Philosophy of Mathematics*, London: Duckworth.

Dummett, M. (1993), *Origins of Analytical Philosophy*, London: Gerald Duckworth & Co.

Eldrige, R. (2004), 'Rotating the Axis of Our Investigation: Wittgenstein's Investigation and Hölderlin's Poetology', in J. Gibson and W. Huemer (eds.), *The Literary Wittgenstein*, pp. 211–28. London and New York: Routledge.

Engelmann, M. (2013), *Wittgenstein's Philosophical Development: Phenomenology, Grammar, Method, and the Anthropological View*, New York: Palgrave Macmillan.

Feigl, H. (1980), 'The Wiener Kreis in America', in R. S Cohen (ed.), *Inquieries and Provocations: Selected Writings 1927–1974*, pp. 57–94. Dordrecht: D. Reidel.

Ferreirós, J. (2007), *Labyrinth of Thought. A History of Set Theory and Its Role in Modern Mathematics*, second revised edition, Basel-Boston-Berlin: Birkhäser.

Floyd, J. and F. Mühlhölzer (2020), *Wittgenstein's Annotations to Hardy's Course of Pure Mathematics: An Investigation of Wittgenstein's Non-Extensionalist Understanding of the Real Numbers*, Nordic Wittgenstein Studies, Cham: Springer.

Frascolla, P. (1994), *Wittgenstein's Philosophy of Mathematics*, London and New York: Routledge.

Frascolla, P. (1998), 'The Early Wittgenstein's Logicism', *Acta Analytica*, 13 (21): 133–8.

Frascola, P. (2017), 'Early Philosophy of Mathematics', in H.-J. Glock and J. Hyman (eds.), *A Companio to Wittgenstein*, pp. 305–19. Oxford: Wiley Blackwell.

Frazer, J.G. (1922), *The Golden Bough: A Study in Magic and Religion*, Abridged edition, London: Macmillan Press.

Frege, G. (1953), *The Foundations of Arithmetic: A Logico-Mathematical Enquiry into the Concept of Number*, trans. J. L. Austin, 2nd rev. edn, New York: Harper Brothers.

Frege, G. (1984), *Collected Papers on Mathematics, Logic and Philosophy*, ed. B. McGuinness, Oxford: Basil Blackwell.

Frege, G. (1986), *Die Grundlagen der Arithmetik*, hrsg. von Ch. Thiel, Hamburg: Meiner Verlag.

Frege, G. (1993), *Begriffsschrift, eine der arithmetischen nachgebildete Formelsprache des reinen Denkens*, hrsg. I. Angelelli, Hildesheim, Zürich and New York: Georg Olms Verlag.

Frege, G. (2013), *Basic Laws of Arithmetic: Volumes 1 & 2*, ed. and trans. P. A. Ebert and M. Rossberg with C. Wright, Oxford: Oxford University Press.

Gibson, A. and N. O'Mahony, eds. (2020), *Ludwig Wittgenstein: Dictating Philosophy to Francis Skinner – The Wittgenstein-Skinner Manuscripts*, Cham: Springer.

Gier, N. (1981), *Wittgenstein and Phenomenology: A Comparative Study of the Later Wittgenstein, Husserl Heidegger and Merleau-Ponty*, Albany: SUNY Press.

Glock, H.-J. (1990), '*Philosophical Investigations*: Principles of Interpretation', in J. Brandl and R. Haller (eds.), *Wittgenstein – Towards a Reevaluation*, pp. 152–62. Vienna: Hölder-Pichler-Tempsky.

Glock, H.-J. (1996), *A Wittgenstein Dictionary*, Oxford: Blackwell Publishing.

Hacker, P.M.S. (1981), 'The Rise and Fall of the Picture Theory', in I. Block (ed.), *Perspectives on the Philosophy of Wittgenstein*, pp. 85–110. Oxford: Basil Blackwell.

Hacker, P.M.S. (1986), *Insight and Illusion: Themes in the Philosophy of Wittgenstein*, Oxford: Clarendon Press.

Hacker, P.M.S. (1993), *Wittgenstein. Meaning and Mind.* Volume 3 of An Analytical Commentary on the Philosophical Investigation: *Part I: Essays*, Oxford: Blackwell Publishing.

Hacker, P.M.S. (1996), *Wittgenstein's Place in Twentieth-Century Analytic Philosophy*, Oxford: Blackwell.

Hacker, P.M.S. (2001), *Wittgenstein: Connections and Controversies*, Oxford: Clarendon Press.

Hacker, P.M.S. (2010), 'Wittgenstein's Anthropological and Ethnological Approach', in J. Padilla Gálvez (ed.), *Philosophical Anthropology: Wittgenstein's Perspective*, pp. 15–33. Heusenstamm: Ontos Verlag.

Hacker, P.M.S. (2013), *Wittgenstein: Comparison and Context*, Oxford: Oxford University Press.

Haller, R. (1988), 'Was Wittgenstein Influenced by Spengler?' in *Questions on Wittgenstein*, 74–89. Omaha: University of Nebraska Press.

Hilmy, S. (1987), *The Later Wittgenstein: The Emergence of a New Philosophical Method*, Oxford: Blackwell.
Hintikka, J. (1991), 'An Impatient Man and His Papers', *Synthese*, 87 (2): 183–201.
Hintikka, J. (1996), *Ludwig Wittgenstein: Half-Truths and One-and-a-Half-Truths*, Dordrecht: Springer-Science +Bissens Media.
Hintikka, M.B. and J. Hintikka (1986), *Investigating Wittgenstein*, Oxford: Blackwell.
Husserl, E. (1968), *Phänomenologische Psychologie. Vorlesungen Sommersemester 1925*, hrsg. von W. Biemel, Dordrecht: Springer-Science +Bissens Media.
Husserl, E. (2012), *Logical Investigations. Volume 1*, trans. J. N. Findlay, London and New York: Routledge.
Hymers, M. (2005), 'Going Around the Vienna Circle: Wittgenstein and Verification', *Philosophical Investigation*, 28 (3): 205–34.
Janik, A. and S. Toulmin (1973), *Wittgenstein's Vienna*, New York: Touchstone.
Kenny, A (1976), 'From the *Big Typescript* to the *Philosophical Grammar*', *Acta Philosophica Fennica*, 28: 41–53.
Kenny, A. (2005), 'A Brief History of Wittgenstein Editing', in A. Pichler and S. Säätelä (eds.), *Wittgenstein: The Philosopher and His Works*, pp. 341–56. Bergen: Working Papers from the Wittgenstein Archives at the University of Bergen.
Kienzler, W. (1997), *Wittgensteins Wende zu seiner Spätphilosophie 1930–1932*, Frankfurt am Main: Suhrkapm.
Kienzler, W. (2006), 'Die Stellung des Big Typescripts in Wittgensteins Werkentwicklung', in S. Majetschak (ed.), *Wittgensteins 'große Maschinenschrif*, pp. 11–31. Frankfurt am Main: Peter Lang.
Kienzler, W. (2013), 'Wittgenstein und Spengler', in J.G.F. Rothhaupt and W. Vossenkuhl (eds.), *Kulturen und Werte*, 317–39. Berlin and Boston: De Gruyter.
Kroß, M. ed. (2008), *'Ein Netz von Normen'. Wittgenstein und die Mathematik*, Berlin: Parerga.
Krüger, H.W. (1993), 'Die Entstehung des *Big Typescript*', in K. Puhl (ed.), *Wittgensteins Philosophie der Mathematik. Akten des 15. Internationalen Wittgenstein-Symposiums. II*, pp. 303–13. Wien: Verlag Hölder-Pichler-Tempsky.
Krüger, H.W. (2014), 'The Determinacy of Sense and Meaning', in L. Albinus, J. Rothhaupt and A. Seery (eds.), *Wittgenstein's Remarks on Frazer: The Text and the Matter*, pp. 101–29. Berlin and Boston: De Gruyter.
Kuratowski, K. and A. Mostowski (1978), *Teoria mnogości*, Warszawa: PWN.
Kuusela, O., M. Ometit and T. Uça, eds. (2018), *Wittgenstein and Phenomenology*, New York: Routledge.
Lugg, A. (2013), 'Wittgenstein in Mid-1930s: Calculi and Language Games', in N. Venturinha (ed.), *The Textual Genesis of Wittgenstein's Philosophical Investigations*, 134–54. New York and London: Routledge.
Lurie, Y. (1989), 'Wittgenstein on Culture and Civilization', *Inquiry*, 32 (4): 375–97.
Majetschak, S. ed. (2006), *Wittgensteins 'große Maschinenschrift'. Wittgenstein-Studien*, Frankfurt am Main: Peter Lang.

Marion, M. (1998), *Wittgenstein, Finitism, and the Foundations of Mathematics*, Oxford: Clarendon Press.
McGuinness, B. (1982), 'Freud and Wittgenstein', in A. Kenny and B. McGuinness (eds.), *Wittgenstein and His Times*, pp. 27–4. Oxford: Basil Blackwell.
McGuinness, B. (2002), *Approaches to Wittgenstein*, London: Routledge.
McGuinness, B., ed. (2012), *Wittgenstein in Cambridge: Letters and Documents 1911–1959*, Malden and Oxford: B. Wiley-Blackwell.
Medina, J. (2002), *The Unity of Wittgenstein's Philosophy*, New York: State University of New York Press.
Methven, S. J. (2015), *Frank Ramsey and the Realistic Spirit*, Basingstoke: Palgrave Macmillan.
Misak, C.J. (2005), *Verificationism: Its History and Prospects*, New York: Routledge.
Monk, R. (1991), *Wittgenstein: The Duty of Genius*, London: Vintage.
Monk, R. (1999), 'Wittgenstein's Forgotten Lesson', *Prospect Magazine*, 7. Available online: www.prospectmagazine.co.u/magazine/ray-monk-wittgenstein/#. Ur.Guo42zccs.
Monk, R. (2014), 'The Temptation of Phenomenology: Wittgenstein, the Synthetic a Priori and the Analytic a Posteriori', *International Journal of Philosophical Studies*, 22 (3): 312–40.
Moore, A. W. (1991), *Infinity*, London: Routledge.
Mühlhölzer, F. (2008), 'Wittgenstein und der Formalismus', in M. Kroß (ed.), *'Ein Netz von Normen': Wittgenstein und die Mathematik*, pp. 107–49. Berlin: Parerga.
Mühlhölzer, F. (2010), *Braucht die Mathematik eine Grundlegung? Eine Kommentar des Teils III von Wittgensteins 'Bemerkungen über die Grundlegung der Mathematik'*, Frankfurt am Main: Vittorio Klostermann.
Munson, T.W. (1962), 'Wittgenstein's Phenomenology', *Philosophy and Phenomenological Research*, 23 (1): 37–50.
Nedo, M. (1994), 'Einleitung', in Ludwig Wittgenstein, *Wiener Ausgabe*, Bd. 1, ed. M. Nedo, pp. VII–XIX. Wien: Springer.
Nedo, M. (2000), 'Einleitung', in Ludwig Wittgenstein, *Wiener Ausgabe*, Bd. 11 *The Big Typescript*, ed. M. Nedo, pp. VII–XI. Wien and New York: Springer-Verlag.
Nedo, M. (2020), 'Wittgenstein's Philosophy: Reorientating Science', in S. Wuppuri, N. da Costa (eds.), *Wittgensteinian (adj.). Looking at the World from the Viewpoint of Wittgenstein's Philosophy*, pp. 165–93. Cham: Springer.
Needham, R. (2018), 'Remarks on Wittgenstein and Ritual', in G. Da Col and S. Palmié (eds.), *The Mythology in Our Language*, pp. 227–50. Chicago: Hau Books.
Park, B-C. (1998), *Phenomenological Aspects of Wittgenstein's Philosophy*, Dordrecht: Springer-Science+Business Media.
Perloff, M. (1996), *Wittgenstein's Ladder: Poetic Language and the Strangeness of the Ordinary*, Chicago and London: The University of Chicago Press.
Perloff, M. (2011), 'Writing Philosophy as Poetry: Wittgenstein's Literary Syntax', in V. Munz, K. Puhl and J. Wang (eds.), *Language and World: Part Two. Signs, Minds and Actions*, pp. 277–96. Heusenstamm: Ontos Verlag.

Peursen, C.A. van (1959), 'Edmund Husserl and Ludwig Wittgenstein', *Philosophy and Phenomenological Research*, 20 (2): 181-97.

Pichler, A. (2004), *Wittgensteins 'Philosophische Untersuchungen': Vom Buch zum Album*, Amsterdam and New York: Rodopi.

Pichler, A. (2018), *Wittgenstein on Understanding: Language, Calculus, and Practice*, in D. Stern (ed.), *Wittgenstein in the 1930s: Between the* Tractatus *and the* Investigations, 45-60, Cambridge and New York: Cambridge University Press.

Pichler, A. and S. Säätelä, eds. (2005), *Wittgenstein: The Philosopher and His Works*, Bergen: Working Papers from the Wittgenstein Archives at the University of Bergen.

Preston, J., ed. (2008), *Wittgenstein and Reason*, Oxford: Blackwell.

Preston, J. (2017), 'Wittgenstein, Herz, and Bolzmann', in: H.-J. Glock and J. Hyman (eds.), *A Companion to Wittgenstein*, pp. 110-25. Oxford: Wiley-Blackwell.

Putnam, H. (2007), 'Wittgenstein and the Real Numbers', in A. Crary (ed.), *Wittgenstein and the Moral Life: Essays in Honor of Cora Diamond*, pp. 235-51. Massachusetts: The MIT Press.

Rhees, R. (1974), 'Note on Editing', in Ludwig Wittgenstein, *Philosophical Grammar*, ed. R. Rhees, 487-91. Oxford: Basil Blackwell.

Rhees, R., ed. (1984), *Recollections of Wittgenstein*, Oxford: University Press.

Ramsey, F. (1923), 'Critical Notice of L. Wittgenstein's *Tractatus Logico-Philosophicus*', *Mind*, 32 (128): 465-78.

Ramsey, F. (1950), 'General Propositions and Causality', in F. Ramsey (ed.), *The Foundations of Mathematics and Other Logical Essays*, ed. R.B. Braithwaite, 237-56. London: Routledge.

Rodych, V. (1995), 'Pasquale Frascolla's *Wittgenstein's Philosophy of Mathematics*', *Philosophia Mathematica*, 3 (3): 271-88.

Rodych, V. (2000), 'Wittgenstein's Critique of Set Theory', *Southern Journal of Philosophy*, XXXVIII: 281-319.

Rothhaupt, J.G.F. (2010), 'Wittgenstein at Work: Creation, Selection and Composition of *Remarks*', in N. Venturinha (ed.), *Wittgenstein After His Nachlass*, pp. 51-64. New York: Palgrave Macmillan.

Rothhaupt, J.G.F. (2016), 'Wittgensteins "Bemerkungen über Frazeres *Golden Bough*". Verortung im Gesamtnachlass – Einbindung in die Philosophietradition – Editions – und Publikationsgeschichte', in J. Albinus, J. Rothhaupt and L. Seery (eds.), *Wittgenstein's Remarks on Frazer: The Text and the Matter*, pp. 11-85. Berlin and Boston: De Gruyter.

Rothhaupt, J.G.F. and W. Vossenkuhl, eds. (2013), *Kulturen und Werte*, Berlin and Boston: De Gruyter.

Rotter, K. (2006), *Gramatyka filozoficzna w dobie sporu o podstawy matematyki. Eseje o drugiej filozofii Wittgensteina*, Opole: Wydawnictwo Uniwersytetu Opolskiego.

Russell, B. (1917), *Mysticism and Logic and Other Essays*, London: George Allen & Unwin Ltd.

Russell, B. (1993), *Introduction to Mathematical Philosophy*, New York: Dover Publications.

Schalkwyk, D. (2004), 'Wittgenstein's "Imperfect Garden". The Ladders and Labyrinths of Philosophy as Dichtung', in J. Gibson and W. Huemer (eds.), *The Literary Wittgenstein*, pp. 55–75. London and New York: Routledge.

Schulte, J. (1998), 'Review of Wolfgang Kienzler *Wittgensteins Wende zu sejner Spätphilosophie 1930-1932*', *European Journal of Philosophy*, 6: 379–85.

Schulte, J. (2013), 'The Role of the Big Typescript in Wittgenstein's Later Writings', in N. Venturinha (ed.), *The Textual Genesis of Wittgenstein's* 'Philosophical Investigations', pp. 81–93. New York: Routledge. Macmillan.

Schlick, M. (1969), *Gesammelte Aufsätze 1926–36*, Hildesheim: Georg Olms Verlag.

Schroeder, S. (2014), 'Mathematical Propositions as Rules of Grammar', *Grazer Philosophische Studien*, 89 (I): 23–38.

Sellars, W. (1997), *Empiricism and the Philosophy of Mind*, Harvard: Harvard University Press.

Shanker, S. (1987), *Wittgenstein and the Turning-Point in the Philosophy of Mathematics*, London and New York: Routledge.

Spengler, O. (1920), *Der Untergang des Abendlandes*, vol. 1. München: C.H. Beck.

Spengler, O. (1926), *The Decline of the West: Form and Actuality. Vol. I*, trans. Ch.F. Atkinson, New York: Alfred A. Knopf.

Spiegelberg, H. (1968), 'The Puzzle of Wittgenstein's Phänomenologie (1929–?)', *American Philosophical Quarterly*, 5: 244–56.

Spiegelberg, H. (1981), *The Context of the Phenomenological Movement*, Dordrecht: Springer.

Stenlund, S. (2018), 'Frege's Critique of Formalism', in G. Bengtsson, S. Säätelä & A. Pichler (eds.), *New Essays on Frege: Between Science and Literature. Nordic Wittgenstein Studies*, vol. 3, pp. 75–86. Chem: Springer.

Stern, D. (1991), 'The Middle Wittgenstein: From Logical Atomism to Practical Holism', *Synthese*, 87: 203–26.

Stern, D. (2005), 'How Many Wittgensteins?', in A. Pichler and S. Säätelä (eds.), *Wittgenstein: The Philosopher and His Works*, 172–88. Bergen: Working Papers from the Wittgenstein Archives at the University of Bergen.

Stern, D. (2015), 'The Middle Wittgenstein Revisited', in D. Moyal-Sharrock, V. Munz & A. Coliva (eds.), *Mind, Language and Action: Proceedings of the 36th International Wittgenstein Symposium*, 205–23. Berlin, Munich and Boston: De Gruyter.

Stern, D., ed. (2018), *Wittgenstein in the 1930s: Between the* Tractatus *and the* Investigations, Cambridge and New York: Cambridge University Press.

Stern, D., B. Rogers and G. Citron, eds. (2016), *Wittgenstein's Lectures, Cambridge 1930-1933: From the Notes of G.E. Moore*, Cambridge: Cambridge University Press.

Thompson, J.M. (2008), *Wittgenstein on Phenomenology and Experience*, Publication from the Wittgenstein Archives and the University of Bergen, No. 21.

Venturinha, N., ed. (2010), *Wittgenstein after His Nachlass*, New York: Palgrave Macmillan.

Venturinha, N., ed. (2013), *The Textual Genesis of Wittgenstein's* Philosophical Investigations, New York and London: Routledge. (Kindle edition).
Vrahimis, A. (2014), 'Wittgenstein and the Phenomenological Movement: Reply to Monk', *International Journal of Philosophical Studies*, 22 (3): 341–8.
Waismann, F. (1930), 'Logische Analyse des Wahrscheinlichkeitsbegriffs', *Erkenntnis*, I: 228–48.
Waismann, F. (1977), 'A Logical Analysis of the Concept of Probability', trans. Hans Kaal, in F. Waismann, *Philosophical Papers*, ed. B. McGuinness, 4–21. Dordrecht and Boston: D. Reidel Publishing Company, 1977.
Weisberg, A. (2006), 'Auffassung der Mathematik im *The Big Typescript*', in S. Majetschak (ed.), *Wittgensteins 'große Maschinenschrift'*, 247–69. Frankfurt am Main: Peter Lang.
Wittgenstein, L. (1967), *Lectures and Conversations on Aesthetics, Psychology, and Religious Belief*, ed. C. Berrett, Oxford: Basil Blackwell.
Wittgenstein, L. (1979), *Wittgenstein's Lectures: Cambridge, 1932–1935*, ed. A. Ambrose, Oxford: Basil Blackwell.
Wittgenstein, L. (1980), *Wittgenstein's Lectures: Cambridge, 1930–1932: From the Notes of John King and Desmond Lee*, ed. D. Lee, Chicago: University of Chicago Press.
Wittgenstein, L. (1993), *Philosophical Occasions*, ed. J. Klagge and A. Nordmann, Indianapolis: Hackett.
Wittgenstein, L. (2016), *Wittgenstein: Lectures, Cambridge 1930–1933. From the Notes of G.E. Moore*, ed. D. Stern, B. Rogers and G. Citron, Cambridge: Cambridge University Press.
Wright, C. (1980), *Wittgenstein on the Foundation of Mathematics*, London: Duckworth.
Wright, G.H. von (1982), *Wittgenstein*, Oxford: Basil Blackwell.
Wrigley, M. (1989), 'Origins of Wittgenstein's Verificationism', *Synthese*, 78 (3): 265–90.
Wrigley, M. (1998), 'A Note on Arithmetic and Logic in the *Tractatus*', *Acta Analytica*, 21: 129–31.

Index

Locators followed by "n." indicate endnotes

analytic geometry (Descartes) 92
anthropological view 4–5, 7, 11, 134, 139, 146, 153, 194 n.10
anti-psychologism 115, 124
Aristotle 85
arithmetic (mathematics) 3, 56–7, 63–6, 68
　applications 57–8, 67–9, 185 n.3, 185 n.4, 186 n.5
　arbitrariness of 57
　arithmetical law 90
　axiomatization 78, 188 n.20
　equations, double role 69–71
　formal and contenual 68
　generality 185 n.10
　infinite expansion 89
　irrational/rational numbers 189 n.28, 189 n.33

Bemerkungen zur philosophischen Grammatik (*Remarks towards Philosophical Grammar*, Wittgenstein) 66
Bernays, Paul 91–2
The Big Typescript, BT (Wittgenstein) 3–8, 11–12, 19, 22, 32, 34–6, 46, 51, 64, 66, 72, 86, 90, 98, 103, 108, 110, 124, 126, 129–30, 133, 157, 188 n.25, 192 n.20
　Dedekind's method in 89
　expectation and wish 8, 127, 130–1
　form and content 114–18
　intention and depiction 8, 127–8
　'Mathematics Compared to a Game' 3, 66
　meta-logical quality in 126, 132
　middle Wittgenstein 110–13
　'On Set Theory' 86
　philosophy as working on oneself 119–22
　surveyable notation 38, 117
　thinking 8, 116, 126, 130
　Umarbeitungen 109
　understanding 7–8, 64, 114–16, 124–7, 130, 132
　write, intention to 107–10
Blank, Andreas 185 n.14
The Blue and Brown Book, BB (Wittgenstein) 5–7, 10–12, 52, 110, 113, 118, 127, 158, 166, 168, 181 n.13, 185 n.12
Boltzmann, Ludwig, *Populäre Schriften* 17
Bouveresse, Jacques 140
Brouwer, Luitzen 45, 74–5
　intuitionism 45–6
　'Mathematik, Wissenschaft und Sprache' 45
Brusotti, Marco 143, 155, 159–60, 194 n.15
　causal theory of meaning 156
　Wittgenstein, Frazer und die 'Ethnologische Betrachtungsweise' 155

calculation game (*Rechenspiel*) 56, 58, 66, 72
calculus (*Kalkül*)
　language as 1–5, 7, 35, 72, 112–13, 117, 175
　and prose (set theory) 81–101
Cantor, Georg 75, 76, 80–2, 85, 104–5, 188 n.22, 189 n.37, 190 n.39, 190 n.43
　diagonal method, Wittgenstein's criticism 82, 92–102
　Grundlagen einer allgemeinen Mannigfältigkeitslehre 85
　as scientific charlatan 103
　set theory (*see* set theory)
　super-system of higher-order 97
　suspect generality (*verdächtige Allgemeinheit*) 93, 101

Carnap, Rudolf 41, 181 n.7
  Der Logische Aufbau der Welt (*The Logical Structure of the World*) 16–17
  Die physikalische Sprache als Universalsprache der Wissenschaft 108
  Intellectual Autobiography 41
Cavell, Stanley 167–70
chess, game of 2–3, 57–9, 61, 64, 66–9
Cioffi, Frank 139, 147–9, 193 n.8. See also obscurantism
  historical and hermeneutic matters 152
  interpretation and objections 151
class theory (TLP) 76–9
  "and so on" concept 78
  formal concepts 79
  infinity 78–9
  logical space 79
  negation operation 77
  number, concept of 77–8
cogito principle 119
collage method 13, 107–8
colour exclusion problem 22–3, 31, 39, 44, 47–8, 53, 111–12, 182 n.15
colour octahedron 145, 193 n.7
'Communication of Personal Experience' 181 n.13
community of life 150
contenual arithmetic 68
context principle 62, 187 n.15
cultural symbolic system 150
culture 76, 137, 163, 166, 173, 179
  language 166
  Spengler 153, 165
  vision of (PI, Cavell) 167–70
Culture and Value, CV (Wittgenstein) 164, 176

Dawson, Ryan 102
DeAngelis, William J. 169
Dedekind, Richard 75, 80, 82, 102, 105, 189 n.29, 189 n.33
  cuts (rational numbers) 82, 88, 90–1, 98, 189 n.33
  infinite set, definition 86–8, 103, 190 n.45
  irrational numbers 88–9
  principle of continuity 88, 91
  and real numbers 86–92, 189 n.33
  Stetigkeit und irrationale Zahlen (*Continuity and Irrational Numbers*) 92
Dostoevsky, Fiodor 160
Drury, Maurice 133, 165
Dummett, Michael 45–6, 59, 186 n.5, 186 n.10

Eldridge, Richard 195 n.7
Elementare Theorie der analytischen Functionen einer complexen Veränderlichen (*Elementary Theory of Analytical Functions of a Complex Variable*) 56
Emile (Rousseau) 168
empirical propositions 98, 117, 119, 157
Engelmann, Mauro 4–6, 11, 22–3, 29–30, 182 n.17, 182 n.19
  external properties 22–3, 182–3 n.19
  internal properties 22, 182–3 n.19
Engelmann, Paul 192 n.20
ethics and religion 159–60
ethnological approach 155, 157–8, 161
Euclidean (physical) space 6, 29, 38, 183 n.23
evolutionary emotions (Darwin) 142

Feigl, Herbert 45, 53
Ferreirós, José 188 n.22
Findlay, John N. 16
finite class 87
formal arithmetic (*formale Arithmetik*) 56–7, 59, 68
formalism, critique of (Frege) 55–61, 64, 185 n.2, 186 n.8
  game and theory 58, 69, 72
  logicism and 65–6
  rule and equation 71
  Wittgenstein's defence 60–74
form of life (*Lebensform*) 4, 104, 163, 166–70, 179
Frazer, James George, *The Golden Bough* 8, 133–47, 150, 157, 192 n.1. See also 'Remarks on Frazer's *Golden Bough*', RGB (Wittgenstein)
Frege, Gottlob 1, 6–7, 43, 60, 75–6, 79, 115, 177, 185 n.3, 186 n.5, 186 n.12
  applicability (*Anwendbarkeit*) 57–8
  Begriffsschrift 72, 182 n.17

critique of psychologism 67, 185 n.2
formale Arithmetik (formal arithmetic) 56–7, 59, 68
formalism, critique of (*see* formalism, critique of (Frege))
game theory, rules 58–9
Grundgesetze der Arithmetik (*The Basic Laws of Arithmetic*) 56, 62, 66, 69, 186 n.5
Grundlagen der Arithmetik 187 n.15, 187 n.21
immense intellectual effort 68
infinite sequences and irrational numbers 59–60
metatheory 58–9, 73
sense (*Sinn*) and meaning (*Bedeutung*) 7, 62–3, 65, 73, 186 n.10
Freud, Sigmund 166, 168, 190 n.43

game
of chess 2–3, 57–9, 61, 64, 66–9
language as 1–4, 10–12, 35, 112–13, 117, 123
mathematics and 67–8
mere game (*müßiges Spiel*) 62
and theory 58–9, 69–70, 72, 186 n.8
genetic method 4–5, 11
genuineness of expression 175
genuine propositions (*eigentliche Sätze*) 50, 79, 185 n.10
Gibson, A. 10
Glock, Hans-Johann 4, 187 n.5
axiom of finitude 81
Goethe, Johann Wolfgang
Dichtung und Wahrheit 176
Die Metamorphose der Pflanzen (*The Metamorphosis of Plants*) 145–6, 153
secret law 145–6
grammar 4–6, 11, 18–19, 23–4, 27, 33, 97, 116–18, 123, 156, 180 n.5
colour-octahedron 193 n.7
of ordinary language 36, 116, 118, 123, 194–5 n.2
phenomena themselves 23, 36, 38–9
phenomenology as 34–9
system of rules 39, 157–8
true circle 37
verification as 52–4
visual space 37–8
Großes Format 109

Hacker, Peter M. S. 44, 126, 152, 175
Catholic confession of sins 152
doctrine of isomorphism 43, 128
historicism without history 158
language as calculus 1–2
method obscurantism 152–3
Hegel, Georg Wilhelm Friedrich 103, 188 n.22
Heine, Eduard 56, 63, 72
Hertz, Heinrich, *Die Prinzipien der Mechanik* 17
Hilbert, David 65, 69, 72, 74–5, 80–1
Formelspiel 185 n.1
'technique of our thinking' 69
Hilmy, Stephen 113, 115
Hintikka, Jaakko 34–5, 110, 123, 181 n.11, 183 n.24
Hintikka, Merrill B. 35, 123
hints, philosophy 9
Hjelmslev, Johannes 183 n.23
Hölderlin, Friedrich 176
'Bread and Wine' 170–2
poverty (*Dürftigkeit*) 170–2
Wittgenstein and 170–5, 195 n.7
Horror Infiniti 80–1
Husserl, Edmund 14–16, 36, 124–6, 181 n.11, 183 n.26
epoché 183 n.26
Logical Investigations 16, 124
Hymers, Michael, 'Going Around the Vienna Circle: Wittgenstein and Verification' 53
hypotheses and mathematical propositions 50–2

immediate and propositional knowledge 125
immediate presence of meaning 125
infinite class 87
infinite/infinity, mathematical 1, 46, 82–4, 100, 188 n.20
actual 60, 79, 85–6, 89, 100–1, 103, 188 n.22
finiteness and 84
possibility 84–5, 97, 100
potential 59, 78, 85, 103, 188 n.22
qualitative 188 n.22
and quantification 80–1, 188 n.23
infinite series 95, 97, 100
infinite sets 84–9, 92, 94, 96–7, 100, 103, 190 n.45

intention and depiction (BT) 114, 127–8
    logical interest 128
    of reality 128–30
intuitionism (Brouwer) 45–6
irrational numbers 59, 88–92, 95–8, 189 n.28

Kant, Immanuel 32, 172–3, 189 n.28
Kenny, Anthony 110
Kienzler, Wolfgang 108, 182 n.17, 185 n.4, 186 n.8, 186 n.12, 191 n.2
    dichten 195 n.10
Kierkegaard, Søren 168
Klein, Felix 183 n.23
Kraus, Karl 177
Kronecker, Leopold 103
    veritable hostility 76
Krüger, Heinz Wilhelm 194 n.16

language 1, 55, 64, 72–3, 120, 127, 157, 159, 161, 163, 178, 186 n.13. See also phenomenological language
    as calculus (*Kalkül*) 1–5, 7, 35, 112–13, 117, 175
    expression (*Ausdruck*) 124–5
    as game 1–4, 10–12, 35, 112–13, 117, 123
    grammar 35–8, 118, 130
    infinite possibility in 84
    pictorial conception 5
    picture-comparisons 130
    rules of 65, 175, 180 n.5
    and world 69, 116, 120, 132
    Zeichenspiel/Rechenspiel 66
language-calculus analogy 112
language games 1, 4, 10–12, 66, 72, 98–9, 104, 113, 143, 156–7, 166–9, 173, 176, 179
    dead forms 169–70
    limits of 169
language–world relationship 35
laws of nature 50, 68, 144, 173
'A Lecture on Ethics,' LE (Wittgenstein) 155, 157, 159–60
Lectures and Conversations on Aesthetics, Psychology, and Religious Belief, LCA (Wittgenstein) 190 n.43
Lee, Desmond 34
Leibniz, Gottfried Wilhelm 76, 188 n.22
Lichtenberg, Georg 177

limits obscurantism 148, 152
logical atomism theory 17, 53–4, 128, 185 n.14
lucid symbolism 22, 28, 30
Lugg, Andrew 2–3

Mach, Ernst 17–18, 33, 39, 181 n.11
    The Analysis of Sensations 25
manuscripts and typescripts 8, 11–14, 51, 107–9, 156, 180 n.2, 191 n.7, 194 n.16. *See also specific manuscripts and typescripts*
Marion, Mathieu 186 n.9, 189 n.33
Maschineneschritf (Wittgenstein) 109
mathematics 3, 6, 45–6, 55–7, 60, 64, 76, 91, 104, 116–17, 123, 163–4, 186 n.12, 188 n.5. *See also* arithmetic (mathematics)
    applicability of 59, 186 n.5
    and game 67–8
    logic and 60, 75–6, 118, 188 n.6
    possibility of correlation 87–8
    priori statements 59
    propositions 46, 50–1, 59–60, 66–7, 72–3, 98, 100, 117
    symbols/symbolism 64–5, 84–5, 101
May Term lectures 133, 142–3, 153, 160, 193 n.2, 194 n.15
McGuinness, Brian 54, 193 n.8
    Azande poison oracle 193 n.8
Merleau-Ponty, Maurice 184 n.26
meta-philosophical comments 119–20
method obscurantism 148, 151–2
Mittag-Leffler, Gösta 103–4
molecular propositions 187 n.5
Monk, Ray 35–6, 174, 181 n.4, 182 n.15, 183 n.26
Moore, George 9–10, 107, 142, 193 n.2, 194 n.15
Mühlhölzer, Felix 55, 186 n.12, 189–90 n.37
Müller-Lyer illusion 28
Munson, Thomas W. 14
music 128, 163–4, 174–5

Nachlass (Wittgenstein) 14, 16, 171
natural number 60, 65, 69, 77–8, 80, 89, 93–7, 102–3, 187 n.4
Nedo, Michael 191 n.7
Needham, Rodney 194 n.10

Newton, Isaac 76, 144
Nietzsche, Friedrich 168, 176–7
Notebooks, 1914–1916, NB (Wittgenstein) 77–8
Notes on Logic (Wittgenstein) 119–20

objects 37, 57, 63, 102, 154, 184 n.26
  of immediate experience 31
  infinity of 79, 93
  physical 25, 29, 34, 101
  theory of 16
  vagueness of 25
obscurantism 147–51
  limits 148, 152
  majesty of death 149–50
  method 148, 151–2
  Nemi ritual 149
  primal practices 149
  rejection of anthropological data 153
  sensibility 148
Ogden, Charles K. 156
ordinary language 1, 8, 22, 100, 112–13, 115–16, 124, 169, 182 n.17, 184 n.26. *See also* phenomenological language
  appearance and reality in 49
  grammar of 36, 116, 118, 123, 194–5 n.2
  phenomenological language *vs.* 19–20, 22–34
  propositions of 21, 51

Park, Byong-Chul 181 n.7, 183 n.24
perspicuous representation 8, 38, 117, 144–7, 153, 155, 157, 159, 179, 193
Pfänder, Alexander 14
pharmakon 170
phenomenological language 4, 6, 8, 13, 38, 47–8, 50, 52, 111, 123, 132, 182 n.17
  appearance *vs.* reality 29
  immediate experience of meaning 21, 23–6, 30–3, 39, 48, 52, 125, 183 n.26
  immediate sense perception 19, 22–3, 26–7, 29, 32–3, 52
  Müller-Lyer illusion 28
  non-linguistic reality 33–4
  vs. ordinary language 19–20, 22–34
  propositions 31–2
  Sellars and myth 31–4
  on visual space 18, 23–4, 26–9, 39

phenomenology 1, 4, 6, 11, 13–14, 17, 26, 29, 33, 47, 52, 110, 114–15, 117, 123, 181–2 n.11, 181 n.4, 182 n.15, 183 n.24, 183 n.26. *See also* phenomenological language
  1929–9 18–24
  as *Aufbau* 181 n.7
  genesis of 15–18
  as grammar 34–9
  physics and 18–19
  prima facie 33
Philosophical Grammar, PG (*Philosophische Grammatik,* Wittgenstein) 109–10, 129, 191 n.8
Philosophical Investigations, PI (Wittgenstein) 1–3, 5, 7–12, 14, 31, 34, 54, 55, 72, 74, 110–11, 113, 118–19, 121, 127, 132–3, 144, 155–7, 159, 175, 180 n.5, 190 n.44, 194 n.16
  aphoristic style 177
  conceptual investigations 173
  forms of life 156–8
  history without history 178
  poverty (*Dürftigkeit*) 166, 170–2
  preface 164, 166, 170
  as vision of culture (Cavell) 167–70
philosophical neutrality 5
philosophical problems 5, 9, 12, 103, 120–1, 155, 180 n.5
Philosophical Remarks, PR (*Philosophische Bemerkungen,* Wittgenstein) 13–14, 45, 107, 109, 164
'Philosophy of Psychology – A Fragment' (Wittgenstein) 175
physics 17–19, 26, 68, 92, 99
Pichler, Alois 4, 7, 12, 108–9
picture theory 182 n.15
The Pink Book (Wittgenstein) 7
Poicaré, Henri 103
primary cultural objects 16
primary propositions (*primäre Sätze*) 50
primitive rituals 114, 121, 143, 146–7, 154, 178, 193 n.8
Principia Mathematica 17
propositional system (*Satzsystem*) 2, 21, 23, 31–2, 44–5, 48, 58, 60, 66–7, 72–3, 77, 79, 111–13, 115–16, 130, 182 n.15, 185 n.8, 185 n.10
  bipolarity 43

infinity 84, 87
kinds of 50–2 (*see also specific kinds of propositions*)
logical multiplicity of 185 n.14
quantification 80
with reality 53
vs. verification 47–8, 123
proto-picture 121
psychoanalysis 190 n.43
psychological concepts 115–18, 132
psychological notions 114
psychologism, critique of (Frege) 67, 185 n.2
Pure Civilization 169
pure intermediary 31–2
Putnam, Hilary 82, 92, 97, 103, 188 n.20, 189 n.29
  points in space and numbers 92
  scientific knowledge 103

qualitative infinity 188 n.22
quantification, infinity and 80–1, 188 n.23

radial method 9
Ramsey, Frank 8, 20, 55, 75, 111
  'General Proposition and Causality' 80
  on infinity and quantification 80–3
  variable hypotheticals 80
rational numbers 86, 88–94, 96, 101, 189 n.33
real language 4, 117
real numbers 95–6, 98, 103
  Cantor and 93, 96–7, 102
  Dedekind and 86–92, 189 n.33
Rehberg, August W. 189 n.28
'Remarks on Frazer's *Golden Bough*', RGB (Wittgenstein) 142–4, 148, 154, 160, 194 n.10, 194 n.16
  ancient sources 134
  Beltane festival 137–41, 146, 151, 153, 193 n.2
  family resemblance (*die Familienähnlichkeit*) 142–4, 153, 160
  game and beauty 142–3
  historical explanations 136–8, 140–2, 145, 150
  human sacrifice 138–9, 142, 146
  instrumental rationality 135

late philosophy 154–61
magical and religious beliefs 134–6, 143, 146
Nemi ritual 134–5, 141, 146, 150, 153, 160, 194 n.13
perspicuous representation 8, 144–7, 153, 155, 159, 193 n.4
Rain-King function 135–6
Rex Nemorensis 134
Remarks on the Foundations of Mathematics, RFM (Wittgenstein) 75, 91, 94–5, 97, 103, 117, 190 n.37
Renan, Ernst
  Histoire du peuple d'Israël (*History of the People of Israel*) 133, 154
  La Pretre de Nemi 194 n.13
Rhees, Rush 10–11, 13–14, 107, 109–10, 133, 164, 191 n.7, 191 n.8, 193 n.2, 194 n.15
Rodych, Victor 188 n.23
Rothhaupt, Josef 192 n.1, 193 n.2
Rotter, Krzysztof 188 n.6, 190 n.45
Russell, Bertrand 60, 75–7, 107, 110, 115, 156, 177
  The Analysis of Mind 192 n.20
  infinity axiom 79
  numerical equivalence 78
  'On Scientific Method in Philosophy' 192 n.17
  quantification 80
  theory of types 72, 81, 182 n.17, 187 n.16

Schlick, Moritz 15–17, 41, 43–4, 47, 54, 111, 183 n.23, 186 n.13
  in critique of formalism 61, 63
  verification in conversations 48–52
Schulte, Joachim 4, 109, 114, 175
science
  of logical forms, philosophy as 120
  philosophy and 173–4, 176
  and technology 165, 173
Sellars, Wilfrid 31–4
  'Empiricism and the Philosophy of Mind' 31
  myth of given 31–4
sensibility obscurantism 148
sensory perceptions 18–19, 22–4, 27, 32, 52

set theory 6, 75–6, 93, 99, 101, 103–4, 123, 187 n.1
   and behaviourism 104
   calculus and prose 81–2, 95, 99, 101–2
   Dedekind and real numbers 86–92
   errors of 83
   intensional and extensional contexts 82–6
   Mengenlehre 103
Shanker, Stuart 44–5, 189 n.29
sign-rule (*Zeichenregel*) 131
Skolem, Thoralf 75
solitary mental life 124–5
sources (verificationism) 41
   Brouwer's intuitionism 45–6
   propositional system 44–5
   Vienna Circle 42–3
Spengler, Oswald 104, 144, 165, 195 n.10
   anti-scientistic approach 145
   civilizations 165–6
   The Decline of the West 144–5, 153, 157, 165
   externalization 168
   spiritual alienation/history 163–7
Spiegelberg, Herbert 16–17, 35–6, 38
   'The Puzzle of Wittgenstein's Phänomenologie' 14–15
St Augustine
   Confessions 178
   language as child 168
Stenlund, Søren 186 n.13
Stern, David 4, 180 n.5
subjectivity, theme 195 n.7

theory of objects 16
Thomae, Johannes 56–7, 59, 61, 63, 65, 69, 72, 187 n.13
Thompson, James M. 181 n.7, 182 n.15
Tractatus Logico-Philosophicus, TLP (Wittgenstein) 1, 4–5, 7–9, 14, 17–21, 23, 34, 41–5, 48, 52–3, 55, 60, 62, 71–4, 75, 80, 83, 88, 107, 110–13, 115–18, 120–1, 124, 127–30, 132, 144, 157, 163, 177, 182 n.17, 182 n.19, 187 n.16, 194 n.2
   class theory (*see* class theory (TLP))
   elementary propositions 8, 18, 20–1, 35, 39, 43–4, 47–8, 53, 77, 111, 113, 184 n.8, 187 n.5

protocol sentences 18
reality through language 128
sign and symbol 186 n.13
spatial statements 19
T-F notation 39
universalist perspective 155

understanding, views (BT) 7–8, 64, 114–16, 124–7, 130, 132, 174

verification/verificationism 1, 41, 123, 184 n.5, 185 n.10, 185 n.14
   in conversations with Schlick and Waismann 48–52
   as grammar 52–4
   propositional system *vs.* 47–8, 123
   sources 42–6
Vermischte Bemerkungen 163
Versuch text 12
Vienna Circle 17, 38–9, 42–4, 53
visual field 19, 24–5, 28, 112, 184 n.26
visual space 18, 23–4, 28, 91, 183–4 n.26, 183 n.23
   and Euclidean (physical) space 6, 29, 38, 183 n.23
   grammar 37–8
   phenomenological language 26–7, 39
von Wright, Georg Henrik 104, 163, 167, 187 n.3, 191 n.8
   'Wittgenstein in Relation to His Times' 104

Waismann, Friedrich 41–2, 69, 108, 183 n.23
   in critique of formalism 61, 63
   'A Logical Analysis of the Concept of Probability' 42
   Thesen 42
   verification in conversations 48–52
Watson, William Heriot 109
Western civilization, spirit 164–6
Weyl, Hermann 75, 91
   Das Kontinuum 189 n.28
whole, philosophy as 180 n.8
Winch, Peter 176
Wittgenstein, Ludwig 1–4, 13–15, 41, 54, 55, 75, 107–8, 110, 123, 133, 163, 182–3 n.19, 192 n.20
   aphorisms 177

defence of formalism 60–74
eigentlich nur dichten 176–9
hocus-pocus 75, 96, 98, 190 n.37
and Hölderlin 170–5, 195 n.7
late philosophy 154–61, 191 n.2
and obscurantism 147–51
pure thought, rejection 67
with Schlick and Waismann (verificationism) 48–52
Sellars and myth of given 31–4
series of forms 60, 77–8, 80, 187 n.4
'Some Remarks on Logical Form' (SLF) 20–2, 36, 39, 48, 139, 184 n.8
'Some Remarks on the Foundations of Mathematics' 179
works (*see specific Wittgenstein's works*)
Wittgenstein's Nachlass: The Bergen Electronic Edition 180 n.2
Wittgenstein Source Bergen Nachlass Edition 180 n.2
Wright, Crispin 184 n.5
Wrigley, Michael 43

www.ingramcontent.com/pod-product-compliance
Lightning Source LLC
Chambersburg PA
CBHW062220300426
44115CB00012BA/2155